# The Economics of Time and Ignorance

"The title of this valuable work . . . comes from a remark of J. M. Keynes: 'The social object of skilled investment should be to defeat the dark forces of time and ignorance which envelop our future.' The moral of this work, however, is that time and ignorance are not so much dark forces to be defeated as unavoidable aspects of the human condition that must be lived with. . . . The major task of the authors, which they have accomplished with considerable success, is to integrate the Austrian, subjective approach to economic theory with that of its close relations in post-Keynesians and a few of the lone rebels against neoclassical orthodoxy."

Kenneth Boulding, *American Journal of Sociology*

"Perhaps now the Austrians will be allowed to help renovate economics."

*The Times Literary Supplement*

"*The Economics of Time and Ignorance* was a watershed event in the history of the Austrian revival. [A]fter 1985 [the original publication date] it would be impossible to think of Austrian economics as anything but the economics of time and ignorance."

Karen Vaughn, *Austrian Economics in America: The Migration of a Tradition* (Cambridge University Press 1994)

*The Economics of Time and Ignorance* is one of the key works in the development of modern Austrian economics. Building on the work of Menger, Hayek and Lachmann, its authors developed a powerful critique of neo-classical economics, in particular of its deterministic models and its pretence of knowledge. The book was effective both in stimulating new work in the Austrian tradition, and in developing connections between Austrians and others exploring similar approaches.

The work is reprinted here in full and is supplemented by a substantial new introductory essay which outlines the major developments in the area since the book's original publication a decade ago.

FOUNDATIONS OF THE MARKET ECONOMY
Edited by Mario J. Rizzo, *New York University* and
Lawrence H. White, *University of Georgia*

A central theme of this series is the importance of understanding and assessing the market economy from a perspective broader than the static economics of perfect competition and Pareto optimality. Such a perspective sees markets as casual processes generated by the preferences, expectations and beliefs of economic agents. The creative acts of entrepreneurship that uncover new information about preferences, prices and technology are central to these processes with respect to their ability to promote the discovery and use of knowledge in society.

The market economy consists of a set of institutions that facilitate voluntary cooperation and exchange among individuals. These institutions include the legal and ethical framework as well as more narrowly 'economic' patterns of social interaction. Thus the law, legal institutions and cultural or ethical norms, as well as ordinary business practices and monetary phenomena, fall within the analytical domain of the economist.

*Other titles in the series*

THE MEANING OF MARKET PROCESS
Essays in the development of modern Austrian economics
*Israel M. Kirzner*

PRICES AND KNOWLEDGE
A market-process perspective
*Esteban F. Thomsen*

KEYNES' GENERAL THEORY OF INTEREST
A reconsideration
*Fiona C. Maclachlan*

*LAISSEZ-FAIRE* BANKING
*Kevin Dowd*

EXPECTATIONS AND THE MEANING OF INSTITUTIONS
Essays in economics by Ludwig Lachmann
Edited by *Don Lavoie*

PERFECT COMPETITION AND THE TRANSFORMATION OF ECONOMICS
*Frank M. Machovec*

ENTREPRENEURSHIP AND THE MARKET PROCESS
An enquiry into the growth of knowledge
*David Harper*

# The Economics of Time and Ignorance

Gerald P. O'Driscoll, Jr.

*and*

Mario J . Rizzo

*with a contribution by*

Roger W. Garrison

*and a new introduction*

ROUTLEDGE

London and New York

First published in 1985 by Basil Blackwell Ltd

Reissued by Routledge 1996
11 New Fetter Lane,
London EC4P 4EE

Simultaneously published in the USA and Canada
by Routledge
29 West 35th Street, New York, NY 10001



Typeset in Times by
Keystroke, Jacaranda Lodge, Wolverhampton

Printed in Great Britain by
TJ Press (Padstow) Ltd, Padstow, Cornwall



*British Library Cataloguing in Publication Data*
A catalogue record for this book is available from the British Library

*Library of Congress Cataloguing in Publication Data*
A catalogue record for this book has been requested

ISBN 0-415-12120-5

This book has been sponsored in part by the
Austrian Economics Program at New York University

To
Ludwig M. Lachmann

# Contents

# Acknowledgements

Many individuals have either read and commented on drafts of chapters of this book or otherwise assisted in the project. We are grateful to all of them. Mark Perlman commented on a paper given at the 1980 American Economic Association meeting, 'What is Austrian Economics?', which became the basis of this book. His kind comments and helpful suggestions gave us the courage to persevere in the early days. Ian Steedman was crucial in bringing that paper to the attention of our publisher, and we are obviously very happy that he did so. We also wish to thank Walter Grinder for his part in the process.

The following have commented on various chapters in the book, in various stages of completion: James Buchanan, Bruce Caldwell, Richard Ebeling, Roman Frydman, Roger Koppl, Stephen Littlechild, Lyla O'Driscoll, James Pearce, G. L. S. Shackle, Jeremy Shearmur, Louis Spadaro, Lawrence H. White, John Wood, and Leland Yeager. We appreciate their comments and apologize to them for not heeding all of their suggestions. We also wish to thank the members of the Austrian Economics Colloquium at New York University, who read and commented on almost the entire book. Members of the Economics Department at George Mason University also provided useful comments on two of the chapters, for which we thank them. Finally, participants in the Liberty Fund Colloquium on Economics as a Process were exposed to some of the ideas in this book and made helpful suggestions.

Sanford Ikeda prepared the master bibliography for this work and also assisted in other ways. We also owe a great debt of gratitude to Mark Brady for his editorial assistance.

Richard Langlois, our former colleague at New York University, was, as it were, present from the beginning. An embarrassingly large proportion of this book owes whatever merit it has to his keen insight, penetrating criticism, and persuasive arguments.

Israel Kirzner also played a special role in the writing of this book. His insightful questions made us reassess many of our positions. If we have not come around to his view on all matters, we have benefited from his criticisms. We also want to thank our publisher, René Olivieri, for his patience with this oft-delayed book and his continued support.

We are also indebted to the Scaife Family Charitable Trusts and the Earhart Foundation for financial support.

Finally, we are profoundly indebted to Professor Ludwig Lachmann. It has been a pleasure and an honor to be his colleagues at New York University. With deep admiration, we dedicate this book to him.

# Introduction

## Time and Ignorance After Ten Years

Mario J. Rizzo[1]

> [W]e all try hard to avoid error . . . Yet to avoid error is a poor ideal: if we do not dare to tackle problems which are so difficult that error is almost unavoidable, then there will be no growth of knowledge. In fact, it is from our boldest theories, *including those which are erroneous*, that we learn most. *Karl Popper (1979, p. 186)*

In her recent history of the contemporary Austrian school, Karen Vaughn says that after 1985, the original publication date of the present book, "it [was] impossible to think of Austrian economics as anything but the economics of time and ignorance" (1994, p. 134). While it would be too generous to attribute this development primarily to our book, her statement does express an important truth. Austrian economics has changed in the past ten years and that change has been positive. Austrians have now become among the most creative, innovative and least doctrinaire of economists.[2] While the neoclassical mainstream continues to spin its wheels, "Austrians" (meaning the broad subjectivist and market-process school of thought) are asking and answering deep questions at the frontier of social-scientific knowledge.[3] They understand that application of the mechanistic model of nineteenth-century physics may well have reached the limits of its useful contributions. They are not afraid to challenge many widely, but passively, accepted beliefs among economists. They know that the twentieth century is almost at an end and that not all of its intellectual developments have been beneficial. They understand that a new century will demand not only "new" techniques (perhaps many of them being old techniques) but also new divisions among academic disciplines (Rizzo, 1992, pp. 246–8). The questions and answers proffered by many of today's economists might comfortably find a home as a kind of "social physics" (Comte, 1988: p. 13).[4] On the other hand, some of the efforts of Austrians and others whose conception of economics is rooted in the realistic intentions and purposes of agents might be appropriately considered, without derogation, a "philosophical" economics.[5]

For our present purposes, however, it is important to understand the sense in which Austrian economics has become the economics of time and ignorance. The reader will recall that the term "economics of time and ignorance" is derived from Keynes' "dark forces of time and ignorance." Of course, this does not mean that Austrian economics has become the economics of John Maynard Keynes. (How ironic that would be!) Although we find elements in Keynes' analysis that are subjectivist, deeply insightful and congenial to our way of thinking, we are not Keynesians. We choose Keynes' expression because he understood, at least much of the time, the importance of the basic problems with which real time confronts individual actors. To say that Austrian economics is the economics of time and ignorance is to say that it is the economics of *coping* with the problems posed by real time and radical ignorance. Although individuals are not paralyzed by these problems, they do not automatically or completely overcome them. The behavior generated by this predicament in which human beings find themselves is a source of market phenomena and institutions. It is also the source of prudential limits to our institutions, both markets and governmental. Human beings are "prisoners of time" (Shackle, 1970, p. 21). This prison acts not only as a constraint (the allocational aspect of time) but also as a formulator of experience, thus generating and limiting our knowledge.

If we take time seriously, it is hard to imagine Austrian economics as merely "a supplement to neoclassical economics." This represents the least the Austrians have to offer (Vaughn, 1994, pp. 165–8). Some neoclassical economists may be able to make improvements in their analyses by formalizing (and thus transforming) the insights to Menger, Hayek or others. But this is not the essence of the Austrian contribution to knowledge about the social world. Austrians ask different kinds of questions and provide different kinds of answers. This is not to say that they may not sometimes ask the same or similar questions or that their vocabulary might not be at least superficially similar to that of the neoclassical mainstream. It is to say, however, that Austrian economics is essentially a different enterprise from neoclassical social physics.

The ways in which Austrian economics has changed over the past ten years focus, as we shall see, on the ideas of time and ignorance. *Why* have time and ignorance become so important within Austrian economics?

Most, if not all, Austrians have argued that subjectivism, as a substantive doctrine and as a method, lies at the heart of the unique Austrian contribution. The theory of subjective value as pioneered by Menger, Böhm-Bawerk and Wieser was the first lesson the Austrians taught the economics profession. The subjectivism of value soon expanded into a more general *verstehende* approach in which the actor's problem situation is defined as he[6] perceives it to be. (This is not to say, of course, that his perceptions bear no relation to an underlying reality.) As Austrian economics increasingly became concerned with the coordinative properties of entrepreneurship and discovery, questions of real time had to surface. Coordination is not simply a matter of meshing activities at a point in time or across a time span frozen by the absence of unexpected change. So the central issue emerged: the meaning of subjectivism in a world of real time.

Subjectivism in time ("dynamic subjectivism") encompasses what Edmund Husserl (1964) called "internal time consciousness" and Henri Bergson called "la durée réelle" or real duration (1910, pp. 99–128).[7] This is consciousness of the passage of time or of the flow of events. As such it requires that consciousness of the present moment manifest within itself a dynamic tendency. Both the past and the future must inhere in that moment through memory and expectation. In the static conception of time the present is a virtual stop – the very negation of passage or flow. In the dynamic conception it is virtual movement from past to future or, more precisely, from memory to expectation. The mnemic link to the past is responsible for the continuity of the flow. But the flow itself arises out of the contrast between the remembered past and the expected future. Without the novelty of the future (seen as "novel" only in contrast to the remembered past) there could be no sense of temporal passage.[8] Thus, subjectivism in time or time consciousness entails novelty[9] and its correlative, ignorance. On the other hand, characterizing time as strictly homogeneous, that is, without novelty, leads to a denial of time consciousness or subjectivism in time.

The denial of time consciousness is inherently self-contradictory from the perspective of the agent. This is because the instantaneous (or mathematical) present is "specious." "Where is it, this present? It has melted in our grasp, fled ere we could touch it, gone in the instant of becoming" (James, 1890, p. 608). We simply cannot perceive a present apart from memory and anticipation. The perceptible present, on the other hand, "is the vivid fringe of memory tinged with anticipation" (Whitehead, 1961, p. 116). Thus, "[t]here is no sharp distinction either between memory and the present immediacy or between the present immediacy and anticipation" (p. 112). Time consciousness or real duration must be a flow because, without the *continuity* associated with the span of memory to anticipation, there is no temporal perception, no action and hence no subject-matter for economics.

Outside of real time, all that is perceived would appear as if it were at a single instant, including all causes and effects.[10] Since action must presuppose causal efficacy, the simultaneity of cause (i.e., human agency) and effect amounts to a denial of the possibility of action. If every effect we as agents (or causes) desire to bring about has already been brought about, then there is no need or possibility of action. Static models thus contain two concepts implicitly at war with each other: the specious present and action. While self-contradictory models can sometimes be useful (Mises, 1966, p. 236), they are obviously not ideal because any attempt to think through all of their implications can lead us into an intellectual quagmire.

A relatively simple example will show, from another perspective, the incompatibility of the specious present and action. Consider a buyer responding to a fall in the price of an intertemporally substitutable product. Should he purchase more now or should he wait because the fall in price is just a sign of further declines to come? The behavioral implications of a change in the current variable depend on the agent's expectation of the future value of that variable. This expectation is, in turn, partly dependent on the agent's previous experience or, more precisely, on his memory of it (Lindahl, 1939, p. 36; Starbuck and Milliken, 1988, p. 40). So the present which has meaning for action is not a specious present, but a present extended to encompass both memory and anticipation.

Austrian economics has become the economics of time and ignorance, not only for "essentialist" reasons such as those discussed above, but also because of its practical attempt, discussed below, to deal with problems of coordination and entrepreneurship. This requires analysis in time, thus implying novelty and ignorance. Given the entrepreneurial turn in Austrian economics (real) time and ignorance *had* to be the next step.

What changes have the ideas of time and ignorance wrought in Austrian economics and in related areas? Before we can answer this question the reader must consider three general points.

First, Austrian economics is still in the process of self-creation so no narrow definition of the subject will capture the significant changes under way. If we were to define Austrian economics so narrowly as to include only the work of those few whose honest vision is fairly restricted, then much of what we say would be untrue about such an Austrian economics.

Second, more importantly, a difficulty in defining Austrian economics narrowly is that it would constitute a stagnant and uninteresting school. It is a consideration such as this, as well as the related capacity for growth in knowledge, that should be paramount in identifying a school. Austrian economics *is* broad because it *needs* to be broad in order to be interesting and in order to grow in the knowledge it conveys. Narrow Austrian economics cannot ask interesting questions and cannot give interesting answers.

Third, in many respects developments in the broader area of subjectivist economics are more important for the future of Austrian economics than those within a narrower range of such thought. This is because gains from intellectual interaction are greatest when, among approaches within the same or similar research programs, there are important differences in perspective. Lawson (1994b, pp. 534–5) suggests, for example, that, substantive differences notwithstanding, Institutionalism, Post Keynesianism and Austrian economics share a common philosophical perspective and "perhaps . . . it is time for some fuller reconciliation between [these] traditions."[11]

In the past ten years there have been many important developments in Austrian and related thought. It is impossible to list them all here (and exclusion of some should not necessarily be taken as disapproval), but there are four developments that appear to be fecund and that are closely related to the themes of this book.

(1) *A more profound recognition of the importance of disequilibrating*[12] forces. While most of the older work in Austrian economics certainly did recognize that not all market adjustments are equilibrating, very little emphasis was placed on this recognition and its implications were certainly not explored. It was as if disequilibration were not an "essential" feature of the market economy: equilibration is essential, while disequilibration is random or "accidental." Whatever incentive-driven asymmetries between equilibration and disequilibration exist (*viz*, agents seek profits and not losses), error is not an accidental feature of a world in real time. The subjective perception of the passage of time inherently or essentially involves genuine surprise. Unless we quite artificially restrict the system to favorable surprises

only, error and disequilibration will be inevitable and therefore an essential part of market "adjustment."[13]

Today many, if not all, Austrians accept the importance of disequilibrating tendencies in markets (Vaughn, 1994, pp. 139–61; Prychitko, 1993a, pp. 372–4). These tendencies are not simply the result of changes in the exogenous data but emanate from the source of equilibrating behavior, that is, the indeterminate or creative response to perceived profit opportunities. "The same active mental processes which are taken to adjust to change once it has occurred, will also originate change" (High, 1986, p. 115).[14] The very process of adjustment – or rather attempted adjustment – will produce errors that undermine equilibration. If this were not the case and if only systematic equilibrating tendencies existed, then money and, more generally, market institutions would tend to disappear (Boettke, Horwitz and Prychitko, 1994, p. 64). Since data changes would then be the only reason for the continuance of institutions, we should expect them to be relatively unimportant in stationary or traditional societies. In fact, just the opposite is the case.

Israel Kirzner, who for many years resisted acknowledging the importance of disequilibrating tendencies, has now undergone somewhat of a change in thinking, as we shall see farther below. The original exposition of his theory of entrepreneurship is completely spatialized. Profits emerge from the price differentials for a single product in a single market at a single moment in time. "For me the changes the entrepreneur initiates are *always* toward the hypothetical state of equilibrium" (Kirzner 1973, p. 73, emphasis added). Without changes in the underlying data, the long-run movement of the market is toward equilibrium or a state of zero arbitrage differentials. In Kirzner (1982, pp. 153–4) this position is reaffirmed even in an analysis of uncertainty: "It should be clear that nothing essential is lost [in the original model] when our picture of the market is expanded to include many commodities and, in particular, the passage of time." An atemporal market "process" is alleged to be essentially the same as a market process in real time. Such a view is plausible because the adjusting changes are seen to have no impact on the data to which they are adjusting. Thus Kirzner can make the even more amazing claim that it is on the tendency for (presumably constant) opportunities to be noticed that "our belief in a *determinate* market process is founded" (1976b, p. 121, emphasis added). The market process is determinate in the sense that all systematic movements are in the direction of the implicit equilibrium corresponding to the initial data.

In the final analysis, however, this equilibration-always view is untenable. A plausible (albeit moderated) case for it can be made only in circumstances where disequilibrating forces are exogenous in origin. Then we might say that entrepreneurial changes, while not *always* in the direction of equilibrium, tend in that direction – in the sense that, with frozen data, the system may ultimately become consistent with that data. This, however, is not a stable intellectual position. If economics is truly part of a more general humane science of rational choice ("praxeology") then more and more of the data will continue to be transformed into endogenous "variables". We have already witnessed the endogenzation of technological choice, knowledge of resource availability – as well as the production of resources themselves, tastes defined over market goods, and, of course, the institutional setting itself. If change does not emanate from outside the system (because there is nothing outside), then either (1) there is no change at all, or (2) change is generated entirely from within, and hence equilibrium must be ruptured by endogenous processes. To the extent, therefore, that the equilibration-always view eschews endogenous disruption of coordination, it must degenerate into the complete-stasis position of extreme neoclassical economics. There will be no exogenous shocks to which entrepreneurial adjustments must be made. As a consequence, the task of economics will be quite rightly seen as moving from a framework in which entrepreneurship is important to one in which it is of no (or little) importance. Economics would, in this view, progress only to the extent that it reduces its dependence on the entrepreneurial function.[15]

Kirzner has not, to my knowledge, fully understood the difficulty into which he has gotten himself. Nevertheless, he has recently emphasized the impact of erroneous entrepreneurial acts on the process of adjustment (Kirzner, 1992, pp. 31–7). He carefully distinguishes "true" (objective) underlying future realities from "mistake-induced" realities. The former reflect consumer preferences that are uncontaminated by the latter entrepreneurial mistakes along the adjustment path. Consider an example discussed by Kirzner (1992, pp. 29–31). Suppose that the objective situation (the initial data) is that there exists significant unsatisfied demand for shoes. Some entrepreneurs, however, misjudge the data and construct, instead, factories to satisfy the less urgent demand for bicycles. *After these factories are built*, other entrepreneurs sell the additional steel that is needed to make bicycles. Kirzner asks the question: Is the activity of the sellers of steel "coordinating" even though resources should have been used, in the first instance, to build shoe machinery? His answer is "yes" because the steel entrepreneurs are responding to the data that is currently relevant – the new data involving the mistaken entrepreneurial judgement to build bicycle factories. "The most useful place *now* for the steel is in fact in the bicycle industry. The original realities . . . have no relevance *now*, and have, indeed correctly now failed to influence the allocation of resources" (Kirzner, 1992, p. 30). The original error – the construction of bicycle factories – is the basis for the emergence of profit opportunities that direct resources into the production of bicycles.

As we see it, sometimes errors that occur in the market process are self-reinforcing in a special sense. Entrepreneurial errors along the adjustment path can lead to a cumulative departure away from the equilibrium implicit in the initial data, that is, the data which exists in putative independence of market adjustments. While it may be true that once the first entrepreneurial error is committed, further "errors" relative to the initial data are warranted from a short-run welfare point of view, this is not the central issue here.[16] What is at stake is whether the market, to a greater or lesser extent, generates its own equilibria or, in other words, whether equilibrium is "defined in the process of its emergence" (Buchanan, 1986, p. 73). In Kirzner's story above, the shoe market will not be moving in the direction of the equilibrium implicit in the initial data. It will, instead, be moving in the direction of an equilibrium that has *endogenously undergone change*.[17] The equilibrium has changed because of entrepreneurial errors in the process of adjusting to the initial data. Thus this example supports, albeit unintentionally, Buchanan's insight concerning the emergent nature of equilibria.

Despite this recent development in his views, Kirzner does not appear to believe that entrepreneurial errors are a necessary part of processes in real time. One gets the impression that, unlike the coordinating activities of entrepreneurs, errors are just so much happenstance. Moreover, the market process is still portrayed as moving in the direction of *an* equilibrium even if it is not the initial equilibrium. Regardless of where we situate Kirzner in the growing recognition of the importance of disequilibrating forces, many other Austrians have, as we have seen, participated in this intellectual change.

It is sometimes argued that this development has not been salutary because too much emphasis has been placed on disequilibration and the possibility of disorder. G.L.S Shackle and Ludwig Lachmann, for example, were accused by some of intellectual nihilism. There is a profound misunderstanding here (for which these authors were partly to blame). In Lachmann's earlier work (1977, pp. 181–93) there was a clear understanding of both equilibrating and disequilibrating forces with an invitation to examine the properties of various markets in terms of the relative strength of these forces.[18] If in later years Lachmann's emphasis (1986) shifted to an examination of disequilibrating forces, the most plausible explanation is that his (largely) Austrian audience needed to hear this far more than another lesson on the equilibrating character of markets. A similar point might be made about Shackle since his intended audience was the (neoclassical) profession-at-large which needed the disequilibration lesson even more than the Austrians needed it.[19]

The ultimate significance of this more profound recognition of the importance of disequilibrating forces is an increasing focus on the conditions necessary for equilibrating behavior, and, ultimately, on the different senses of equilibrium.

(2) *Greater attention to the prerequisites for equilibrating behavior.* If equilibration cannot simply be taken for granted, in the sense that profit opportunities – in and of themselves – are sufficient to ensure movements toward equilibrium, then it is necessary to discover the cooperating conditions that are needed to make equilibration more (or less) likely. But before this can be done we must understand that different concepts of equilibrium have different knowledge requirements. These requirements differ not only in the content but also in their severity, and therefore in the likelihood that an economic system will move in the direction of the equilibrium described by the concept. The more complex the knowledge requirements in equilibrium the more complex the knowledge requirements of successful moves *toward* that equilibrium.

At one end of the "continuum" the concept of individual equilibrium, without common knowledge across individuals, is almost a tautology. (The qualifier "almost" is used because under conditions of uncertainty there is an entrepreneurial element in discovering the most efficient means to ends.) Maintenance of such an individual equilibrium over time, requires that the data generated by the economy does not disrupt the agent's expectations. In the absence of common factual knowledge, agents can have their individual expectations confirmed while holding incompatible theories.

Interpersonal equilibria, on the other hand, have more stringent knowledge requirements. Market-day coordination on the stock market, for example, requires knowledge of offers to buy and offers to sell. Yet there are, and indeed must be, divergent expectations about the future value of the stock. Mutual compatibility of individual plans *over time* requires convergent expectations among those who are engaged in exchange (otherwise their plans would be based on inconsistent premises). Finally, a *full* plan coordination not only requires mutual compatibility of plans of exchanging agents but also the complete exhaustion of gains from trade. The prerequisites for equilibration will thus vary in content and likelihood depending on the concept of equilibrium in use. A detailed examination of these is beyond the scope of this Introduction. Our attention shall be largely focused, therefore, on the more general considerations common to a wide variety of equilibrium concepts.

Some of the conditions prerequisite to equilibration can be analyzed at the aggregate level while others are more obviously and fruitfully analyzed at the individual level. At the aggregate level, we can think of institutions as "points of orientation" (Lachmann, 1971, p. 38) that are likely to lead to relatively compatible actions and expectations. At the individual level, we can assess the information requirements for increased coordination (e.g., Hayek's "knowledge of the particular circumstances of time and place" (1948b, p. 80)). The former consists of general or enduring pieces of knowledge, while the latter consists of knowledge relevant for so short a time-period that it cannot have been congealed into institutions.

In a number of articles Peter Boettke (1990a, b; 1994) explores the epistemic properties of alternative institutional arrangements. Institutions are, in an important sense, congealed social knowledge. By following institutionally-sanctioned patterns of behavior, separate individuals are able to coordinate more completely their actions and plans. This is because institutions often limit the options available to an individual thereby reducing the uncertainty about what others are going to do. Furthermore, to the extent that institutions represent approximate, if not optimal, adaptations to the objective environment, the individual plans will also be roughly coordinated with that environment.

On the other hand, institutions which encourage what we call (in chapter 5) "time-dependent uncertainty" can be discoordinating. Suppose speculator *A* expects speculator *B* to place a high valuation on an asset (e.g., the stock of a firm) but neither of them has any idea about how much consumers will indirectly value the firm. It is quite possible that the underlying institutional arrangement, that is, the stock market, will generate a great deal of uncertainty as people try to guess what others are thinking about their thoughts (and so forth). If, however, the speculators are really trying to guess what others are concluding about the current and future decisions of *consumers* and there are some shared beliefs about these, then institutions may decrease, rather than increase, uncertainty. This is because knowledge or knowledge surrogates are disseminated more quickly when price offers and actual transactions are made mainfest in an organized setting.

Institutions are also less likely to enhance coordination in the context of "big players." In a series of papers Koppl and coauthors (Koppl and Yeager, 1994; Butos and Koppl, 1993; Koppl and Langlois, 1994) have argued that the presence of agents who are large and relatively less sensitive to the discipline of profit and loss reduce the reliability of expectations. There are at least two reasons for this. First, the mass of agents must try to predict the idiosyncracies of a single individual (e.g., the timing of short-term interest rate recommendations by the chairman of the Federal Reserve Board). Second, the behavior of big players is more likely to be suboptimal or maladapted than that of players who are more strictly subject to the discipline of profit and loss. Consider, for example, the dubious behavior of a central banker seeking to keep the international value of his currency from falling in the face of accelerating domestic inflation. Furthermore, to the extent that governments try to insulate agents against the possibility of failure, then they can create a big-player effect through relatively small players. Such is the consequence of Federal deposit insurance on the stability of the banking structure. Under this system of "insurance" risk is shifted by the big players (the Federal Deposit Insurance Corporation) from the banks who create it to depositors. This means that the banks will incur more risk than is appropriate and the banking system will become more unstable than otherwise (Clair and O'Driscoll, 1993, pp. 47–8). This instability is ultimately a result of the institution-creating behavior of the big players.

Within a given institutional context, equilibration requires the dissemination and utilization of transient knowledge. The knowledge-enhancing movements that can occur in disequilibrium contexts vary in their complexity and difficulty. The nearer the system is to overall equilibrium, the fewer are the deviations of prices, quantities and expectations from their "appropriate" magnitudes (or the smaller are such deviations). Under these circumstances, individual agents are more likely to make correct or equilibrating decisions. The farther the system is from overall equilibrium, on the other hand, the more complex is the system of deviations from appropriate magnitudes and hence the more likely agents are to err in their adjustments (Rizzo, 1990, p. 25).[20]

It might appear that in far-from-equilibrium situations there will be larger profit incentives to overcome – perhaps completely – the greater information difficulties. If this were true it would not follow (except *ceteris paribus*) that equilibration is less likely far from equilibrium. Information difficulties, however, are not perfectly offset by the greater potential profits. The distance from equilibrium to which we are referring is not primarily that of a single price deviating from its equilibrium value. Instead, we are referring to a situation of many markets in states of disequilibrium. In such a circumstance there will be complex distortions among these many markets. To obtain the large profits associated with significant moves toward equilibrium a number of prices must be changed simultaneously. Even if there were to happen, however, a single decision-maker would not be able to appropriate these large profits. He would earn the smaller profits associated with the movement of a single price because related prices would be beyond his reach.[21]

(3) *Growing attention to the idea of endogenously-produced change.*[22] The essence of the contemporary Austrian research program (or, more precisely, of its positive heuristic) is the development of the idea of endogenously-produced change. This lies at the heart of the "genetic-causal tradition" (Cowan and Rizzo, 1995) in economic thought which, although certainly not confined to Austrian work, received its most self-conscious elaboration by Austrians, especially by the neglected Hans Mayer (1994). Schumpeter (1934, p. 63) was also one of the first to lay explicit stress on the concept of endogenous change, but failed to convince the economic profession as a whole of its importance. A careful examination of the nature and role of "entrepreneurial alertness" in contemporary Austrian theory will show that only by elaborating the idea of endogenously-produced change can Austrians be successful in drawing out the full implications of their contribution and in differentiating their product from that of the neoclassical mainstream. Alertness, that is, the discovery propensity, although exogenous in certain respects, is switched on by profit opportunities within the economic system. Nevertheless, the way in which alert entrepreneurs move from knowledge of the current state of the world to knowledge of future opportunities is largely unexplored. Austrians must show, obviously in general terms, first, how knowledge

is disseminated within a disequilibrium economy and, second, how the economic process itself generates completely new knowledge. Both the dissemination of knowledge ("subjective novelty") and the generation of completely new knowledge ("objective novelty") are sources of change within an economy (Witt, 1992, pp. 223–4).[23] While the first issue is extremely important, our main concern was and is with the second.

Brian Loasby's emphasis on research programs, discussed below, and elaborated recently (1991), is an important step in the direction of understanding the generation of new knowledge. Still more recently, David Harper (1994, 1996) has comprehensively applied the broad Popperian framework to the phenomenon of entrepreneurship. Among many interesting results, Harper shows that since the solution to any given problem necessarily gives rise to new problems, entrepreneurial learning can never cease or settle into a state of rest. Thus, not only will knowledge continually grow but it will grow in a coherent way arising out of the previous problem situation (or, at least, so it would seem most of the time). Attempts to solve current problems, *whether successful or not*, will give rise to new problems and thence to new knowledge. The history of technological change is replete with examples of this phenomenon (Rosenberg, 1969).

There is also an older tradition, to which Loasby (1991, pp. 11–12) refers us, that holds promise for understanding endogenous change. This is the idea of dynamic increasing returns in its original Smithian version. Unlike the more recent version of Brian Arthur (e.g., 1990) changes in technology are not the result of random shocks at some early stage of technological development. In Adam Smith's version the specialization and concomitant division of labor directs the individual's attention to certain problems and hence to certain kinds of solutions. These problems are actually opportunities for increased productive efficiency which intimate knowledge of the productive process (through division of labor and specialization) gives rise. There is nothing automatic about this growth of knowledge. What the (static) division of labor does is make the perception of some technological opportunity for gain ("the problem") more likely and by increasing the agent's understanding of possible technologies renders the solution more likely.

More importantly, it is not only the division of labor, *having already occurred*, that endogenously generates the production of new knowledge. In a world of real time and novelty, the division of labor is not simply a function of the (exogenous) size of the market. Greater division of labor – and hence improvements in technology via Smithian increasing returns – does not need to be generated by an exogenous shock. In real time the homogeneous differentiates into heterogeneity spontaneously.[24] So relatively unspecialized and undivided labor (the homogeneous) becomes more and more specialized and divided (the differentiated heterogeneity) as productive knowledge grows in the passage of time. As a result there will also be continual growth in the technologies inspired by the ever-new divisions and specializations of labor. This is an application of the Principle of the Instability of the Homogeneous. As earlier discussed by Herbert Spencer (1888, pp. 401–2), it did require initiation by an exogenous shock, but in more modern discussions by complexity theorists it became a principle of spontaneous differentiation (Prigogine and Stengers, 1984, p. 38). Thus any *given* division of labor with its consequent opportunities for the growth of knowledge will not simply play itself out and settle in an equilibrium. It will continually generate new divisions of labor which will, in turn, produce ever-fresh discoveries. This is a reason that overall equilibrium is inherently unstable in the long run. Equilibrium makes possible the very circumstances (i.e., divided labor and specialization)[25] that generate a change in knowledge and hence an undoing of the equilibrium. Spencer's law, cited above, is actually the Principle of the Instability of Equilibrium.[26]

(4) *Attention to the reconciliation of equilibrium and unpredictable change.* An economics *in* time must have an equilibrium construct that is in time as well. Hayek tried to marry equilibrium and time. As we show in chapter 5, however, the conception of time was, in his earlier work, largely static. As such, Hayek's first "marriage" was not a happy one; it does not carry us very far along the contemporary Austrian research program. In Hayek's later work (1973, pp. 98–110; 1976, pp. 114–25) the reconciliation among equilibrium, time and unpredictable change is more successful. Hayek distinguishes between the legal framework, upon which the relative certainty of expectations is founded, and the system of market exchanges within that framework, in which there is no certainty of expectations. Because of the law's abstract quality, agents can rely on expectations regarding the typical form or pattern of economic interactions (Rizzo, 1985; Horwitz, 1992, pp. 45–79). In contract law, for example, there are criteria for a valid contract regardless of the price or nature of the goods exchanged; excuses or justifications for breach of contract do not depend on the prices or quantities of economic theory – and neither does the type of remedies for breach. There is a relative order

or "pattern equilibrium" at the level of legal institutions. Within this higher-level equilibrium, however, there is a disequilibrium or continual change in the economic variables. The framework clearly permits agents to change their plans (and hence the prices of whatever they buy or sell) in accordance with new facts about both the external word and other agents. In fact, the stable legal framework makes such change *possible* for without the certainty generated by the institutions of property and contract market exchanges would cease. In facilitating these changes the higher-level pattern equilibrium ensures maximum market coordination. Maximum coordination, however, does not necessarily mean a state that is fairly close to a full or exact coordination (Rizzo, 1990, pp. 25–7). This is because to attain the highest possible degree of coordination we must have (adaptive) change which itself involves a certain amount of discoordination. The very process of coordinating must involve discoordinating. Thus encompassed within an overall pattern equilibrium there is a system of market interactions that endogenously produces a certain degree of disequilibrium – a disequilibrium that is vital to generating whatever degree of market coordination we do in fact enjoy. If we move beyond simple adaptation to the case of technological change, it is clear that an initial change will stimulate still-further technological discoveries and consequently disappointments in expectations. This is because technological changes generate imbalances and bottlenecks in production processes (Rosenberg, 1969, pp. 1–11). These, in turn, create profit opportunities where there were none previously, in associated technologies, as well as disappointments in the expectations of those whose activities were coordinated with the old technology. These effects are discoordinating in terms of the current *behavior* of agents, whatever the long-run consequences for the satisfaction of their underlying preferences.

Another promising, if yet untested, route has been forged by Brian Loasby (1991). He wishes to adapt the concept of equilibrium to the continual process of learning that occurs under conditions of real time and radical uncertainty. For Loasby an equilibrium is something similar to a shared research program, that is, an intellectual structure for learning.[27] A research program contains, among other things, instructions as to how individuals ought or ought not to go about learning. Although the structure is temporarily fixed and relatively predictable, what individuals will learn when applying it is not fixed or predictable. Genuine novelty is not thereby excluded from equilibrium in real time. The most obvious locus for a "fixed" research program is the individual firm, regulated, as it is, by a single or small group of decision-makers. Nevertheless, it is not inconceivable that, at least with respect to general or broad features of the environment, a common and relatively fixed research program may apply across many individuals and firms within an economy.[28]

An equilibrium construct in time has significant implications for the equilibrating process. To the extent that equilibrium can "realistically" be defined only in terms of relatively constant structures of a higher order (e.g., law, research programs) the transmission of knowledge during periods of equilibration must be conceptualized in a radically different way. It no longer makes sense to think of this knowledge as decentralized *facts* about consumer demand, resource availability, etc. This would be more appropriate to a static framework in which knowledge of current facts moves through a system. What kind of knowledge can be transmitted through a system undergoing change? To transmit the data of today is already too late because decisions are future-oriented. In a world of real time, and hence of change, the facts of yesterday or today will not be the same as those of tomorrow. An efficient economic system must therefore transmit not (outdated) facts but effective techniques of coping with change, of solving problems of a certain type.[29] "Evolution selects, therefore, for populations with the ability to learn, rather than populations with optimal, but fixed, behavior" (Allen, 1994, p. 11). This is why "institutions" at the individual or firm levels (routines), as well as at the more general societal level, are very important. At their best, institutions are successful methods of dealing with an unknown future.

The evolution of money made possible the rapid adaptation of the individual's and community's resources to new conditions. The firm-routine of maintaining inventories performs a similar function in a more specific way. Other institutions provide adaptational flexibility, not so much by improving responses once a change is recognized, but by improving recognition or anticipation of change in the first place. While the future is not predictable it is also not entirely novel or undetermined. There are repeated patterns (typicalities) in the world which make certain routines of problem-solving successful even where the content of the problem could not have been predicted beforehand. It is also true, however, that the future is *partially* determined by antecedent conditions. Thus, attention to the "laws" of our world puts us in a better position than we would otherwise be to anticipate at least certain aspects of future developments. The institutionalized methods or techniques of accomplishing all this are vital to the successful functioning of an economic system.

Markets transmit propensities to adapt and to learn through the incentives provided by profit and loss. It is obvious that the kind of "knowledge" to which we are now referring cannot be summarized in a price. Nevertheless, a price system, through the discipline it exerts on actors, can stimulate them to do much to adapt to and partially anticipate the future.

Even after ten years, *The Economics of Time and Ignorance* must be seen as a transitional work. Between the late twentieth-century Austrian revival and the new mature Austrian economics of the twenty-first century must stand an intellectual transition: a series of insights, problems, incomplete and perhaps even messy solutions. We make no pretence that our work is anything more than a small beginning but, we deeply believe, a step that must be taken in order to enter the world of discovery that could be ours.

## NOTES

1 I am indebted to many people, for very helpful comments on earlier drafts, particularly to Gerald P. O'Driscoll, Jr. and Peter J. Boettke. I am also indebted to William Butos, Young Back Choi, Robin Cowan, Andres Garcia, Sanford Ikeda, Israel Kirzner, Roger Koppl, David Harper, Yaw Nyarko, Joseph Salerno, Karen Vaughn, and the Austrian Economics Colloquium at New York University. Responsibility for errors is mine alone.

2 The idea of asking innovative questions is in the Hayekian tradition. See O'Driscoll (1989, p. 345).

3 There has been a world-wide explosion of work in the broad subjectivist tradition, some of which has appeared in the *Review of Political Economy* (Edward Arnold), *Advances in Austrian Economics* (JAI Press), *Review of Austrian Economics* (Kluwer Academic Press), the series of books entitled, "Foundations of the Market Economy," published by Routledge, and the series of books entitled, "The Political Economy of the Austrian School," published by New York University Press. Attention should also be directed toward the "praxeology" school reflected in the sociological journal, *Cultural Dynamics* (E.J. Brill). Moreover, Austrian perspectives in macroeconomics are now receiving recognition side-by-side with mainstream developments. See, for example, Snowden, Vane, and Wynarczyk (1994). Other related intellectual currents are emanating from work on realism in economic thought severally produced by Lawson (1994a, c) and Mäki (1990). There is also a lively Austrian-inspired literature on competitive

banking in the works of White (1989), Selgin (1988), Selgin and White (1994), and Cowen and Kroszner (1994). Similarly, an Austrian (i.e., Böhm-Bawerkian) literature on capital theory has been produced by Faber (1986). In the field of comparative economic systems there is Lavoie (1985), Boettke (1990c, 1993), Prychitko (1991) and Kornai (1992). Evolutionary economics has witnessed attempts to combine Austrian with other strains of thought in the work of Langlois (1992) and Witt (1992). One cannot fail to mention, as well, the international industry devoted to the analysis and criticism of the work of Friedrich A. Hayek. The contributions to this literature are vast. Mention should be made, however, of Birner and van Zijp (1994) and Colonna and Hagemann (1994a, b).

4 In recent years, the theme of economics patterned-after-physics has been examined critically by Philip Mirowski (1989).

5 Although fashionable, a very sharp division between philosophy and science is insupportable. Philosophy is more "scientific" than is commonly supposed, and science is more "philosophical". See Gjertsen (1989). For a discussion of realism in economics, see Mäki (1990).

6 "He" is used in its traditional generic sense. Readers who are uncomfortable with this may mentally replace "he" or "his" with "it" or "its" because the actors, agents or individuals discussed are constructs rather than flesh-and-blood people.

7 We are quite aware that there are important differences on the conception of time among Husserl, Bergson, James and Whitehead (the latter two are cited below). For our purposes these differences are not important. We are making use of the characteristics these ideas have in common to illuminate issues in economics; this is not a detailed work in philosophy. On differences among Bergson, James, and Whitehead, see Capek (1971: passim).

8 In ordinary parlance we reserve the word "novel" for differences that are relatively large or interesting. The change that is a necessary part of our perception of time's flow may be boring. This is, in part, responsible for the mistaken view that it is possible for real time to flow without anything new happening.

9 Cycles may or may not qualify as novel. If agents think and make decisions at the level of the putatively identical cycles, then there is no novelty and hence no time consciousness. If, on the other hand, the cycle is a phenomenon visible only to the analyst, then the agents may experience change within the cycle. For these agents there is novelty and hence time consciousness.

10 The reader ought to keep in mind that we are talking about time *consciousness*, and not physical time.

11 Lawson locates the common perspective at a fairly high level of abstraction in the philosophical tradition of "transcendental realism." This set of ideas holds, *inter alia*, that (1) the world is "structured," that is, not reducible to the events of sense experience, and (2) these structures are "intransitive,"

that is, they exist independently of their identification (Lawson, 1994, p. 513). Burczak (1994, pp. 31–58), on the other hand, discovers a common thread between Hayekian Austrianism and Post Keynesianism in their "postmodern moments." The emphasis here is on "constituted subjectivity" or, more specifically, on the way in which socially-constituted knowledge and meaning affect human action (pp. 34–6). These two conceptions of a common perspective do not appear, at least *prima facie*, to be entirely consistent.

12 "Disequilibrating" refers to a movement away from equilibrium. There are different meanings of the term "equilibrium" in modern Austrian economics. The meaning in this subsection is that of full coordination of plans, i.e., (1) the mutual consistency or compatibility of plans (ex ante and ex post) among agents who are trading with each other; and (2) the exhaustion of profit – arbitrage – opportunities. Thus, even if Jones (seller) and Smith (buyer) are both happy to trade apples at 25 cents each, this is not an equilibrium if Wilson would be willing to buy from Jones at 35 cents each. An equilibrium in this sense is not equivalent simply to maximizing behavior. Furthermore, equilibrium requires more than that the interacting parties have consistent beliefs. There must also be a dissemination of knowledge to all parties to whom it would be relevant.

13 If favorable surprises have implications for action (rather than are simply windfalls) then, as surprises, they will cause disruption of the plans of others, and hence a certain amount of disequilibration. For a view that excludes favorable surprises from the process of equilibration, see Fisher (1983, pp. 86–94) and the analysis of Fisher by Ikeda (1990, pp. 81–4). Consider also, at this point, the statement by Joan Robinson (1971, p. 53): "[I]t is impossible for a system to *get into* a position of equilibrium, for the very nature of equilibrium is that the system is already in it, and has been in it for a certain length of past time." The very factors responsible for the existing state of disequilibrium may make movement into a position of full equilibrium impossible.

14 Compare Franklin Fisher (1983, p. 91): "In an ongoing economy, what constitutes an 'exogenous' shock? How is such an original shock to be distinguished from the 'endogenous' shock brought about by adjustment to the original shock?"

15 For an interesting discussion of the disappearance of the entrepreneur from neoclassical economics, see Barreto (1989).

16 To the extent that the relevant short-run equilibrium is defined largely by mistake-induced "data," then Kirzner's implicit welfare standard is not independent of the analytical standard around which he organizes his description of the market process. This "merger" raises profound questions beyond the scope of our inquiry here. Furthermore, from a long-run perspective the accumulation of many errors along the adjustment path should cause us to revise our conception of the welfare properties of the market to one which is primarily based on the comparison of institutions. For the

original statement of the comparative-institutions approach, see Hayek (1948a, p. 100, 105–6).

17 Vaughn's failure to recognize the importance of this endogenous shift in equilibrium leads her to say that Kirzner has not changed his position (Vaughn, 1994, p. 149).

18 It is instructive to compare Kirzner's more recent approach (1992) with that of Lachmann (1977). Consider, first, Kirzner (1992, p. 35): "Although theory insists on the formal validity of the market coordinating process under all relevant circumstances, it does not claim that the tendencies which make up the process operate with uniform power at all times and in all contexts. It is easy to imagine circumstances where the power of the coordinative market process is completely swamped by the volatility of change and by the high incidence of entrepreneurial error. No doubt there have been moments in capitalist history where this has been the case." The reader should now decide to what extent Lachmann (1977, pp. 189–90) is saying much the same thing "[T]o deny the significance of general equilibrium is not to deny the existence of equilibrating forces. It is merely to demand that we must not lose sight of the forces of disequilibrium and make a comprehensive assessment of all the forces operating in the light of our general knowledge about the formation and dissemination of human knowledge."

19 I am more confident of my understanding of Lachmann's position than of Shackle's. I discussed these issues with Lachmann over a period of many years. Nevertheless, those who believe that Shackle sees no order in economic affairs should read Shackle (1969, pp. 4–5).

20 Any attempt to make the concepts of "nearer" to or "farther" from equilibrium precise is fraught with difficulty. Nevertheless, it seems (intuitively) that there is an important analogy here with the behavior of physical systems whose equilibration properties vary with their distance from equilibrium.

21 The ideas in the preceding two paragraphs bear an obvious relationship to Leijonhufud's concept of the "corridor" (1981, pp. 109–10). Within the corridor, that is, when the economy is near overall equilibrium, deviations bring the system back to equilibrium; outside of the corridor (i.e., far from equilibrium) they move the system farther away.

22 In this section we pay exclusive attention to endogenous change on unhampered markets. On the other hand, Sanford Ikeda (forthcoming) has developed this idea in the context of state intervention in the economy. He shows how endogenous change can propel a system from the minimal state to a highly-interventionist state.

23 The distinction between subjective and objective novelty is important because the first involves pure dissemination and thus can be modelled by the economist in a way that permits a neat separation between the endogenous and exogenous. The to-be-disseminated knowledge can be viewed as given to the analyst (if not to the agents). Its dissemination amounts to discovery of the system's data and thus is modelled as equilibrating. On the

other hand, completely new knowledge cannot be taken as given even to the analyst and should be modelled as disruptive of equilibrium.

24 "Spontaneously" does not mean in a completely undetermined manner. Instead it means *under*determined, that is, the determinants of a particular event do not necessitate its production.

25 A system in overall equilibrium encourages greater division of labor and specialization than a system outside of equilibrium. This is because the division of labor, which makes greater production possible, is limited by the extent of the market. The market has a greater "extent" the more often traders can rely on selling their greater output and the more frequently consumers can buy from the market. Thus the extent of the market varies directly with the degree of coordination among market participants or inversely with the distance from overall equilibrium. See Loasby (1991, pp. 9–13).

26 "Order is desirable not for keeping everything in place but for generating new powers that would otherwise not exist" (Hayek, 1988, p. 79).

27 Young Choi Back (1993) has similarly modelled equilibrium as a "regime of convention" (p. 99) which in turn is based on a paradigmatic learning structure.

28 This, however, is just speculation at this stage of our endeavor. Much more work will be necessary to test this idea. Nevertheless, see the stimulating observations and analysis of Denzau and North (1994).

29 Nathan Rosenberg (1969, p. 1) observed this phenomenon in his study of the inducements to technological progress: "One of the things which is perfectly obvious about societies which have achieved high degrees of industrialization is that they have acquired unusual skills in problem-solving activities."

# 1

# An Overview of Subjectivist Economics

> The social object of skilled investment should be to defeat the *dark forces of time and ignorance* which envelop our future. *John Maynard Keynes (1964, p. 155; emphasis added)*

> That subjectivists of different schools, that is to say, all those who view the market as a pattern of meaningful utterances of the human mind, will in the future be able to find common ground seems to us to lie distinctly within the realm of possibility. *Ludwig M. Lachmann (1984, pp. 13–14)*

This book began as an attempt to survey and restate the basic features of "Austrian" economic theory. As we examined the fundamental presuppositions of the theory, however, we realized that in order to accomplish our task we had, in a sense, to go beyond it. At the very heart of Austrian economics lies a common ground with some other schools of economic thought. This common ground has long been recognized as the essence of the Austrian contribution to economics: subjectivism. For most economists, unfortunately, subjectivism denotes either exclusively the supposedly complete subjective theory of value or the idea that scientific theories should be personal and hence never subject to testing. Both meanings are, however, thoroughly inaccurate.

On the most general level, subjectivism refers to the presupposition that the contents of the human mind, and hence decision-making, are not rigidly determined by external events. Subjectivism makes room for the creativity and autonomy of individual choice. Dealing as it does with the individual mind and individual decision-making, it is also intimately related to methodological individualism. This is the view that overall market outcomes ought to be explained in terms of individual acts of choice. Thus, for the Austrians, and for subjectivists generally, economics is first and foremost about the thoughts leading up to choice, and not about things or the interaction of objective magnitudes (Morgenstern, 1972, p. 702, Shackle, 1972, p. 66).

In this chapter we first examine the basic implications of subjectivism for economic theory. We then discuss the importance of these implications. In a third section we outline the common ground between Austrians and (post-) Keynesians while, at the same time, recognizing the unique Austrian contributions to subjectivist economics. Finally, we briefly discuss the contents of the remaining chapters.

## TIME AND IGNORANCE

The relative autonomy of individual choice clearly implies the imperfect predictability of the future consequences of choices. When an individual decides to embark upon a particular course of action, the consequences will depend, in part, on what courses of action other individuals are, or will be, choosing. A world in which there is autonomous or creative decision-making is one in which the future is not merely unknown, but *unknowable*. There is nothing in the present state of the world that enables us to predict the future state because the latter is underdetermined by the former. (This, of course, does not preclude the analyst from, *ex post*, making the once-future intelligible on the basis of what happened in the past.) Subjectivism and action under uncertainty are thus inseparable ideas.

There are two complementary ways of conceptualizing the unknowability of the future. The first is to develop the dynamic conception of time (variously known as "real," "historical," or "subjective" time). The other is to explicate the notion of ignorance and its corollary, radical or "genuine" uncertainty. We begin with a discussion of real time.

### *Real Time*

In a certain respect, neoclassical economics has not changed much in the past 50 years. Many of the recent "innovations" in theory simply extend the static maximizing apparatus to allegedly dynamic issues. In particular, time is still most frequently conceived in purely static terms. As such, it is analogized to space: Just as an individual may allocate portions of space (land) to certain purposes, he can also allocate portions of time to certain activities. In principle, time and perfect predictability are compatible. The dynamic conception of time, on the other hand, is time perceived as a flow of events. Implicit in this idea of a flow is that of novelty or true surprise. The individual's experience of today's events itself makes tomorrow's perceptions of events different than it otherwise would be. As an individual adds to the stock of his experiences, his perspective changes and so both the present and the future are affected by the past flow of events. Flows, however, are continuous, and hence the individual's perspective changes right up to the moment of any experience. This renders perfect prediction of the experience impossible. Since all individuals are similarly affected, and since, as we have seen, the consequences of an individual's course of action depends on what others will do, this idea of time has implications for decision-making. Choices made in real time are thus never made with complete knowledge (either deterministic or stochastic) of their consequences. The recognition of this fact by individuals is the source of rule-following behavior and, on a social level, of the development of institutions. We have more to say on this later in the chapter and in future chapters.

### *Ignorance*

In all variants of neoclassical economics there is a presumption of knowledge on the part of economic agents. In its older form the presumption was of perfect knowledge and foresight, and in its more recent form it has been that of perfect stochastic knowledge and foresight. Thus, 30 years ago agents knew with certainty the price charged for a given product in both the current period and in all future periods; today, on the other hand, they are likely to know the probability distribution of current prices and the underlying stochastic structure that generates future prices. Even when agents are assumed not to know the complete probability distribution, such a distribution is hypothesized to "exist" in some objective way. This is then used as the basis of a story about how individuals gradually learn the distribution. None of these approaches, however, captures the idea of ignorance in the sense intended by subjectivists. Ignorance is not something that, at least at some level, can be avoided or overcome. It is not a state of imperfect knowledge that some process asymptotically eliminates. As long as we remain in a world of real time, unexpected change is inevitable and ignorance is ineradicable. Subjectivists therefore are not in sympathy with analytical devices that eliminate this object of study. Ignorance should not be transformed into a variant of knowledge.

The neoclassical method of modeling uncertainty essentially denies the fundamental tenet of subjectivism: the autonomy of individual choice. To portray the uncertain future as an objective probability distribution defined over an exhaustive set of events is to make the claim that the future is merely unknown. Thus, it is in principle knowable because the future exists out there independently of the autonomous choices of individuals. Or, to put it another way, the neoclassical modeling techniques abolish the autonomy of the human mind. This is the central problem inherent in most formulations of rational expectations equilibria.

The movement toward a "subjectivist" theory of probability in some areas of economics has no doubt been an improvement from our perspective. Yet most of this literature neglects a fundamental aspect of ignorance: the (perceived) unlistability of all possible outcomes. It is not merely that we do not know which possibility out of a given set will occur, but the set itself is unbounded. Subjective probability thus reflects subjectivism in its static form; while unbounded possibility sets reflect the essentially dynamic aspect of subjectivism. Real time and ignorance belong together.

## THE IMPORTANCE OF TIME AND IGNORANCE

Does any of this matter? A critic might admit that real time and ignorance do describe aspects of the world in which we live, but he might claim that they are unimportant (or even counterproductive) from the perspective of deriving useful economic implications. Most of the rest of this book is, in effect, an answer to this hypothetical critic. We hope to show in very detailed fashion that subjectivism has important implications for economic theory and, ultimately, for applied economics. It is, however, important to make clear that contemporary economics overemphasizes the importance of "useful implications." This is the consequence of an essentially instrumentalist view of social science. The presupposition is that we really know *nothing* about individual decision-making, aside from what can be corroborated in econometric tests of aggregative (market) data. We reject this naive instrumentalism (Caldwell, 1982, pp. 173–88). While the implications for overall market behavior are important, it is also important to be faithful to the structure of human action as we know it to exist (Mises, 1966, pp. 11–29, 92–142; Rothbard, 1970, pp. 1–66). In this sense, we try to steer a middle course between pure apriorism and pure instrumentalism.

The most fundamental or general implication of time and ignorance, to which we have already alluded, is that economics must abandon its traditional static mold. "[A] theory which takes serious account of time and ignorance must be a theory of processes, not of states – not even dynamic states" (Loasby, 1976, p. 220). Since all action takes place in real time and under genuine uncertainty, the actions of individuals are unlikely to be perfectly coordinated. This means, of course, that people will be frustrated in efforts to achieve their goals. Hence all market activity, as the outgrowth of individual goal-directed action, can be rendered intelligible as a *process of attempting* to correct errors and coordinate behavior. This process will obviously fail at times, and economics must also concern itself with the forces that promote error and discoordination. Sometimes these forces will be the result of purely exogenous changes in the "data," but at other times they will be the result of endogenous changes. Thus, the market process is literally unending.

Time and ignorance not only make economic processes necessary, they also affect the very character of these processes. A process economics differs from one incorporating dynamic states insofar as the former is not deterministic. There is no stable endpoint toward which the process must lead, nor a single path that it must follow. At least on a general level, our view shares much in common with that of Nelson and Winter (1982), who have developed a non-deterministic evolutionary economics. In their approach, as in ours, error and the correction of error are important facets in the dynamic process. In counter-distinction to the neoclassical approach, however, these errors do not wind down to a determinate equilibrium state. Thus, we have process or evolution without traditional equilibria.

A second extremely important effect of the explicit recognition of time and ignorance is a shift away from modeling all behavior as the result of mathematical maximization. The unboundedness of expectations – or, more specifically, of the possibilities and choice set envisaged by the actor – means that traditional maximization techniques are inapplicable (Loasby, 1976, p. 217). Consequently, actors are more appropriately modeled as following rules of thumb or "routines" (Nelson and Winter, 1982, pp. 14–21 and passim) at one end of the behavioral continuum, or as engaging in entrepreneurial discovery at the other end (Kirzner, 1973, 1979).

In the first case, many different perceptions of the environment, as well as different expectations, are each consistent with the same pattern of behavior. Rules provide, as it were, safe bounds for behavior in a relatively unbounded world. Institutions are the social crystallization of rule-following behavior or, in other words, the overall pattern of many individuals following a similar rule (Hayek, 1973, pp. 35–54). Thus, the circle is closed. Time and genuine uncertainty promote the following of rules and the development of institutions. The latter, in turn, serve to reduce, but not eliminate, the unboundedness of the economic system by providing the stable patterns of interaction.

In the second case, entrepreneurial discovery can be seen as an attempt to fill coordinative gaps in the system that arise from existence of time and ignorance. At the individual level, entrepreneurship consists of going beyond a given means–ends framework; it is the act of altering or creating the framework by discovering new ends and means. At the market level, entrepreneurs strive to discover (or create) possibilities that have been generally overlooked by other market participants. Entrepreneurs are, however, themselves subject to the effects of time and ignorance, and hence may often commit errors. These errors can be the source of further unpredictability and instability in the system. Nevertheless, it seems reasonable to believe that a world without profit-seeking entrepreneurial behavior is likely to be more unpredictable and unstable than a world with it.

A third implication of taking time and ignorance seriously is a greater emphasis on spontaneous or unintended consequences of individual action. Neoclassical economics in its purest form is uncomfortable with the idea of spontaneous consequences.

Wedded as it is to one or more species of knowledge, it strives to explain as many market phenomena as possible as the intended outgrowth of individual optimizing. In the economic analysis of law, for example, certain judge-made legal doctrines have been rationalized as promoting efficiency. While the process by which this supposedly comes about is somewhat mysterious, there is a clear implication that judges, at least implicitly, want it that way (Posner, 1977, pp. 15–191). Similarly, in at least one variant of the economics of the political process, tariffs, agricultural subsidies, minimum wages, and the like exist because they are efficient adaptations to individuals' redistributional demands (Peltzman, 1976; Becker, 1976b). Many, though not all, neoclassical rationalizations of aggregative phenomena are thus rooted in the view that "people get what they want."

The subjectivist research program, on the other hand, is to explain overall outcomes as the spontaneous, unintended product of social interactions. Under conditions of ignorance, no individual can predict fully the consequences of a chosen course of action. Hence he is bound to be at least somewhat surprised by the ultimate (aggregate) outcome. The world looks as if it is no part of his doing. The interaction of individuals' courses of action, the market process, is thus a kind of discovery procedure (Hayek, 1978). Through the knowledge that is revealed to him by this process each agent is able to surpass the limits of his own ignorance. No one individual or firm needs to know, or can know beforehand, how best to organize production, what products to produce, or even what raw materials to use. In the course of acting, an individual will learn more about the "environment" in which he operates.

The idea of spontaneous consequences and market discovery has significance for economic policy. It leads us away from the presumption that we can always improve matters by merely applying our (i.e., the planner's) *given* knowledge in the most efficient way. This is the view Hayek (1965) has called "constructivism." In contrast, Austrian subjectivists would argue that state economic planning deprives society of the knowledge gained through the market process and of the ability to surpass the limitations of individual knowledge (Lavoie, 1985). Thus, the ignorance of the individual constrains action at the central planning level to a far greater extent than at the market level.

## KEYNESIANISM AND THE AUSTRIAN CONTRIBUTIONS

### *Keynes*

It is clear from the first epigraph of this chapter that Keynes was no stranger to the economics of time and ignorance. Recognition of the power of the "dark forces" was central to his conception of the economic system. In the first instance, the "state of long-term expectations," which is important in determining the rate of investment, might "be subject to [autonomous] waves of optimistic and pessimistic sentiment . . . where no solid basis exists for a reasonable calculation" (Keynes, 1964, p. 154). As we have seen, a "reasonable" or, more exactly, an optimizing calculation is not possible in an unbounded context. In addition, Keynes saw the importance of subjectivism for short-run output decisions which are influenced by user cost. "User cost" is "the reduction in the value of . . . equipment due to using it as compared with not using it" now "and preserving it to be used later on" (1964, p. 70). The calculation of user cost obviously depends upon subjective guesses as to the future state of the market. Keynes sometimes also recognized that individual choice is the pivotal distinction between the natural and social sciences. In an important letter to Sir Roy Harrod, he said that, if the natural sciences were to be treated as the social sciences, then "it (would be) as though the fall of the apple to the ground depended on the apple's motives" (1973, p. 300).

Despite the evidence presented above, it is only quite recently that the subjectivist aspects of Keynes' thought have been more widely recognized. In part, this is because the reformulation of his work in general equilibrium terms, arising out of the neoclassical synthesis, obliterated the subjectivist component (Davidson, 1981, p. 159). More importantly, perhaps, there exists a deep contradiction in the *General Theory* itself between the mechanical, aggregative method and the non-formalized subjectivist message (Lachmann, 1984, p. 7). Unfortunately, Keynes never resolved this contradiction, and thus it prevented him from seeing the full implications of subjectivism. His statement about the dark forces of time and ignorance was made in the context of advocating government management of major investment decisions. He apparently never saw the limitations that real time and ignorance place on policy-makers.

### *Post-Keynesianism*

In recent years a largely American branch of the Cambridge (UK) school, known as post-Keynesian economics, has arisen to carry forth the subjectivist aspects of Keynes' system. For a long time these had been buried and almost forgotten within the Hicksian neoclassical synthesis. Now, fortunately, they are being revived and developed. Paul Davidson has conveniently summarized the post-Keynesian perspective in three propositions (1981, pp. 158–61):

(1) the economy is a process in historical (real) time;
(2) in a world where uncertainty and surprises are unavoidable, expectations have an unavoidable and significant effect on economic outcomes;
(3) economic and political institutions are not negligible and, in fact, play an extremely important role in determining real-world economic outcomes.

The reader will be hard pressed to find any significant differences between these propositions and the argument of this chapter. What is even more surprising is that Davidson's explication of the meaning of these propositions increases, rather than reduces, the area of overlap. It is evident that there is much common ground between post-Keynesian subjectivism and Austrian subjectivism. Cross-fertilization between these two schools is, however, exceedingly rare, although the possibilities for mutually advantageous interchange seem significant.

### *Austrian Contributions*

We have already discussed what may be the most important distinctive contribution of the Austrian variant of subjectivism. Austrians have stressed the view of the market process as an engine of discovery. Just as real time implies genuine uncertainty about the future, it equally implies that truly novel things can be learned by economic agents. One interpretation of the statement that we live in a world of real time and ignorance is simply that we cannot predict the knowledge we shall gain in the future (Popper, 1964, pp. vi–vii). Learning, for Austrians, is not merely plugging in new values of variables in an otherwise unchanged learning function. It involves a structural shift in knowledge, i.e., a change in the learning functions themselves. The market process is both the source and the manifestation of these structural changes. In the absence of such a process, economic planners must address the question of how they can acquire the requisite information necessary to implement their plans successfully.

There are other distinctive Austrian contributions to subjectivist economics. These, however, are less easy to state in summary fashion, but some will be examined in greater detail later in this book. Austrians have made fundamental contributions to, among other areas, interest theory (Fetter, 1977; Rothbard, 1970, pp. 313–86), capital theory (Lachmann, 1956; Kirzner, 1966), the theory of money (Mises, 1953; White, 1984), competition and entrepreneurship (Kirzner, 1973; 1979), and business cycle theory (Hayek, 1969; O'Driscoll, 1977; Wainhouse, 1982). The common thread underlying all of these analyses is the extension of subjectivism beyond the point to which it had previously been developed. This is not to say that in all of these areas the subjectivist approach has been completed or is fully adequate. It is rather to claim that the subjectivist ideas of time and ignorance have been infused into the analyses in a way that changes the basic questions and issues.

## OVERVIEW OF THE REST OF THE BOOK

This book is divided into two parts. In the first we present, in more detailed fashion, the analytical framework that we sketched in this chapter. We discuss subjectivism, knowledge, decisions, time, uncertainty, and equilibrium. In the second part we apply this theoretical framework to specific economic subject areas such as competition and monopoly, political economy, capital theory, and monetary theory. In neither part will the reader find much in the way of explicit formal modeling. This reflects a conscious decision by the authors. In the first place, we believe that presenting the conceptual foundations of our approach is both logically and heuristically prior to any modeling effort. Second, and perhaps more important, many of the formal analytical tools used by economists today necessarily preclude the phenomena in which we are interested. In fact, one of the reasons contemporary economics is still fundamentally static is that the mechanics of optimization and the standard assumptions of equilibrium are not consistent with genuine process analysis.

## *Framework*

In the next chapter we distinguish our concept of subjectivism from the older, static idea that derives from the subjective theory of value. In so doing, we discuss the meaning of creative choice and the role of non-deterministic explanation. Our general conclusion is that we must avoid both the position that creative choice is impossible, and the position that all choice is creative and unbounded. Creativity can exist only within a framework that provides at least some degree of predictability.

In chapter 3 we analyze the problem of knowledge from a subjectivist perspective. Foremost among the issues we discuss are the nature and process of learning, the difference between knowledge of economic actors and knowledge of the scientist, the division of knowledge in society, and the role of knowledge in institutions. The chapter concludes with a re-examination of utility theory. Here the subjectivity of both blades of the Marshallian scissors (utility and cost) is explained and applied to a disequilibrium context.

Chapter 4 is a detailed examination of the differences between "Newtonian" (analytic or static) time and the dynamic conception that we have already briefly mentioned. We discuss the role of each concept of time in specific economic models. In particular, we examine the implications of real time for the study of economic processes. The chapter concludes with a discussion of the conceptual relation between Newtonian and real time.

The fifth chapter explores the most important implication of ignorance: genuine uncertainty. Here the interrelation between uncertainty and equilibrium is explored. We find that genuine uncertainty is incompatible with traditional ideas of equilibrium, including that of stochastic equilibrium. In this context we spend a good deal of time analyzing the "endogenous" uncertainty in Keynes' famous beauty contest and Morgenstern's Holmes–Moriarity story. An alternative equilibrium construct is proposed ("pattern coordination") that is consistent with endogenous or genuine uncertainty.

*Applications*

Chapter 6 is a detailed study of our claim that the market process is a discovery procedure. We trace the logical evolution of the concept of competition from that of a state of affairs to a process of attaining or approaching equilibrium to, finally, a ceaseless "mechanism" of discovery. We then go on to show that market processes, in the widest sense, consist not only (or even primarily) of optimizing behavior but also of rule-following behavior. The latter is, of course, ultimately related to the social role of institutions. Both rules and institutions are, in turn, as we have seen, consequences of the conditions of ignorance under which individuals face the future.

In chapter 7 we apply the theoretical structure developed in the previous chapter to a number of important issues in political economy. Real time, ignorance, and genuine uncertainty, as we have seen, have significant implications for economic policy. In this chapter we apply those general insights to pollution control through tax policy and to antitrust regulation. Our general conclusion is that much regulation, in order to be effective, presupposes the kind of knowledge available only through market processes. Paradoxically, then, the regulators need the very process that their regulation is at least in part, designed to supplant.

Chapter 8 applies subjectivist ideas to the theory of capital goods and associated "macro" and monetary issues. The Austrian concept of a production structure is introduced and the nature of capital complementarities within that structure is explored. The heterogeneity of capital goods is shown to be crucial to any theory of economic processes. Specifically, the whole process of capital recombinations or changes in the production structure is obliterated by neoclassical theories of capital homogeneity. In those theories there is nothing to recombine and no production structure to change. Therefore, subjectively perceived differences in capital goods are intimately related to the dynamic market process.

Chapter 9 begins with an analysis and application of the Mengerian theory of the origin of money. As we shall see, Menger's theory embodies almost every important aspect of subjectivist economics: methodological individualism, emphasis on expectations, and a market process of discovery. One important conclusion we draw from his theory is that even a basic economic institution like money is a part of the ongoing market process. Hence, attempts by government to modify or regulate monetary institutions must take account of this process. The final part of chapter 9 discusses the Wicksell–Mises–Hayek theory of economic fluctuations. Here the subjectivist theory of capital goods and the production structure, developed in chapter 8, is integrated with a theory of the cycle. The chapter concludes with a review of new evidence corroborating the Austrian cycle theory, as well as an analysis of the relevance of rational expectations to this theory.

Chapter 10 is a concluding chapter in which we identify some areas of future research and suggest applications of the approach developed in the previous nine chapters.

# Part I

# Framework

# 2

# Static versus Dynamic Subjectivism

Economic theory is unending, because we are confronted with an *open system*. The idea we could have a (closed) "system of economic theory", say, of the Walrasian type, is a futile one. *Oskar Morgenstern (1972, p. 702)*

## THE QUESTIONS

Proponents of different schools of economic thought have traditionally emphasized the conflicting answers that their respective schools have given the great economic questions. Recently, however, it has become evident that what really separates schools of thought is, in large part, the asking of different questions (Robinson, 1977). Therefore, it seems appropriate to begin our discussion of subjectivist economics in general, and the Austrian approach in particular, with a precise statement of the class of questions that we propose to ask. Specifically, it is necessary to address two issues: (1) What is the "level of reality" in which we are interested? (2) What is our research policy – what precisely are the questions within the chosen level of analysis?

### *Subjective Meaning as the Phenomenon*

Each science specifies, implicitly or explicitly, the level of reality in which it is interested. "Levels" demarcate the different aspects of what, from a more general point of view, might be considered the same phenomenon. Man, for example, may be studied from the perspectives of physics, physiology, medicine, chemistry, biology, and many other disciplines. The level of reality in which we are interested is the realm of purposes, plans, valuations, and expectations. In other words, we are interested in the realm of *subjective meaning.*[1] The objects of economic activity are thus not even definable except in terms of what actors perceive them to be. A price is not merely a number placed on a label but, more fundamentally, the conditions of exchange on which A and B purposefully interact. This world of subjective meaning is inextricably bound up with the world of everyday life. It rests on our "experience of the existence of other human beings and of the meaning of their actions," which "is certainly the first and most original *empirical* observation man makes" (Schutz, 1954, p. 265; emphasis added).

Having identified the domain of relevance, the economist is now in a position to observe, at least in a preliminary way, patterns of social interaction. These patterns are not the physical coordinates of commodity stocks or quantities of capital goods. Rather, they are the coherent ways in which individuals who are attempting to achieve various goals typically interact. Speculative markets, for example, can be understood as attempts by individuals with different expectations each to "buy low and sell high." No amount of study of the physical attributes of the commodities in question will make such markets intelligible. It is impossible even to conceive of the term "speculative" in purely physical terms. Recognition of the realm of subjective meaning is therefore a prerequisite for identification of the organized phenomena in which we are interested.

## *General Research Policy*

The task of economics goes beyond the preliminary recognition of certain patterns of interaction based on subjective meaning. There are, in addition, the three further, yet closely related, tasks: (1) more precisely identifying interaction patterns; (2) specifying their logical or static "origins"; and (3) explaining the historical or causal processes that give rise to them.

A science of subjective meaning permits a more precise recognition of interaction patterns than is possible on the basis of preliminary or commonsense observational theories (Hayek, 1955, pp. 55–6). A more exact understanding of the concepts of rent and supply elasticity, for example, places us in a position to see a common element in exchanges that are far removed from the original context of land transactions. Rent can thereby be seen as an ubiquitous economic phenomenon. None of this involves a denial of the original subjective meaning contexts with which we began our pattern recognition. On the contrary, we are simply engaging in the refinement of our ability to recognize such patterns.[2] The abstract concept of rent is thoroughly suffused with subjective meaning because, apart from that, no sense can be attached to constitutive terms like transfer price and the perception of alternative opportunities on which the latter is based.

To understand the subjective meaning of a price is not automatically to understand the relation of that price to the valuations of all individuals in a market. How does it come about that consumers and producers with a myriad of different valuations can create or tend to create a single price? The theory of price determination under static conditions enables the economist to "build up" the market price from given individual valuations. This does not specify causal processes in which learning and the transmission of information are involved. However, it does demonstrate how the aggregate phenomenon and its subjective meaning is, in turn, built up from the meanings of many individuals (Hayek, 1955, pp. 36–42).

Finally, to understand the subjective meaning of a price and how it can, in a static sense, be recomposed from the valuations of individuals is only the first step toward a genuine causal explanation. Causal explanations involve the description of processes through time and hence must allow for learning. A dynamic theory theory of price formation consists not only of showing how individual valuations interact to form prices but also how the acquisition of knowledge and the projection of expectations are involved. Again, none of this requires any deviation from the subjectivist character of our discipline because learning and expectations are pre-eminent subjective-meaning concepts.

In the foregoing paragraphs we have outlined, in effect, three major steps in our research program.

1. On the basis of commonsense observational constructs, the empirical reality of intended meanings is perceived. In a preliminary way, patterns of social interaction (e.g. money, prices, etc.) are identified.

2. Further refinement of these patterns and identification of still others is achieved by a more precise conceptualization of the

commonsense observational categories. The scientist eliminates their concrete associations and builds up an abstract or general framework of subjective meaning. Substitution, complementarity, elasticity, money, prices are all examples of such abstract subjective-meaning concepts. They are essentially constructs of commonsense constructs (Schutz, 1953) i.e., the distillation or typification of everyday concepts.

3. The final stage of analysis is achieved when the economist recomposes or builds up, either statically or dynamically, the overall pattern (viewed as a "social fact") from its individual elements, i.e., the meanings of individual actors. The main feature that takes us beyond mere description of the phenomena is the attempt of the research program to show how these are the unintended outgrowth of purposeful behavior. More precisely, our self-imposed question is: *How can individuals acting in the world of everyday life unintentionally produce existing institutions or, more generally, the overall patterns of social interactions?*[3] (Compare Menger, 1963, p. 146.) The subjective meanings of actors do not directly, as by mere command, bring economic events into existence. Instead, there is a complex chain of mutually reinforcing actions that produces results beyond those that can be individually apprehended or intended.[4]

In the remaining sections of this chapter we shall examine the central features of subjectivism as a method. In particular, we shall contrast the method's two important forms: the traditional static subjectivism that emanates from the standard theory of consumer choice, and the more recent thoroughgoing variety that affirms the "creativity" of human decision-making. In a final section, the relationship and interdependency of these approaches will be examined. We shall conclude that both are necessary for a comprehensive analytical framework.

## THE METHOD OF SUBJECTIVISM

The mere posing of our question determines, in large part, the method that will be used in answering it. The methodological subjectivist constructs a model of an individual mind or a fictitious consciousness that is endowed with certain goals, constraints, knowledge and expectations. This *mind construct* (see the similar terms in Machlup, 1978a, p. 221) is then portrayed as engaging in activity that must bear an "understandable" relation to the phenomenon we wish to explain (Schutz, 1953). The familiar economic concepts of the consumer, producer, firm, and entrepreneur are all examples of a mind construct. Our preliminary investigation of the subjectivist method will then be centered around the following two issues: (1) the permissible contents that can be attributed to the mind construct, and (2) the meaning of an "understandable" relation.

Since we are concerned not with an actual real-world individual but only with a model of such an individual, the contents of its mind need be only those things necessary to generate the appropriate behavior. Whether it believes in the Virgin Birth is presumably irrelevant to an explanation of why the price of lima beans has risen. Thus, the imputed contents of our fictitious consciousness must satisfy a *minimum sufficiency* requirement.

The creator of the mind construct cannot attribute any type of knowledge to it that will ultimately rationalize the phenomenon in question. The construct ought to possess only that knowledge which, in terms of its position or what it deems relevant, would have been reasonable to acquire.[5] It is not appropriate to attribute to a farmer construct, for example, knowledge of demand and supply conditions in the steel industry or of the general equilibrium prices of the commodities he grows. Nevertheless, at some point we needn't explicitly account for the knowledge possessed by our construct if that is so general as to be warranted by merely its existence in a given society or its "human" character.

An "understandable" relation must be understandable in the structural terms of commonsense interpretation of everyday life. Hence the scientific constructs must be *consistent* with, although not identical to, the mental constructs of everyday life (Schutz, 1953). This follows from our statement of the research program's central question: How can we relate action in everyday life to the overall patterns of social interaction?

The above consistency requirement is met by preserving the basic structure of decision-making but not the individualized contents of particular decisions or plans. This structure moves beyond the mere logical implications of human action to include some of the typical contexts of such action. An incomplete, but illustrative, list of the common structural components of decision-making can be stated in five propositions.

(1) The decision to take a specific course of action is the outcome of a process of projecting and weighing the consequences of the various courses of action.
(2) This projecting is based on a stock of knowledge, part of which is individually acquired and part of which is socially transmitted through institutions.
(3) An individual's chosen courses of action fit into an overall plan.
(4) The social world consists of many such acting individuals.
(5) There is a social distribution of knowledge and plans and, consequently, of chosen courses of action. Not all individuals know or do the same things.

In the subsequent sections of this book these important components of decision making will be extended and integrated into a coherent theory of individual action. This theory, in turn, will be the basis for our overall analysis of the market process.

## DIMENSIONS OF SUBJECTIVISM

In the previous section we discussed the subjectivist method of mind constructs without acknowledging the two different forms that method can take. The first form is most closely related to the traditional subjective theory of value and we shall call it "static subjectivism." In this case, the mind is viewed as a passive filter through which the data of decision-making are perceived. To the extent that this filter can be understood, the whole process of decision-making is perfectly determinate. The second form, on the other hand, views the mind as an active, creative entity in which decision-making bears no determinate relationship to what went before. Here, decision-making is literally a "cut," a new beginning (Buchanan, 1982a). This form of subjectivism we shall call "dynamic subjectivism."

Static subjectivism is perfectly consistent with the well-known covering-law model of scientific explanation (Hempel and Oppenheim, 1965, pp. 246–51). In this model, explanation proceeds by way of an explanatory apparatus, consisting of logically antecedent conditions and a general ("covering") law. From the conjunction of the conditions and law, a statement of the event we are attempting to explain is logically derived. Thus, from the antecedent conditions of tastes and knowledge of the relevant constraints in conjunction with the law of constrained utility maximization, we are able to derive a statement of the consumer's bundle of choices. The explanatory schema appears to determine exactly the particular outcome. In principle, the outcome could have been predicted given complete knowledge of the antecedent conditions and appropriate laws before occurrence of the event (Hempel and Oppenheim, 1965, p. 243). This determinism-in-principle is closely related to the "apodictic" praxeological theorems of Mises (1966, pp. 30–71) and the "exact laws" of Menger (1963, p. 218). For both of these economists, there was a variant of subjectivism that had much in common with the rigidly deterministic systems of classical mechanics.

The deterministic ideal is not, however, a fully realizable research program. The most obvious problem is that it is rarely possible to specify the antecedent conditions and relevant law completely. All sorts of difficulties, both conceptual and pragmatic, stand in the way of such an achievement. Thus, static subjectivists must offer explanations that are incomplete even in terms of the theoretical framework in which they appear. A perfect fit between the explanatory schema and the relevant phenomenon is consequently out of reach.

Still more important are several considerations that make deterministic explanation unachievable *even in principle.* Recall that, from a statement of initial conditions and a general law, we derive a statement of the particular event. It is clearly impossible to relate this *statement* in a deterministic fashion to the actual real-world event. D. J. O'Connor explains this point concisely:

> No prediction can distinguish the predicted event in such a way as to discriminate it from any of the other possible events that could fall under the same set of measurements . . . . The statement which expresses our prediction is never capable of identifying without ambiguity one and only one event whose occurrence would satisfy the prediction, for a description can do no more than specify a *class* of closely similar events, whose differences lie beneath the threshold of discrimination . . . . (O'Connor, 1957, p. 313)[6]

A second reason why attempts at purely deterministic explanations must, in principle, fail arises from the fact that the "economy" is an open system (Morgenstern, 1972, p. 709). Conditions at the boundary of our analysis are always changing, thus upsetting our best efforts at prediction. For example, economists cannot explain the formation of tastes, and hence when these change the predicted effects of supply shifts may prove entirely wrong. To "close" the system would require building a model of an order of complexity far in excess of what the human mind seems capable. Everything that could possibly interact with the "economy" would have to be accounted for in a precise quantitative way. This, of course, cannot be done. As a consequence, explanations of a fairly complex phenomena usually must be limited to general "explanations of the principle" or of the class of such phenomena (Hayek, 1967b, 1967c) and hence cannot be deterministic.

The formidable obstacles in the path of rigid determinism have not, however, led to the abandonment of static subjectivism or the covering-law model of explanation. Machlup, for example, views determinateness as an ideal characteristic of a well constructed model (Machlup, 1978b, p. 280). All theoretical models should be deterministic in the sense that the statement of the phenomenon we wish to explain can be logically derived from the explanatory apparatus. Determinism is thus a feature of the model and not of the world. The applicability of a model in any given instance, on the other hand, is not determinate but may, in fact, be highly uncertain. From Machlup's perspective, then, indeterminism has no role in the context of model-building itself but presumably does have a role in the empirical application or testing of a model. As we argue next, this view is tenable *only* if indeterminism were unimportant to those whose behavior we are trying to explain. In such circumstances indeterminism could be treated as a residual unexplained variation in the relevant phenomena that is of interest only on the level of the analyst-observer. In principle, this cannot be the case, and thus we must reject Machlup's position.

The essential premise of dynamic subjectivism is that decisions are not the determinate result of clearly specifiable causes (Shackle, 1969, pp. 3–7). This fundamental premise manifests itself both in the learning process and in the formation of expectations. Genuine learning is not merely the result of a determinate processing of what is already known. It must go beyond those narrow confines and include unpredictable shifts in the method of processing itself. Similarly, expectations must not be confined to the discovery of an already-determined future. Much of the future is the result of the free, indeterminate decisions of actors and hence is actually created by them. Dynamic subjectivism is incompatible with rigid determinism and perfect predictability.

Dynamic subjectivism requires that the models themselves embody non-deterministic processes in an essential way. This is in sharp contrast to Machlup's suggestion that indeterminism be viewed as a feature of the model's applicability rather than of its structure. The reason for this difference is not merely a matter of taste. We contend that the actor *must* see his own decision-making as indeterminate and, hence, cannot be in a position to predict his actions. As a consequence, it is logically impermissible to develop mind constructs in which decisions are purely deterministic. This can be demonstrated in two useful ways.

Our first argument is derived from Karl Popper's demonstration that it is impossible for an individual to predict his own future knowledge (Popper, 1950, pp. 117–33, 173–95; O'Hear, 1980, p. 141). Because actions are based on the individual's stock of knowledge, if he cannot predict his future knowledge, he also cannot predict his future decisions.

Suppose P (predictor) has complete knowledge of his initial circumstances at $t_1$ as well as of the appropriate theories of learning, and wishes to predict his knowledge at $t_3$. Can this be done? P will take some finite amount of time, say until $t_2$, in order to deduce his state of knowledge at $t_3$. However, the knowledge gained at $t_2$ will affect P's state at $t_3$. Again, it will take a finite amount of time, until $t_3$, to determine precisely how this will affect his state at $t_3$. But then complete self-prediction of future states of knowledge is obviously impossible.[7] If P cannot have his knowledge at $t_3$ until $t_3$, he also cannot know exactly what he will *decide* at $t_3$ until $t_3$.[8] Thus, no individual can have total foreknowledge of his decisions.

A second, similar, argument is based on the proof that the ability to foresee one's own decision at $t_2$ *logically precludes* the ability to decide at $t_2$ (Schick, 1979, pp. 240–2). Suppose an individual, P, is both "deductively thorough" – that is, he believes all of the logical consequences of his initial beliefs – and "belief-retentive" – that is, between the point of attempted prediction and the point of choice he will not change his beliefs. Let us further suppose that at $t_1$ P knows his preferences, prices and income at $t_2$. Because he is deductively thorough at each instant in time, he also knows that he will decide X at $t_2$. Therefore, P believes at $t_1$ that it is true that X is the case. Because P is belief-retentive, he will also believe that X is the case at the moment of his decision. If X is *already* the case, then where are the options at $t_2$? Clearly, there can be none, and hence the decision was already made at $t_1$, the moment of the "prediction." Hence self-prediction of a decision can only be made simultaneously with the decision. This, of course, means that self-prediction is impossible.

From the foregoing two arguments, we draw an important general conclusion. Mind constructs that yield the required behavior as a determinate implication of initial conditions and a theory cannot be genuinely dynamic. If we allow time to pass, then we must in effect be claiming that the individual can predict his own decisions. Consider, for example, a determinate choice-theoretic model of a process. This would require the postulation of a mind whose decisions at $t_2$ are perfectly determined by its own self-conscious[9] state at $t_1$. If this is logically impossible, as we have argued, then such a model would be inconsistent, or, more exactly, would be based on inconsistent foundations. "Surprise" is thus integral to the lives of individual actors.

The covering-law model, therefore, does not provide an adequate form of explanation for dynamically subjectivist theories. An essential feature of these theories is that logical deducibility of the statement of the relevant decision or phenomenon is no longer possible. This, of course, does not mean that explanation is no longer possible, but merely that one variety of explanation has been excluded. "Not deducibility, but intelligibility constitutes the basic feature of the logic of explanation" (Yolton, 1959, p. 207; see also Lachmann, 1971, pp. 36–38; Lachmann, 1943, p. 14). One clear and useful meaning we can attach to the intelligibility relationship is that the choice-theoretic explanatory schema must render the given phenomenon more likely than if the particular model had not been presented. This does not imply predictability, or even a high likelihood, but merely *increased* likelihood of occurrence.[10] "The need [is] for favourable relevance rather than high mathematical probability" (Cohen, 1977, p. 300). Thus, within a mind-construct model a number of alternative decisions can be seen as possible, but, given the model, that which actually did occur is rendered more likely than it would have been given some alternative model. On this view of the role of a theoretical explanation, the observed decision need not be the most likely of the various alternatives. Even the least likely of these can, if it were to occur, be explained by the model so long as there is "favourable relevance."[11]

Favorable relevance may be viewed from either an *ex ante* or *ex post* perspective. In an *ex ante* sense, the hypothesis will have a certain *marginal* predictive value. What might have appeared highly unlikely before the hypothesis was proffered may now appear somewhat less unlikely. From an *ex post* perspective, on the other hand, the relationship between an event, after it has already occurred, and an explanation will be such that the "retrospective likelihood" of an event is increased in the light of the explanation (Rizzo and Arnold, 1980, p. 1408 and passim; Rizzo, 1981, p. 1030). One of the main differences between a retrospective calculation of likelihood and an *ex ante* calculation is that, *ex post*, we may know more about what has happened to conditions at the boundary of the system. Thus, after the price of soybeans rises we may know, at least indirectly, what happened to tastes or expectations. Consequently, it might be possible to construct an explanation with favorable relevance only after the event has occurred and not before. In either situation, the explanation can render the event more intelligible.

There is another method of relating an explanatory schema to a given event that is consistent with dynamic subjectivism. This is captured in the idea of "pattern explanation" or "pattern prediction" (Hayek 1967b). If a model yields a determinate implication for a *class* of phenomena, each element of that class will be perfectly consistent with the explanatory schema. Thus, with respect to the specific event itself, the schema is not deterministic. Other events in the class could have occurred without producing any change in the proffered explanation. This concept of non-deterministic explanation is consistent with the favorable relevance view discussed above in the case where the competing hypothesis entirely excludes the event in question. Then, of course, the likelihood of that event will be greater on the accepted hypothesis than on its competitor. In most cases, however, the two methods are not identical. Nevertheless, for the broad purpose of specifying principles of explanation consistent with dynamic subjectivism, both the favorable relevance and pattern explanation ideas are acceptable.

## RELATIONSHIP BETWEEN STATIC AND DYNAMIC SUBJECTIVISM

While there are extremely important differences between static and dynamic subjectivism, there are also important logical dependencies and interrelations between them. This section will be devoted to an analysis of that relationship. We shall divide the discussion into two arguments.

(1) Within a broader perspective, both the static and dynamic approaches are consistent.
(2) The static form of decision-making (or, more precisely, its real-world analogue) is a necessary empirical foundation for "creative" decision-making.

The static subjectivist view is that four factors determine choice: (1) the ordinal ranking of goals or wants, (2) knowledge of the relationship between courses of action (or commodities) and want satisfaction, (3) knowledge of prices, and (4) knowledge of the income constraint. This is determination in a purely logical sense. The four factors are mental constructs: we have recomposed the choice in terms of its constituent parts. So the choice is determined in a causal sense by itself; or, more precisely, the theory does not tell us what the causal determinants are. This has been recognized in terms of the ranking of wants by Schutz – "goals do not exist at all before the choice" (1967, p. 67) – and by Mises – "The scale of value is nothing but a constructed tool of thought" (1966, p. 102) – but the principle clearly applies to the other three factors as well.

If the determinants of choice do not exist except as constituent parts of the choice, how do individuals choose? Goals in a disembodied sense can exist prior to choice; it is only the finalized ranking that does not. The individual, in his imagination, projects the likely consequences of different courses of action, including what must be sacrificed to achieve them. This "phantasying" takes place sequentially, with each fantasy informing and affecting the other (Schutz, 1967, p. 38). In this process, the individual clarifies his ranking of the imagined consequences, his knowledge of the relationship between particular courses of action and those ranked consequences, and his perception of prices and income. The point at which the ranking and perceptions are finalized *is*, or constitutes, the point of decision. They exist simultaneously, and thus this four-pronged apparatus does not determine the decision in any causal sense, for that would require temporal priority of the cause.

What an individual decides to do depends, in large part, on what he expects other individuals to decide. Therefore, it is impossible to examine adequantely the nature of decision-making without paying attention to the content of expectations. Unless an individual can expect a great deal of predictable decision-making on the part of others, he will find it impossible to make a meaningful choice.

### *Single-valued Expectations*

For simplicity, let us begin our analysis with the case in which expectations are of one, and only one, possible outcome. Where an individual does not envisage a probability distribution over a set of possible outcomes, the only criterion of forecasting accuracy is how far the single-valued estimate deviates from the actual outcome. In such a world there must be a base of "tolerably" predictable or habitual actions. These actions need not be automatic reflex motions but can be purposeful activity whose contents have been routinized (Berger and Luckmann, 1966, p. 53). "Habituations" are the empirical counterparts to static decision-making. In such cases the logical constituents of a decision remain unchanged from period to period.[12] Therefore, the tastes and knowledge of the previous period can be viewed *as if* they causally determined the choices of the current period. In the final analysis, however, this is merely an illusion of determinism, because the individual is actually freely choosing to repeat his activity. Since this type of activity provides the necessary predictable foundation for all forms of decision-making, including the most creative and spontaneous, static analysis is itself the necessary foundation for dynamic theory.

In a world of univalued expectations in which the individual must be able to predict fairly accurately in order to make meaningful decisions, all activity still need not be habitual. Truly creative, indeterminate decisions are possible so long as they do not too heavily disappoint the expectations of most decision-makers. In fact, creative activity can disappoint some expectations while at the same time ensuring the fulfillment of others. The lure of profits as the reward for facilitating the activities of other individuals means that sometimes creative activity will make the decision-making environment more stable, on balance, than otherwise (Kirzner, 1982).

### *Multi-valued Expectations and Decision Weights*

The single-value expectations approach is ultimately an inadequate portrayal of the position of the decision-maker. Normally, there are many *possible* actions that could be undertaken by other relevant parties. Not only is that number probably quite large, but, more importantly, the particular combination of of such actions will affect the consequences of the decision-maker's choice. A still further element of complexity emerges when we realize that the "order" of such actions also matters. The particular identity of the individuals who engage in certain actions will itself have an effect since some individuals are closer than others, in an economically relevant sense,[13] to the original decision-maker. Hence we must be concerned with the total number of permutations of the possible actions. Even in a very small society this number will be extremely large. Thus, it is imperative that people be able to weight these various possibilities in terms of their likelihood in order to make the process of decision-making humanly manageable.

Weighting possible actions of others does not necessitate being able to specify all the possible outcomes. If an individual feels that one or more decisions might be made of which he knows absolutely nothing, his own decision-making can proceed unimpeded if he places a low weight on these. Such a requirement may seem a bit awkward at first because the individual is expected to know something about the likelihood of unknown eventualities. This, however, is not at all implausible because the contrary assumption would paralyze all action. We cannot be blocked by the mere possibility that something just might happen to upset our plans.

The weights that we have been discussing are, like the determinants of choice under certainty, logical constructs used to identify the constituents of a decision. They are fully subjective attributes of the methodological mind construct. To say that they are "subjective" does not mean, however, that there is nothing in the objective world to which they refer. In order to see this, let us analyze three possible views of decision weights.

1. The weights refer to nothing objective: they are merely arbitrary and personal, like tastes. If this is so, then decision-making is almost entirely a leap of faith. Not only are sufficient grounds for choice thereby eliminated, but any grounds, in the sense of interpersonal justification, are impossible. The consequences of any course of action would be limited only by wishful thinking. Furthermore, in this kind of world any degree of *ex ante* coordination of plans could occur only by sheer accident. Presumably, then, exchange and social institutions as we know them would be virtually impossible.[14]

2. The weights are *only* social conventions. Again, even the most casual observation refutes this view. If this were the case, then no amount of disappointment would ever lead people to change their weights. The real world would provide no useful feedback of any kind, and hence learning would be impossible.

3. The weights are *attempts* to perceive objective propensities (Popper, 1959b). If we say that a great deal of what individuals will do is affected by objective propensities, then the requirements of meaningful decision-making are met. The huge number of possible consequences of different courses of action can be pared down by a weighting scheme. This scheme, in turn, is something that bears a relationship to the external world and is not merely self or social delusion. Thus, there must be a base of "loosely determined" behavior. With respect to this base, although something completely unexpected could happen, it is not likely. And what is not completely unexpected is more or less likely to happen as specified by underlying objective propensities.

On this base of loose determinism, there can be erected a domain of creative decision-making. This is determinate in neither the strict nor the loose sense. Yet it is possible only because it is limited. In a stimulating passage of an introductory mathematics book, Alfred North Whitehead comes to a very similar conclusion:

> It is a profoundly erroneous truism, repeated by all copy-books and by eminent people when they are making speeches, that we should cultivate the habit of thinking of what we are doing. The precise opposite is the case. Civilization advances by extending the number of important operations which we can perform without thinking about them. Operations of thought are like cavalry charges in a battle – they are strictly

limited in number, they require fresh horses, and must only be made at decisive moments. (Whitehead, 1939, p. 61)

Creativity in decision-making that is both unbounded in degree and quantitatively unlimited is a contradiction. No decisions at all can be made when the future is completely unpredictable. Yet this does not imply that creativity must be unimportant. Like Whitehead's cavalry charges, it can occur at decisive moments and hence be of profound importance. The key behavioral aspect of its limitation must be that it does not render decision-making pointless. Whether decisions are to be viewed as efficacious or not is obviously a determination that only acting individuals can make. The maximum amount of indeterminism consistent with genuine choice is not a subject that can be addressed on purely *a priori* grounds.

### *Institutions*

One of the main focal points of habituations are institutions. Outside of the special theoretical case of univalued expectations, institutions do not perfectly determine the behavior of their participants. Instead, they "[posit] that actions of type X will be performed by actors of type X" (Berger and Luckmann, 1966, p. 54). For example, the institution of the post office enables us to predict the actions of the ideal typical postman (e.g., he will pick up the mail, deliver it, etc.) Similarly, typical firemen, butchers, doctors, and so on can be counted on to engage in certain predictable patterns of behavior. For any given real-world individual, institutions enable us to narrow the range of possible actions to some specifiable class[15], perhaps even to rank the elements of that class in terms of their likelihood. Thus, institutions reduce but do not eliminate uncertainty; they provide, as it were, "points of orientation" (Lachmann, 1971, pp. 38, 49–91).

## CONCLUDING REMARKS

The discussion of dynamic subjectivism in this chapter has established a theme that will be pursued throughout most of this book. The creative aspects of human decision-making appear in many forms in subjectivist economic theory. The process of learning, the characterization of time and uncertainty, the construction of a useful equilibrium concept – all must entail appreciation of the non-mechanistic and indeterminate aspects of individual action. The development of this theme even in the more applied areas later in the book will reveal its importance. Practical issues such as antitrust law and government regulation of industry can be seen in a new light from a dynamically subjectivist perspective.

## NOTES

1 "Praxeological reality is not the physical universe, but man's conscious reaction to the given state of this universe. Economics is not about things and tangible material objects; it is about men, their meanings and actions" (Mises, 1966, p. 92).

2 "Theoretical economics has the task of presenting not merely the *laws*" of economic phenomena to us but also their '*general nature*.' A presentation of the above science, for example, which would, to be sure, enlighten us on the laws, but not on the *nature*, of goods, of value and the various forms in which value appears, of economy, of price, of ground rent, or income on capital, of speculative gains, of money, etc., would at any rate have to be designated as incomplete" (Menger, 1963, p. 198).

3 This definition of the economic question is intentionally broad since the boundaries between economics and the other social sciences are, to a great extent, merely conventional.

4 It is conceivable that institutions could be the *intended* consequences of human action. This may, in fact, be true in certain selected cases. However, in general, considerations such as the divergence of individual plans and the social division of knowledge make it unlikely that complex outcomes could be completely intended.

5 "My knowledge of everyday life is structured in terms of relevances. Some of these are determined by immediate pragmatic interests of mine, others by my general situation in society" (Berger and Luckmann, 1966, p. 45).

6 The quotation continues: "We can indeed make this class smaller and smaller without limit by making our description more and more detailed. But however far we go, it is a necessary consequence of the nature of language that we can never make the description perfectly determinate" (O'Connor, 1957, p. 313).

7 This doesn't depend on how the periods are divided (Ackerman, 1976, p. 45).

8 It makes no sense to argue that P will decide at $t_3$ on a course of action on the basis of what he knows only up to $t_2$. Why should P ignore information that, by assumption, he has on hand?

9 How could a mind not be conscious of what, *ex hypothesi*, has been attributed to its consciousness?

10 For a development of this principle in the area of legal causation see Rizzo and Arnold (1980, p. 1410 and passim) and Rizzo (1981, p. 1022).

11 In principle, there may be many theories that increase likelihood or provide favorable relevance. Choice among them must proceed, *inter alia*, on some notion of relative degrees of likelihood and the ability of a theory similarly to explain other phenomena.

12 Some habituations are merely the result of the same maximization exercise being repeated time after time while others are non-maximizing rules of thumb. The former can be approximated under roughly static conditions. The latter are consciously followed as an alternative to maximization under non-static conditions. See chapters 5 and 6 for further discussion.

13 People with whom one expects to engage in one exchange per year may be of less importance to the success of one's plans than people with whom one trades every day.

14 We would also never observe actors spending resources to learn what is more or less likely. They could merely "conjure up" the relevant weights.

15 On this idea of prediction in general see Popper (1965, p. 73) and Hayek (1967b, and 1967c).

# 3

# Knowledge and Decisions

> We are not simply acquiring knowledge about a static system which stays put, but acquiring knowledge about a whole dynamic process in which the acquisition of knowledge is itself a part of the process. *Kenneth Boulding (1966, p. 9)*

The all-encompassing importance of the individual's state of knowledge was implicit in our analysis of the mind construct in the last chapter. In this chapter, we probe more deeply into the nature of that knowledge and the process of learning. In addition, we focus explicitly on an extremely important, though widely misunderstood, feature of decision-making: cost. In a subjectivist framework, cost must be seen in a way that takes account of both its foundations in utility theory and its forward-looking orientation.

## SUBJECTIVISM AS CONTENT: KNOWLEDGE

In recent years the economics of knowledge has received considerable attention. It is not our purpose to retrace its development. Instead, we shall concentrate on a number of critical issues that have not been explored in this literature. The neglect of these issues stems from the non-subjectivist perspective adopted by most information theorists. Our analysis will stress precisely those subjectivist themes that tend to be absent in the conventional approaches. Specifically, we shall divide our discussion into four subsections: (1) the context of the individual's knowledge; (2) the nature of learning; (3) the division of knowledge in society; and (4) the difference between scientific and nonscientific knowledge.

## *The Context of Knowledge*

An individual's knowledge always arises in the context of a problem situation (Popper, 1979b). The static version of "situational analysis" consists simply of a precise statement of a problem, the background to that problem, and the framework of its solution. From the economic perspective, the problem situation is interpreted as focusing around a means–ends relationship. Consider, for example, the problem of want satisfaction. The background to this is knowledge of the relationship between commodities or courses of action and want satisfaction. The framework is the assumed motivation of utility maximization and the price–income constraints. Thus, from the point of view of situational analysis, the task of the economist is to reconstruct the situation of the actor in terms of achieving the *rational* solution to a problem *as the actor saw it*.

The emphasis on the rational solution to a problem differentiates this form of analysis from a *psychological* subjectivism that often appeals to notions of "irrationality." In addition, our approach differs from that of individual psychology insofar as there is no real-world individual-by-individual investigation of perceptions. Instead, there is only a conjecturing of the perceptions of an ideal-typical individual or mind construct. More generally, because no direct observation of what the individual "sees" is possible, the problem situation must be *hypothesized* in the context of the overall outcome the analyst wishes to explain.

Situational analysis need not imply, however, that the behavior of the individual be determinate as the solution of a mathematical problem would be. We must clearly allow for dynamic or nondeterministic situational analysis (Popper, 1979b, p. 178). Fundamentally, the problem-solving logic is a rationalization or reconstruction of a situation. "When we speak of a problem, we do so almost always from hindsight. A man who works on a problem can seldom say clearly what his problem is (unless he has found a solution). . . . " (Popper, 1979a, p. 246). The indeterminism inherent in the actual situation is thus evident when we try to reconstruct matters as the actor saw them *ex ante*. From that perspective, the statement of the problem will not be very precise, and, hence, an exact solution cannot be determined in advance.

### *The Nature and Process of Learning*

Merely to confine ourselves to rational reconstruction of problem situations does not tell us anything about how the individual sets up the problem context. Learning is thus not usefully explained in terms of the logical working out of a given, carefully specified problem. Recall that the consumer's problem under static conditions is reduced to mere computation of a constrained maximum. Because economic agents are assumed always to be rational, they don't even take time to compute such solutions. "True" learning involves more than mathematical computation; rather it consists of the setting up of the problem situation itself or the movement from one problem situation to another This is analogous to Hahn's distinction between different solutions to the same learning function (as the data change) and different functions themselves. Learning takes place when the individual's framework of interpreting external "messages" or stimuli has changed over time (Hahn, 1973, pp. 18–20). At present, we do not have a theory that enables us to say something significant about the move from one problem context to another. Nevertheless, we can go beyond Hahn's remarks and say something about how such a theory might look.

Theories about genuine learning cannot be deterministic. If we try to force learning into such a mold, we shall lose any notion of creative response. We have already seen the inconsistency involved in constructing deterministic theories of processes. In addition, because individuals undoubtedly perceive a non-deterministic element in their learning experiences, this must affect how and why they act. Nevertheless to claim that learning is not deterministic is not thereby to assert that it is purely random. Popper has elucidated, at least in general terms, the idea of a "plastic control" (Popper, 1979a, p. 240) standing between mechanical determinism on the one hand and blind chance on the other. While the details of this idea are based on a theory of scientific progress that we do not entirely share, it is nonetheless important to model the learning process in a way that attempts to formalize Popper's intuition.

Learning in this Popperian sense is evident in the Austrian theory of entrepreneurship. In that theory we assume only the *"tendency* for a man to notice those [facts] that constitute possible opportunities for gainful action on his part" (Kirzner, 1979, p. 29; emphasis added). In addition, "human action involves [merely] a *posture of alertness* toward the discovery of as yet *unpercieved* opportunities and their exploitation" (Kirzner, 1979, p. 109; first emphasis added). The *process* of entrepreneurial learning is neither determinate nor random. With respect to this "in-between" world of plastic control, two important points can be made. First, although what individuals will learn is not determinate, that they will learn something may well be. In fact, this is the fundamental assumption of the theory of entrepreneurship. We are willing to say *a priori* that learning will take place. Second, given the overall context of a change in knowledge, we can show how the move from framework$_1$ ($F_1$) to framework$_2$ ($F_2$) is intelligible, in the sense that a metatheory can be constructed in which a loose dependency on $F_1$ is shown. $F_2$ is more likely (though not necessarily highly likely or probable) given $F_1$ than it would be given some other $F_1'$. On the other hand, we might say that, given $F_1$, many possible alternative frameworks can be ruled out and that only a class of subsequent frameworks (which includes $F_2$) can be determined.

## *The Division of Knowledge*

One of the criteria for the type of knowledge we can attribute to the mind construct is whether it is plausible (intelligible) that the knowledge would have been acquired in the postulated context. Fundamentally, this context is the individual's system of relevances (Schutz and Luckmann, 1973, pp. 182–229) – what he deems important. This, in turn, is dependent on his goals, the perception of opportunities, etc., or, in short, – on the problem situation he faced in the previous period. Primarily because different people face different problems, there is a division or distribution of knowledge in society (Schutz and Luckmann, 1973, p. 306). It is not plausible to argue that, regardless of the situation, individuals find that they will ultimately learn the same things. Further, even if all individuals faced the same problems, they would probably not all have the same ability to acquire knowledge. There would still be a distribution of knowledge, although the "stock" of knowledge would be equally useful to everyone. Merely because people faced different problems does not mean, however, that all of the knowledge acquired by one individual is irrelevant to the others. Hence, knowledge must be communicated.

Consider the case of a reduction in the supply of steel. Those in the industry itself may know that a rise in the price of coal is partly to blame for the increased cost of production and therefore the reduced supply. But the causes of supply reduction may be irrelevant or, at least, less relevant to the builders of houses. They need know only a part of what the steel producers know: merely that steel has become relatively more scarce. Thus, some knowledge will remain uncommunicated while other bits of knowledge will be transmitted. For our purposes there are two important ways for knowledge to be communicated: through prices and through institutions.

*Prices* In the previous example, the price of steel would rise, thus conveying information about the relative reduction in supply (Hayek, 1940). But price signals need not always be correct. Suppose the same steel producers mistakenly believe that there has simultaneously been a decrease in the demand for products using steel as an input. They might actually attempt to lower the price.[1] The issue is not, however, the accuracy of the price signal relative to some external standard of perfection. Prices, we admit, can and will be incorrect. The crucial point is that, overall, more information is conveyed through a market price system than without one (Hayek, 1937, 1935a, 1935b). Further, even "incorrect" (i.e., non-equilibrium) prices convey information by revealing inconsistencies and plan discoordination (Kirzner, 1984).

*Institutions* Information is also conveyed outside the price system through patterns of routine behavior. Institutions may transmit knowledge in two senses. First, if people can rely on others to fulfill certain roles then their expectations are more likely to be coordinated. If, for instance, an individual knows that the sanitation department will pick up his garbage in the morning, then he can make use of the knowledge of garbage disposal that is possessed by others. What is transmitted to him is not that knowledge itself but the knowledge of how to make effective use of skills he will never possess (Sowell, 1980, pp. 8–11).

Second, some have argued (e.g. Hayek, 1973) that institutions also convey knowledge, in the sense that the routine courses of action they embody are efficient adaptations to the environment.

A vague Darwinian process is postulated, which weeds out institutions with inferior survival properties. There are several problems with the view. Unless the nature of these survival properties is made clear, the whole "theory" is a little more than a tautology. Survival properties are, by definition, those attributes that enable an institution to survive. Hence in any "conflict" among institutions those with inferior survival properties must necessarily give way to those with superior properties. Unfortunately, as the theory now stands, a careful specification of what makes societies survive has not been achieved. The second problem with the "Darwinian" view of institutions arises out of indivisibilities. The routine courses of action that comprise an institution are not all independent; the Darwinian process cannot eliminate all but the very best routines and combine them into a consistent or coordinated whole. Some clearly inferior routines must be maintained in order to permit those clearly superior (but dependent) to exist. Furthermore, nature does not throw up an infinite number of institutions out of which only the best will survive. The choice set, so to speak, is normally quite limited. The implication of these considerations is that, in the absence of a clear conception of the nature of survival properties, we cannot know whether any given institution or course of action is the most adaptive. In fact, we know that many institutions will not be the most adaptive possible because of indivisibilities in the evolutionary process.

*Are prices and institutions objective knowledge?* The transmission of knowledge through prices and institutions does not mean that subjectivity is no longer important and knowledge has in effect, become objectified. It is a misconception of subjectivism to assume that it deals with only elements of the individual psyche that can never be intersubjectively communicated. The social world is preeminently an intersubjective world (Schutz, 1954), and the phenomena in which we are ultimately interested rest on this fact. To say that knowledge has been transmitted from A to B means that where there was initially only one mind there are now two. Subjectivism is now more, not less, important than before. The nature of what is transmitted – the thoughts of individuals – is subjective. Similarly, the modes of transmission must be interpreted by those who receive the signals. A price or an institutional code of behavior must *mean* something in order to be an effective communication device. A rise in the price of a given commodity, for example, will have different meanings depending on the "elasticity of expectations" of the receiver. A price rise may signal higher or lower future prices when the subjective context of the date is taken into account.

Although the process of transmission enables individuals to make use of widely dispersed knowledge, it does not eliminate the heterogeneity of individual stocks of knowledge. Because people misinterpret signals, communication is imperfect. What the sender sends is often not what the receiver receives. Furthermore, information transmission is costly. At the very least, individuals must pay attention to prices, and they must recognize or understand how institutions function. Thus, there is an optimal amount of transmission and hence a degree of heterogeneity of knowledge that is irreducible.

But even when it pays to communicate, the sequence or order of knowledge acquisition will probably not be the same for all actors (Schutz and Luckman, 1973, p. 307). If, for example, the individual who directly acquired bits of information $a_1$, $a_2$, $a_3$, $a_4$ did so in that order, another individual might acquire this same information in reverse order, $a_4, \ldots, a_1$. This means, however, that their stocks of knowledge will ultimately be different. The "meta"-knowledge of relationships among these elements can depend upon the order in which they are apprehended. It is also the case that the nature of communication itself makes it impossibe for all heterogeneity to be eliminated. So long as knowledge is communicated rather than directly acquired, the context of its original acquisition will be unkown to some. As a consequence, not all individuals will understand the full context and hence the full meaning of the "communicated" knowledge.

Because of (1) differences in the problem situations that individuals face and (2) the very nature of the communication process, there exists no presumption that knowledge will be uniformly distributed: it will always be divided. Even in equilibrium,[2] then, not everyone will know the same things.

To talk of a "social stock of knowledge" is therefore merely a shorthand way of referring to its distribution across society. This social stock, however, bears no simple relationship to the individual stocks. It is both less and more than their summation. It is less because not everything that is relevant to each individual taken separately is in their common interest (Schutz and Luckmann, 1973, p. 289). It is more because new knowledge arising out of combinations of the old "isolated" elements is now possible.

The relationship between the two stocks of knowledge is compositive. An initial social stock is built up from the individual stocks on the basis of common relevances. Then the individual is able to increase his knowledge still further by establishing interconnections among the now-collected bits. By so doing, the social stock on which individuals can draw is expanded as this new derivative knowledge spreads. The process can continue *even if* underlying objective conditions remain unchanged. There is no end to the enrichment of the social stock of knowledge except the largely unexplored limitations of the human mind. Thus we must reject any notion of a final "equilibrium" state of knowledge.

### *Scientific Knowledge*

In the previous section we explored some fundamental aspects of the individual and social stock of knowledge as "data" of economics. In this section we wish to emphasize the important differences between the subjectivity of the subject matter and the subjectivism of our method of investigation. *Subjectivism as a method is perfectly consistent with objective science.* In order to see this, we must consider two component issues: first, the difference between scientific knowledge and knowledge of the mind construct; second, the possibility of having an objective science of subjective meaning.[3]

The key to the difference between the level of knowledge of the scientist and that of the economic actor or mind construct lies in the different problem situation faced by the two. The typical scientific question investigates the overall, frequently unintended, consequences of individual action. Individuals, on the other hand, are not always interested in those consequences.

Consider, for example, the well-known scientific question: Does capital, labor, or the consumer bear the burden of the imposition of a corporate income tax? For the individual actors this issue can be decomposed into several subissues: savers must decide whether to continue the same rate of saving; investors must decide whether to reshuffle their portfolios; laborers must decide whether to shift jobs in response to any change in wage rates; and, finally, consumers must decide whether to shift product mixes. Each of these actors make their own marginal adjustments without necessarily understanding the interaction and overall result of those adjustments. If, on the other hand, they are faced with the political question of whether to support the corporate income tax, the overall result or net burden may be a part of their problem situation.

This does not mean, however, that the actors understand the relevant scientific theory. A further argument must be constructed that will show that this knowledge can be communicated from scientists to non-scientists. More importantly, actors are normally faced with several models of an economic problem. They must choose among scientific theories. The proponent of the "correct" theory has no assurance that actors will believe his theory instead of an "incorrect" one. There is no reason to think that non-scientists will settle on just that theory adopted by the scientist. In the first place, even scientific standards of theory acceptance or rejection are controversial and highly ambiguous (Feyerabend, 1975; Kuhn, 1970; Lakatos, 1970). So there is a large range of indeterminacy that will surround the choice of theories. In the second place, scientific standards do not necessarily coincide with those of the actors. Suppose, for example, that a model explains the effects of a tax on X and Y. Because of the problem in which the actor is interested, he may be more concerned about inaccuracies in the explanation with respect to X along. The scientist, on the other hand, may be interested in minimizing the sum of the errors with respect to X *and* Y. Hence, each may be led to select a different theory on the basis of different standards of performance.

The second issue concerns the status of an objective science of subjective meaning. The possibility of such a science rests on the method of idealized rational reconstruction (whether deterministic or non-deterministic) of a problem situation. On the must abstract level, the problem situation need not embody reference to any concrete goals or constraints. Instead, we may be content to work out merely the formal implications of purposiveness. The law of diminishing marginal utility, for example, says a great deal about the structure of action in a static context, while completely abstracting from the content of individual ends. Objective science at this level is the development of a *logic* of choice that transcends the context in which particular individuals find themselves.

On an applied level, however, the economist cannot abstract from the typical contents of actors' minds. He must incorporate these into explanations of real-world phenomena. Although direct observation of subjective contents (tastes, expectations, etc.) is not possible, applied economics can still have intersubjective validity. The knowledge attributed to the mind construct must bear an "understandable" relation to the behavior under study. Therefore, our attribution of subjective states is always "controlled" by the real-world action they are meant to illuminate. In addition, the contents of the actor's mind must be assumed to be consistent with one another in the specific sense that no one will *knowingly* believe contradictory things or have contradictory values. Finally, the usefulness of particular subjective states in understanding behavior outside of the immediate context of investigation is important. If, for example, we wish to explain why the price of soybeans has risen, we may want to invoke expectations that the government will impose a general price-increasing regulation on commodities. This specific attribution of content to individuals' expectations will carry greater scientific weight the more *independent* evidence that there is for it. Thus, if the behavior of the prices of other commodities, the information-gathering activities of individuals, and the announcements of the government are all consistent with our expectational hypothesis, then we can assign it some measure of scientific corroboration. At no time, however, do we directly "see" expectations; rather, we merely observe that there are more and more phenomena consistent with the same subjective state.

The objectivity of the subjectivist method ultimately rests both on the level of analysis pursued by the scientists and on the "controlling" effect of the individual's behavior. In the first instance, although the knowledge of the scientist incorporates the subjective contents of the actor's mind, it goes beyond that to a higher level of generalization. This level often concerns the overall unintended consequences of individual actions. Furthermore, even at the individual level, objectivity in the method can be maintained. The imputed knowledge of the mind construct must bear an understandable relation to the behavior we seek to explain. Hence our imputations are controlled at least partially by that behavior.

## SUBJECTIVISM AS WEIGHING OF ALTERNATIVES

For many economists subjectivism means little more than the subjective theory of value. As we have already seen in this and the previous chapter, the nature and implications of subjectivism spread farther and wider than this. Nevertheless, even within the domain of value theory subjectivism has been only partially understood. While value is admittedly subjective, cost has inexplicably been viewed as objective. Thus, the Marshallian blades of the scissor were invented to symbolize the neoclassical fusion of subjective and objective factors. In our view, however, this dichotomization of the value process fails to understand the fundamental principle of subjectivism: valuation is nothing but the *mental* weighing of alternatives. None of these alternatives is a realized event because choices can be made only between images or projections of the outcomes of various courses of action. When an alternative is realized it is already too late to choose (Buchanan, 1969, p. 43). Subjectivism, then, must suffuse both the theory of value and the theory of cost; both blades of the scissor are made of the same material (Schumpeter, 1954, p. 922).

### *Utility Background*

Figure 1 illustrates in schematic form a thoroughly subjectivist view of value theory. The foundation of all value is a basic human want. In the sense originally conceived by Menger (1981, pp. 52, 139) and more recently developed by Becker (e.g. 1965) and Lancaster (e.g. 1966), wants are not directly for observable goods. Instead, they are for the satisfaction of some more basic desire: music (Stigler and Becker, 1977, p. 78), comfortable indoor temperature, health, and delicious meals (Becker, 1971, pp. 47–8) are all examples of basic wants.[4]

With a background of these wants, the individual projects an image of future want satisfaction. These projections are the immediate motivating source of his activity. Because individuals choose among directly observable goods or observable courses of action that produce these goods, there must be some link between the projected want satisfaction and these observables. This link is the individual's knowledge of a commodity's want-satisfying potential, i.e. the perceived production function. The relationship between market commodities and projected want satisfaction is not automatic but depends on the undertaking of a specific course of action to transform the commodity into actual satisfaction. This is the essence of the household production idea, originated by Menger and developed by Becker.

As we have just seen, the relationship between wants and choices

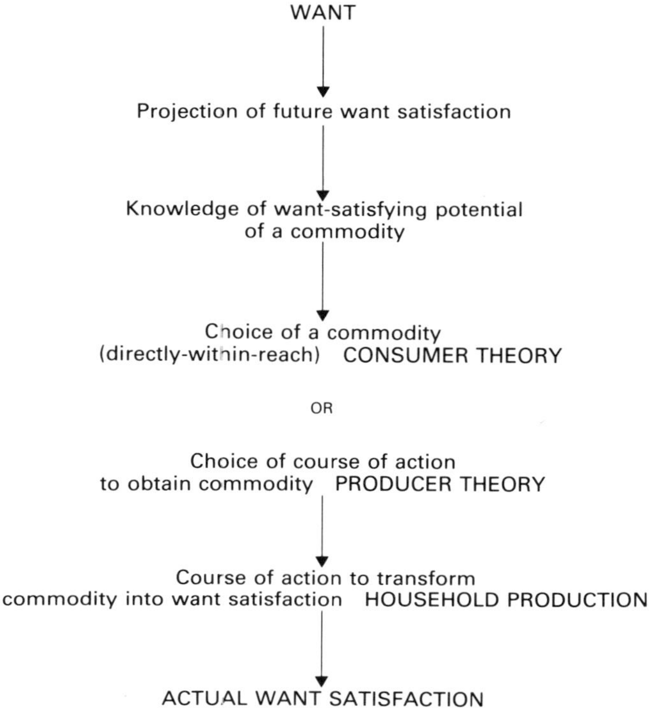


Figure 1 Value theory: a utility scheme

of market commodities is not a simple one. "There is many a slip betwixt cup and lip." The individual may incorrectly attribute want-satisfying potential to a good (Menger, 1981, p. 53; "imaginary good"), or he may ignore such potential when it is actually there. Furthermore, he may find that the costs involved in engaging in a particular plan of household production (in addition to the direct commodity costs) make the achievement of a particular want satisfaction prohibitively expensive.

Utility in this framework refers to the rank ordering of *projected* want satisfactions. An individual may value the prospective satisfaction of his desire for an additional unit of comfortable indoor temperature more than that of his desire for an additional unit of delicious meals. Strictly speaking, he does not rank the wants themselves, because they are mere deprivations and are not valued.

Similarly, he does not rank the market commodities themselves, because they are wanted not for their own sake but only for the satisfaction they indirectly produce.

It is true that, if we viewed the link between commodities and satisfaction as automatic, then little is gained by this separation. The subjectivist view of utility theory must allow, however, for the erroneous perception of such a link. Hence the distinction between commodities and satisfaction is important. Finally, realized (as opposed to projected) want satisfactions cannot be objects over which utility is defined because *ex post* magnitudes occur too late to motivate behavior. It is only projected satisfaction of wants that can provide the motivating force in decision-making.

In a static equilibrium world, the distinctions, on the one hand, between commodities and the projected satisfactions they can create and, on the other hand, between realized and projected want satisfaction lose much of their force. In the first case, no economically relevant error would enter into the perception of a commodity's want-satisfying potential. In the second, images or projections of satisfaction would never deviate from the realized event. Thus, one might quite reasonably invoke Occam's Razor and define utility over market commodities, omitting the intermediate steps.[5] However, in a world of disequilibrium, individuals cannot proceed directly and immediately from goods to want satisfaction. In such a world the distinction made in our utility scheme can be quite useful in highlighting the complexities of the decision process.

### *Cost in Consumer Decision-making*

Cost theory is not really a separate subject from utility theory. The concept of cost follows immediately from the way in which utility is defined. In a subjectivist framework, the cost of choosing any commodity is the highest ranked projected want satisfaction that is perceived to be sacrificed. Cost, just like utility, is defined over projected want satisfaction and not directly over the commodities themselves. The relevant sacrifice cannot be merely the perceived commodity displacement, for the same reason that the relevant motivation for choice cannot be the chosen commodity itself. Commodities are only way-stations to the ultimate satisfaction of basic wants. It is these projected satisfactions that constitute both utility and cost.

The only sense in which cost can influence choice is the perception at the very moment of choice of the satisfactions foregone (Wicksteed, 1967, p. 391). Thus, cost is tied to choice and apart from it has no economic meaning (Buchanan, 1969, p. 43). After a choice is made, retrospective calculations of what the relevant costs "really" were (in the sense of what the actor would have perceived if he had had certain superior knowledge) cannot, of course, be relevant to that prior choice situation. To the extent that conditions are expected to remain the same, however, such calculations can inform future choice situations. Nevertheless, even these historical estimates cannot demonstrate unambiguously what *would* have happened if the individual had chosen another commodity of course of action. It is quite possible that the projected satisfaction associated with a rejected alternative would have never materialized. Thus, even *ex post*, costs cannot be realized. They must remain for ever in a world of projecting, fantasizing or imagining.

Although cost is inextricably bound to the individual's choice context, it is nevertheless possible for one individual to affect the costs of another. If A pollutes the water (a completed act of choice), then the cost to B of obtaining clean water to drink will increase. The nature of B's cost is still subjective: the highest ranked projected want satisfaction that *he* perceives must be sacrificed in order to obtain drinkable water. Nevertheless, this perception is affected by individuals making choices outside of the context in which B's cost itself affects behavior. This is not the same thing as saying that other individuals strictly "determine" or "impose" costs on any decision-maker. While other people can surely affect the environment of choice, it is still the choosing individual who must ultimately perceive the alternatives sacrificed and bear the costs of his choices. In perfectly competitive equilibrium, the three quantitative magnitudes (foregone revenue, outlay cost, and consumers' valuation) are equal at the margin. This equality at the margin does not imply that the conceptual differences disappear but that they are not manifest in competitive markets in equilibrium.

## *Cost in the Theory of the Firm*

For heuristic purposes, cost takes on a somewhat different meaning in the theory of the firm. Here, the relevant meaning depends entirely on the imputed objective function of the firm's decision-maker. *If* the firm seeks to maximize profits, then cost must be defined in terms of foregone revenue and not in terms of foregone want satisfaction. This is because it is analytically convenient to separate the process by which the firm makes its decisions (theory of the firm) from the process by which the decision-maker buys market commodities and transforms them into want satisfaction (consumer theory). To combine the two in every case would make our efforts to understand market phenomena enormously more complicated without yielding any increased insight. Nevertheless, we must always remember that the *ultimate* motivation for all choices is want satisfaction. Profit maximization, sales maximization, and other imputed firm goals are only means to the attainment of more basic ends. Thus, any assumed motivation cannot be viewed as fixed profit maximization might be the best means to achieve want satisfaction in one context, but not in another.

For the profit-maximizing decision-maker, cost is the revenue that the *decision-maker* perceives *he* could have obtained with the same resources in the best alternative line of endeavor (Thirlby, 1973, p. 277). In contrast to this notion of cost, there are at least two conventional non-subjectivist concepts. The first is direct outlay cost: this amounts to the expenditures incurred in acquiring the necessary factors of production. The second is a species of "social cost" (Thirlby, 1973, p. 278), referring to the *consumers'* valuation of the alternative products that *other* decision-makers might have produced had a different course of action been undertaken. In perfectly competitive equilibrium, all three notions of "cost" collapse into each other. Assuming that a decision-maker is not restricted to any given industry, his costs will be equal at the margin to the market prices of the resources that he employs.[6] This follows because, under competitive conditions, these prices will be bid up to the value of the resources in their best alternative use, regardless of where in the economy that might be. The decision-maker's costs will also equal the consumers' valuation of the alternative product because the total value of a commodity on the output market will be the same as its value on the resource market.

In disequilibrium, however, these notions of "cost" need not bear any systematic relation to one another. Therefore, the analyst's choice of which one he will use is of paramount importance. To understand the decision-making process of the firm, only the first, thoroughly subjectivist, view of cost (the firm's anticipated foregone revenue) will be useful. Only costs as perceived by the decision-maker in terms of his own options are relevant to understanding his behavior. Direct outlay cost in conjunction with the implicit market value of factors owned by the decision-maker will, on the other hand, be useful in calculating entrepreneurial profit. The difference between total revenue and these expenses represents profit from the market point of view. Finally, a comparison of the consumer valuation of alternative products and the costs as perceived by the firm tells us something about how well the market is satisfying consumer demands. When firm decision-makers view alternative A as preferable to B, and consumers favor B over A, then we have imperfect market coordination.

The three concepts that are conventionally lumped together as "cost" are really very different in analytical function outside of competitive equilibrium. As a consequence, it would seem better to allocate different names to these ideas, reserving the term "cost" for the concept that arises directly from the theory of choice. Implicit or explicit expenses (outlays) and consumer valuations are unambiguously handled by these other terms, and calling them "cost" only creates confusion.

## CONCLUSION

In this chapter we have discussed issues of knowledge from a perspective different from that normally pursued in the economics literature. We view knowledge as inherently decentralized and its acquisition as necessarily non-mechanistic. In addition, we have found that the transmission and growth of knowledge is a never-ending process. In the next chapter, this continual increase in knowledge will be linked with a dynamically subjectivist conception of time. Real time and changes in knowledge belong together. In chapter 5, an equilibrium construct will be developed that is firmly embedded in real time. Thus, the continual growth of knowledge will occur even in equilibrium.

We have also seen that decisions made on the basis of the individual's knowledge contain fully subjective components. Not only is utility subjective, but costs are as well. The theoretical developments of this idea in the current chapter will lay the foundation for a more thoroughgoing critique of economic policy presented in chapter 7.

## NOTES

1 Of course, their error need not manifest itself if there are sufficient speculative purchasers of steel who are correctly informed.

2 Here the term "equilibrium" is being used in the sense of no tendency to change rather than in the dynamic Hayekian sense of plan coordination. See the discussion in chpaters 5 and 6.

3 Schutz (1953, pp. 334–5) poses this question but does not appear to answer it very clearly.

4 How exactly basic wants ought to be defined depends on what is useful in the context; there is no unique way to do this.

5 Although even here the distinction between basic wants and market goods can be useful in some contexts, as Becker (1976a, p. 5) has claimed.

6 We assume that he owns no factors and hires or purchases everything he uses. If he owns any factors then they must be included at their implicit market price as part of the firm's "outlays."

# 4

# The Dynamic Conception of Time

> The element of time. . . is the centre of the chief difficulty of almost every economic problem. *Alfred Marshall (1961, p. vii)*

In the two previous chapters we presented an overview of the methodological and substantive importance of subjectivism. In this chapter we shall extend and deepen dynamic subjectivism by applying it to a critical concept in economic theory: time. The non-subjectivist method of neoclassical economics has not been able to handle time in a satisfactory manner. The core of orthodox theory is beset with temporal paradoxes and inconsistencies. As long ago as 1934, Kaldor saw that in equilibrium theory "the formation of prices must *precede* the process of exchange and not be the result of it" (1934, p. 127). Recently, Bausor more precisely diagnosed the problem when he concluded that in general equilibrium theory there is a "logical *simultaneity* between current decisions and current prices" (1981, p. 6; emphasis added). Thus, cause and effect, present and future are all laid out instantaneously. Even models that purport to take time seriously fail. Intertemporal general equilibrium theory has also effectively annulled time. As Hahn admitted, "The assumption that all intertemporal and all contingent markets exist has the effect of collapsing the future into the present" (1980, p. 132). Decisions are all made in a single primordial instant: the future is merely the unfolding of a tapestry that exists *now*.

In recent years, a number of articles have emphasized both the neglect of time by neoclassical economics and the importance of incorporating it into our models (e.g., Hicks, 1976). Nevertheless, much of this critical literature fails to pinpoint the exact source of the problem and, more importantly, to indicate the character of a possible solution. In this chapter we attempt to remedy that situation by, first, critically analyzing the orthodox treatment of time and, second, presenting an alternative, thoroughly subjectivist, conception of time.

The chapter is divided into five sections. The first is an analysis of Newtonian time and its implications for economic theory. The second is a contrasting study of the implications of real or subjectivist time. In the third section we clarify the relationship among real time, planning, and action. There follows a development of the consequences of real time for economic processes and the characterization of uncertainty. Finally, we examine the interrelation between Newtonian and real time and specify their respective analytical roles.

## NEWTONIAN TIME

The Newtonian conception of time is spatialized; that is, its passage is represented or symbolized by "movements" along a line. Different dates are then portrayed as a succession of line segments (discrete time) or points (continuous time). In either case, time is fully analogized to space, and what is true of the latter becomes true of the former. Neoclassical theory has uncritically adopted this idea and used it in almost every systematic treatment of the temporal aspects of economics. In fact, almost all work on the economics of time is plagued by an excessive dependence on this analogy. Theorists treat a mere analogy as if it were the reality to which all models had to be faithful.

While the Newtonian view of time has doubtless been useful for many purposes, it nevertheless abstracts from some of the most important problems with which contemporary economics must deal. In order to support this conclusion, we shall begin by analyzing the central features of Newtonian time and the particular ways in which they manifest themselves.

### *Central Features of Newtonian Time*

Newtonian time can be characterized in many ways, but for our purposes there are three aspects that are especially important: (1) homogeneity, (2) mathematical continuity, and (3) causal inertness (Capek, 1961, p. 36–48).

*Homogeneity* In the geometry of lines each point is identical to all others, except for its position. In fact, position is really all that constitutes a point. Analogously, spatialized time is merely *temporal* position. It is an empty point or "container" that can (but need not) be filled with changes. Just as matter occupies empty space, changes occupy points or instants of time. Since a point is, by construction, empty, time must in principle be independent of its contents. In other words, Newtonian time can elapse without anything happening. The Newtonian conception thus transforms time into a static category.

One implication of this is that time can pass without agents learning. In the Arrow–Debreu model, for example, all decisions are made on some initial day. Although time passes and agents eventually find out which of the various contingent states of the world occur, they never learn anything that would cause them to want to change the decisions made on day one (Radner, 1970, pp. 480–4). Agents are completely constrained to the view of the world held at the beginning of time.

*Mathematical continuity* This is not continuity in the sense of an interrelation between successive instants but merely continuous divisibility. Just as a line can be divided and subdivided without end, the intervals of Newtonian time can be made arbitrarily small. In addition, no matter how finely we divide time and how close the resultant points are to each other, there is always some space between them. Each instant of time is isolated or, in principle, independent of the others, for points on a line can never touch.

Gunnar Myrdal (1939) saw the significance of mathematical continuity. If economic adjustments occur at points or durationless instants, all dynamic problems are evaded and hence left unsolved. In temporary equilibrium models, for example, adjustments occur at "the timeless points dividing the periods form each other" (p. 44). This, then, must neglect both the learning that accompanies processes and, more specifically, the order of each element in a process (since they are modeled all to occur at once). Furthermore, adjustments must have an infinite velocity and resources must be infinitely mobile for a process to take place at a mere instant. Here, of course, is the heart of the Newtonian paradox: if adjustment is instantaneous, why is change ever necessary? Things should be "right" from the beginning. Indeed, Myrdal put it more strongly, "The occurrence of change is contradictory to the idea of a timeless point" (1939, p. 44). This difficulty has been noted in the literature on price adjustments. Any stable *disequilibrium* adjustment process must occur instantaneously. Stability of the adjustment functions implies the predictability of the entire process. Consequently, if the process were to take time, pure profit opportunities would emerge. Entrepreneurial response to these opportunities would ensure that prices immediately adjusted (Gordon and Hynes, 1970, p. 372; White, 1978, p. 9).

Nevertheless, Newtonians have attempted to represent change "as a series of states, each of which is homogeneous. . . and consequently does not [itself] change" (Bergson, 1911, p. 163). Hence, any movement must emanate from outside the system; that is, if must be exogenous. A Newtonian system is merely a stringing together of static states and cannot endogenously generate change. Each period (or point) is thus isolated. Consequently, either we have the mere continuation of a period (no change) or we have change without the ability to show how it could be generated by the previous period. This is the fundamental problem with the comparative dynamics method that derives from Lindahl's temporary equilibrium theory (Hicks, 1965, pp. 68–9). Since each period is in temporary equilibrium, we can examine change only by asking what the "new" equilibrium would be if an alternative set of data were exogenously imposed on the system.

*Causal inertness* That the mere elapse of time does not produce or cause anything is obviously just another way of looking at homogeneity: the independence of time from its contents. More importantly, however, if there are any changes, then they must be determined from the beginning. The initial state of the system must contain within it all that is necessary to produce "change"; *time adds literally nothing.*

The causal inertness of time is especially evident in the deterministic treatment of learning in neoclassical models. The passage of time does not produce change in the method of processing exogenous messages. In equilibrium an agent's "theory" is "independent of the date *t*" (Hahn, 1973, p. 19). Therefore, given an exogenous message, we definitely know what the agent learns from it. More specifically, given his present information, we know what his expectations are. Neoclassical learning is merely a series of cross-sections over a surface or function depicting the *existing* state of knowledge.

### *The Illusion of Change*

Change or the succession of events is not "genuine" in Newtonian time. Just as the points on a line coexist or are simultaneously given, so too must the future that the Newtonian model is intended to portray. In our previous example of neoclassical learning, the entire learning function exists "now" or, more exactly, is outside of time. Thus, there is no analytical difference between the various cross-sections being spread out over what we call successive instants and those same cross-sections being spread out over different regions at one instant in time (Shackle, 1969, pp. 16–17). It is perfectly possible for $t_1, \ldots, t_n$ to be compressed into a single conscious present.

### *The Eradication of Time*

As we stated in the introductory section of this chapter, the explicit compression of change into a single instant is an important feature of neoclassical economics. No doubt this often results in greater mathematical tractability and the elimination of such problems as false trading (since equilibrium prices and exchanges are simultaneous), but, as we shall see, it also *negates the very problem the economist ostensibly has set out to solve*. This is the inevitable outcome of the causal inertness of Newtonian time and its consequent determinism. If *all* of the causes are present at $t_1$, why must we wait until $t_2$ for the results? In this section we shall examine three cases of the explicit elimination of time and the resultant undermining of the essential problem at hand.

*Capital theory* The classic Clark–Knight theory of capital is an important illustration of the neoclassical treatment of time. Throughout the 1930s and 1940s this theory was contrasted with the Austrian approach to capital. The latter placed heavy emphasis on variations in the time structure of production. Knight, however, fundamentally disagreed with that emphasis, for "under equilibrium conditions production and consumption are simultaneous" (1946, p. 387). There is no time structure in Knight's theory because he fully adopted the Newtonian conception of time. The Clark–Knight view collapses the time structure of production into a cross-section of the economy's "stages." Once again, the future is spread out over instantaneous space.

*Intertemporal general equilibrium* The purpose of the Arrow–Debreu construction was to refine and extend the simple Walras–Pareto model of general equilibrium. The latter had been criticized for neglecting intertemporal relations and uncertainty. A simple and ingenious analytical device incorporating contingent futures markets was used to remedy these defects. But even though commodities are made available on different dates over an indefinite future, the analysis is still essentially static. There is no real difference between a given physical commodity at two dates and at two geographic locations. The further complication of adding a contingent state of the world (e.g., "if it is cold") to the physical description, location, and date changes little. All we have done is expand the number of commodities over which the individual maximizes.

Change, rather than mere uncertainty, is the *true* effect of time. Suppose, for example, that all of the "future" commodities were spread out in space at a single instant. Then we could view contingent markets as merely the uncertain prospect of what *now* is actually in a given container (perhaps ice cream, perhaps hot soup, etc.). The incompleteness of knowledge is not the sole element of a genuinely temporal model.

*Tight prior equilibrium* The most dramatic case of the abolition of time is the research program described by Reder (1982, esp. pp. 11–13) and ostensibly practiced by Chicago school economists. The core of this approach is the maintained hypothesis that "in the absence of sufficient evidence to the contrary, one may treat observed prices and quantities as good approximations to their long-run competitive equilibrium values" (p. 12). Despite a considerable amount of confusion as to which long-run model Reder is referring to, the main thrust of this approach is clear. Agents are assumed to "treat long-run equilbrium values of all endogenous variables as parameters" (p. 18). Thus, permanent rather than transitory income explains variations in consumption; security prices fully incorporate all relevant information at (almost) every instant in time; agents "rationally" expect the distribution of prices generated by the long-run stochastic structure of the model; and all decisions can be effectively executed, that is, all decisions are immediately pre-reconciled.

This position is the most thoroughgoing and consistent application of the Newtonian conception of time in contemporary economics. The "Tight Prior Equilibrium" framework thus reduces all economic theory to a set of comparative static propositions (Reder, 1982, p. 12) that are assumed to hold instantaneously. The question of time as change does not arise, much less is it answered, in this world.

## *The Measurement of Time*

The eradication of succession is intimately related to the way in which Newtonian time is measured. Strictly speaking, there is no such thing as the succession of Newtonian moments. Time is measured by the "counting of simultaneities" (Bergson, 1911, p. 338) and not of successive events. Suppose, for example, that T is a mobile that moves along its trajectory. Then the dating of a movement ("change") of T is by reference to the *simultaneous* position of another mobile, T′. Thus, if T moves by one unit simultaneously with T′ moving by one-half a unit of distance, then T can be said to have moved (or "changed") by one unit in one-half a unit period of *time* (as measured by the movement of the second mobile). Now, compress the *psychological* duration separating the trajectory positions, $T_1$ and $T_2$, etc., into one instant, and nothing has really happened. The change of T is dated by comparing simultaneous positions of T′. If mobiles $T_1$, $T_2$ $T_3$ . . . , all coexist, they can still correspond to the positions of other mobiles $T_1'$, $T_2'$, $T_3'$, . . . , which also coexist. Hence, even in the measurement of Newtonian time, succession, as opposed to juxtaposition, is inessential.

Hood (1948, p. 462) gives a simple example of the instantaneous measurement of time. Consider three continuous and differentiable functions: $y = f(t)$, $x = g(t)$, and $y = F(x)$, where $t$ is the trajectory of the mobiles X and Y. Time can be measured in terms of either X or Y. Suppose we choose to measure it by movements in X. Let's assume that $dy/dt > dx/dt$. This then implies (since the relationship $y = F(x)$ was established) that $dy/dx > 1$. Now if $dy/dx = 2$, we can conclude the Y changes by 1 unit in ½ unit measure of time (which is analogous to our result in the previous paragraph). This conclusion, however, is really just a convention or stipulation. A system based on differential equations is actually concerned with *present* or *instantaneous* rates of change: neither the past nor the future is involved. Newtonian time is thus measured by simultaneous correspondences with a static moment.

As a final illustration, consider the adjustment model discussed by Hood (1948, p. 463) in a somewhat different connection. Let the rate of price change, $dp/dt$, be a function of excess demand:

$$dp/dt = K[D'(P_0) - S'(P_0)]\ (P_t - P_0)$$

where K = constant; $D'$, $S'$ are the slopes of the demand and supply curves respectively; $P_0$ is the equilibrium price; and $P_t$ is the current price. Time is here measured in terms of the absolute value of the changes in excess demand. The simultaneities counted then are the changes in the quantities supplied and demanded and the changes in price. Thus, the above equation determines the instantaneous (present) rates of change in prices for various present changes in excess demand. All of these changes literally refer to a single moment. The formal model effectively collapses diachronic and synchronic changes; that is, the temporal cross-section distinction is obliterated.

## REAL TIME

Along with other economists, Austrians have stressed the importance of real time. Often, however, the main features of this alternative concept have not been made precise. From our discussion of the Newtonian framework, it ought to be evident what real time is not. In this section we shall go beyond the previous discussion and present the central features and consequences of non-Newtonian time.

Following the work of the philosopher Henri Bergson (1910), we distinguish between spatialized time and the subjective experience of the passage of time. Bergson called the latter concept "la durée" or duration, but we shall generally use terms more congenial to economists: "real" or "subjective" time. Time, in this sense, is not the static subjectivist concept used in planning or reflection. Instead, it is a dynamically continuous flow of novel experiences. This flow is not *in* time, as would be the case from a Newtonian perspective; rather, it *is* or constitutes time. We cannot experience the passage of time except as a flow: something new must happen, or real time will cease to be.

### *Features of Real Time*

There are three interrelated features of our alternative view of time: (1) dynamic, rather than mathematical, continuity; (2) heterogeneity; and (3) causal efficacy (Capek, 1971, pp. 90–1).

*Dynamic continuity* This form of continuity can most easily be grasped by an aural analogy. Hearing only one note of a melody, for example, is insufficient to capture the experience of music. This is because our perception involves memory of the just-elapsed phases (or notes) and anticipation of those yet to come. The actual experience is thus more than a mathematical instant; it is impossible to subdivide continuously a piece of music without fundamentally altering or negating the experience. The dynamic structure of real time consists, then, of two aspects: *memory* and *expectation* (Shackle, 1958, p. 16). On this view, the present is in principle linked with other periods through the perceptions of the individual. Memory and expectation are the structural components of real time accounting for its dynamic continuity. Although the physical or mathematical time that a given experience takes can be continuously subdivided, these durationless instants are not, from a subjectivist viewpoint, independent of or isolated from one another. Real time thus implies the very linkages from which Newtonian time abstracts.

All purportedly dynamic models postulate some kind of connection between successive periods. The existence of linkages per se, however, does not mean that Newtonian time has been abandoned. The exact character of the intertemporal relationship is very important. For example, Hicks (1965, p. 32) links periods in a dynamic analysis by the "stock of *physical* capital that is handed on from one single period to its successor" (emphasis added). Similarly, Hey (1981, p. 52) discusses a dynamic optimization model in which the present is linked to the past through the "inherited" value of wealth; but, given that value, the individual's optimal strategy is independent of time. Thus in both the Hicks and Hey models, "the future always looks the same irrespective of from where it is viewed" (Hey, 1981, p. 52). The central difference between this form of intertemporal connection and the dynamic continuity of real time is that the latter necessarily involves a change in perspective. The future must look different depending on from where it is viewed. In a somewhat different context, Hahn (1952, p. 805) has made a similar point: "The experience of the first situation must always enter as a new parameter into the second situation."

*Heterogeneity* If memory is the component of our experience that links the past to the present, it is also the factor responsible for the continuous differentiation of each successive moment. As time passes, the individual's memory is continually enriched and thus the subjective standpoint from which he experiences the world undergoes change. As a consequence, each phase of real time is novel *precisely because* it is linked to previous periods by memory (Capek, 1971, p. 127). The dynamic continuity and heterogeneity of real time are thus not separable features, but are merely two aspects of the same phenomenon.

The heterogeneity of time sheds considerable light on the limitations of agents' forecasting abilities. Suppose that an individual tries to predict an event. Paradoxically, even if it occurs "exactly" as predicted, it will not be *experienced* exactly as predicted. The simple reason is that before he made the forecast his standpoint was different. Afterwards, his memory incorporated the forecast and this changed his perspective (Schutz and Luckmann, 1973, pp. 240–1). This is a limiting case of the general phenomenon of a prediction interacting with and changing the object of prediction. The focus of this interaction, however, is on the subjective standpoint (state of knowledge) of the agents and not on a physical event. Thus, where the predicted event is dependent on a subjective state of affairs, such as the expectations of individuals, the *event itself* may be altered by predictions. If an oligopolist, for example, decides to change his price, this decision will in part depend on his expectation of the prices to be charged by competitive firms. But the prices that they will charge depend on their expectations of the price he will charge. Therefore, the competitors must determine his expectations about their expectations of his expectations. If he were to make a "wrong" prediction, then their predictions and hence actions would in fact be different. This phenomenon is well known in the literature of oligopoly models. In the next chapter we discuss in greater detail the particular form of uncertainty engendered by a similar example.

*Causal efficacy* This follows immediately from heterogeneity. The mere elapse of time, as distinct from physical change, is a source of novelty. As we saw in the previous section, the swelling of memory alone changes the perspective from which the world is seen. Hence time is causally potent and creative. This implies that all economic processes must involve the transmission and growth of knowledge. In this framework, for example, competition is no longer merely the name given to a certain equilibrium state. Instead, as we demonstrate later in this book, the process of competition is literally a discovery procedure. The growth of knowledge is the endogenous force that endlessly propels the system.

### *General Consequences of Real Time*

There are two important consequences of adopting our non-Newtonian concept of time. First, real time is irreversible. There can be no return to a previous period. Thus, "movements" along supply and demand curves do not mirror real temporal changes. Strictly speaking, as soon as we move away from a given point on such a curve there is no going back to it. Second, the passage of time involves "creative evolution"; that is, processes produce unpredictable change. A process is not a mere rearrangement of *given* factors, as it is portrayed in deterministic models of "change." If change is real, it cannot be completely deterministic: there must be scope for surprise.

## REAL TIME, PLANNING, AND ACTION

The concept of time directly incorporated in plans is Newtonian. The planner can imagine units of time that are isolated, empty, and as small as convenient. These homogeneous units can then be filled with specific activities. If completed plans were the only important aspects of economics, then Newtonian time would be quite sufficient as a tool of analysis. However, the *process* of planning must take place in real time. As we contemplate a course of action and project its consequences, we continually refine and refocus our tentative plans. Knowledge must be gained in the process of projecting. If this were not so, we could never go from a state of indecision to one of decision. Something must have changed during the process in order to account for the individual's eventual ability to decide (Bergson, 1910, p. 171).

In a plan, the individual projects a completed act (e.g., the ditch as already dug) (Schutz, 1967, p. 58), and so, as we have seen, the plan itself is static and hence compatible with spatialized time. In the process of acting (e.g., digging), however, the individual experiences things. These experiences are novel if only because he approaches the world from subjective standpoints continually changed by the memory of what has been occurring. Moreover, *exogenous* factors are also affecting the system and upsetting the individual's prior decision framework.

Neoclassical economics conflates the plan with the process of planning, the completed act with the process of acting. Furthermore, in its perfect-foresight version, the plan, and completed act are conflated. This is equivalent to the assumption that all plans can be successfully executed and that there are no coordination problems. In such a world, there is no room for real time.

Novel experiences acquired in planning or acting are significant only to the extent that they engender plan revisions or alterations in the course of action. Thus these experiences must be connected with changes in the stock of knowledge. Knowledge, unlike pure experience, has applicability beyond the individual case that gave rise to it and thus can affect the future. In order to show that the growth of experience can be significant for our purposes, we must show its interrelation with the growth of knowledge. This can be demonstrated in alternative ways. From an inductivist perspective, agents can infer universal statements from statements of particular experiences. If all past increases in the money supply were ultimately associated with higher interest rates, then agents might infer the universality of this relationship. Therefore, as they "collect" more particular experiences they strengthen (or perhaps change) their theoretical understanding. Even from the now dominant hypothetico-deductive perspective, it is conceded that experiences "suggest" certain hypotheses or interpretative frameworks. In addition, experiences can overturn or refute existing hypotheses. As a consequence, any change in (addition to) the stock of experience will give rise to new conjectural frameworks. Necessarily, then, it will also generate revised anticipations of the future because these are based on the current tentative framework. Hence growth in the stock of experience leads, via growth in the stock of knowledge, to alterations in both memory and expectations (the intertemporal links).

These alterations can never be deterministic. The connection between experience and new knowledge is not logically airtight. In the first instance, induction is a logically insufficient basis for any generalization. The fact that past expansions in the money supply were associated with higher interest rates does not justify a law covering all future occasions (Popper, 1964, pp. 27–30). Second, since many hypotheses are consistent with the same data (Friedman, 1953, p. 9), any given experience will not point uniquely to a particular generalization. Finally, even the elimination of hypotheses is not absolute. A particular observation may be incorrect, or further data may reinstate a previously refuted hypothesis (Popper, 1964, p. 50).

Real time is important because in the course of planning and acting the individual acquires new experiences. These new experiences then give rise, in a non-deterministic way, to new knowledge. On the basis of this new knowledge, the individual changes his future plans and actions. Thus the economic system is propelled by purely endogenous forces. The "natural" state of an economy in time is change and not rest, for "as soon as we permit time to elapse we must permit knowledge to change" (Lachmann, 1959, p. 73).

## ECONOMIC PROCESSES AND UNCERTAINTY

The most important implications of real time are for the modeling of adjustment processes and the characterization of uncertainty. No process can fit comfortably within a purely Newtonian construct. As we have seen, a world of instantaneous adjustment is really a world without process. If, on the other hand, adjustment takes time, then knowledge can grow and novel outcomes can emerge. Real time also affects the characterization of uncertainty. Risk analysis, whether objective or subjective, is essentially a weighting of possibilities already known. Genuine uncertainty, however, allows for the unpredictable growth of these possibilities and thus for "gaps" in agents' probability distributions.

### *Reality of Succession and Indeterminacy of Processes*

Since the essence of real time includes novelty and causal efficacy, the future cannot be logically derived from the present because the former has not yet been created (Capek, 1971, pp. 106–11). Recognition of the creative aspect of time reinforces the position we adopted in chapter 2 that decision-making is not deterministic. Conventional utility maximization, or what Kirzner calls "Robbinsian maximizing" (1973, p. 38), is a mere rearrangement or computation of things already known. To model processes in these terms is to render the analysis completely mechanical. In real time the situation must be different. Although the stages of a choice-theoretic process must be dynamically continuous (memory and expectation link the periods), these stages cannot *ineluctably* give rise to one another. The relationship between stages will be understandable even though each stage will not be completely predictable given its predecessor.

*Examples* In the Arrow–Debreu construction an agent knows with certainty his response to every possible contingency. Although the future states of the world are uncertain, nevertheless, *given* any such state, the agent views his response as certain. Pye (1978) developed a model embodying at least one aspect of real time: a decision-maker can predict only stochastically his response to hypothetical future situations. This is a reasonable feature for models in which the individual can be expected to learn during the course of time. Such a feature implies indeterminism in any sequence of decisions. Even if the consequences of the first decision and the exogenous state of nature at the moment of the second decision were perfectly predictable, we still could not predict exactly that second decision. Hence, the second decision does not follow inevitably from the first and the connection between stages in the process is stochastic. Winter (1971, pp. 254–6) depicts the stochastic evolution of an industry, and Radner (1975, pp. 198–205) discusses a stochastic process of cost reduction. And a general theoretical analysis of probabilistic processes is examined in substantial detail by Howard (1971).

In Schotter (1981, pp. 13–14), a possible framework is described for processes that are both non-deterministic and non-stochastic. There, a game is constructed for which two stable institutional arrangements can be construed as solutions. Because each arrangement is really a class of possible specific solutions, the theory delimits classes rather than exact imputations. This type of outcome is typical of many game–theoretical analyses. "The complete answer to any specific problem consists not in finding a solution, but in determining the set of all solutions" (von Neumann and Morgenstern, 1947, p. 44).

This view has been more recently echoed by Hayek (1967b) in his idea of pattern predictions. Theories of complex phenomena can be expected to predict only the overall pattern of outcomes (e.g., the kind or type of institution) rather than the exact outcome (e.g., the particular variant of the institutional type). If we model a social process as a series of such games, that process will be indeterminate. Even if we know the outcome of the first game and the nature of the second, we cannot say what the particular outcome of the second will be. We can only delimit a class of outcomes given the first outcome.

### *Genuine Uncertainty*

We shall postpone the main discussion of uncertainty to the next chapter. However, it is important to understand that real time implies a characterization of uncertainty that is fundamentally different from that prevalent in neoclassical economics.

Ordinary treatments of uncertainty depict it as a weighted arrangement of already-known possibilities. This is simply a given framework under static uncertainty (Langlois, 1982b). As we have seen, genuine uncertainty involves an open-ended set of possibilities. At the moment of choice, the individual will have conceived of a certain number or range of possibilities. Nevertheless, he is fully aware that in a world of change something might happen that he could not list beforehand. So he perceives his choice set as, in principle, unbounded in at least certain respects.

Genuine uncertainty is inherently ineradicable in the sense that additional knowledge may not enable the individual to overcome it (Dahrendorf, 1968, p. 238). Recall the forecasting example where the forecast altered the predicted event itself. In more general terms, since action takes place in real time, any activity designed to deal with uncertainty may merely transform that uncertainty. The source of uncertainty is thus endogenous in a world in real time.

## NEWTONIAN AND REAL TIME: THE INTERRELATION

Until now, we have merely presented two concepts of time and examined the different implications of each. The impression thus given is of alternative and irreconcilable perspectives. Newtonian and real time, however, are each special cases in a more general temporal analysis. While it is true that these extreme cases are quite distinct, some types of human activity tend more in the one direction and others in the other direction (Bergson, 1911, p. 200). The deciding characteristic is the strength of the mnemic and exceptional link between time periods. As we shall see, creative decision-making (e.g., the setting up of frameworks of analysis) tends in the real-time direction. Ordinary maximizing behavior, on the other hand, tends in the Newtonian direction. Therefore, the actual content of the thought or decision-making process determines the appropriateness of the particular concept of time.

### *Individual Entrepreneurship*

What is commonly called "creative" activity or "insight" involves solving a problem or seeing a solution in a single leap (Bergson, 1920, p. 20). After this undivided insight is gained, an analyst may *reconstruct* the solution in a series of steps that others, at least in principle, are capable of following. The original leap can then be portrayed as the condensation of the reconstructed steps into a single, undivided, one. From the perspective of the less creative activity that follows these explicit steps in time, the more creative activity involves the compression of the past preliminary stages into the present final stage (the problem's solution), and hence a very wide mnemic link.

This is precisely Schumpeter's concept of entrepreneurship. For Schumpeter entrepreneurial success depends on "the capacity of seeing things in a way which afterwards proves to be true, even though it cannot be established at the moment" (1934, p. 85). A creative leap cannot, by definition, be conclusively "established" because it literally leaps over the requisite logical steps. Through this intuition the entrepreneur may be able to discover better technologies, new products and new resources. Similarly, Kirzner (1979, pp. 158–92) has analyzed entrepreneurship at the individual level in which the central task is to formulate the "given" means–ends framework. This framework is logically prior to ordinary maximizing behavior.[1] It is the result of a creative insight or relatively condensed activity.

This analysis has important implications for the agent's perception of the rapidity of time change. In entrepreneurial or creative activity the preliminary stages in a problem solution are seen as part of the very recent past or, in the limit, as an aspect of the subjective present moment. In contrast, the less creative the activity under study, the more distended those stages become, or, equivalently, the narrower the mnemic link between them. Each stage becomes relatively more isolated. Reduction in the degree of creativity is thus associated with a relegation of the stages to the more remote past. Increasing the degree of creativity and the consequent widening of the mnemic link results in a subjective quickening of time. For any given interval of clock time, more is happening *relative to* the less creative state. Thus, the entrepreneur will perceive clock time as passing relatively more quickly (cf. Capek, 1971, p. 200).

### *Maximizing Behavior*

Less creative activity takes each step at a time so that each phase more nearly resembles a Newtonian time period. The steps are relatively isolated from one another and thus the mnemic link is attenuated. This "Newtonization" of time is greater the more the agent's actual solution to a problem is broken down into explicit steps. Solving a problem is made fully explicit when the steps that lead up to the solution are logically sufficient, i.e., when the framework yields determinate implications. In this form of activity there is no place for "creative leaps." Pure Robbinsian maximizing is an example of an explicit step-by-step and determinate technique applied to decision-making. Thus, maximization analysis is compatible with the essential features of Newtonian time.

Since the mnemic link for explicit maximization has a relatively narrow span, the perceived present will encompass a smaller range of activity. This in turn means that, *ceteris paribus*, maximizers perceive clock intervals as passing relatively less quickly. In other words, there is a subjective lengthening of time (cf. Capek, 1971, p. 200).

### *Rules of Thumb*

Routine activity, such as following rules of thumb, moves us still closer to the Newtonian end of our continuum. It is of the essence of a rule of thumb that the individual will perform certain actions without seeing how they fit into an overall picture. Thus, even more than with maximizing behavior, each step in what may appear to the observer a coherent process is relatively isolated and fragmented from the agent's perspective. Thus the mnemic span is further narrowed and subjective time is further slowed.

None of the foregoing discussion of the degrees of real time makes any sense from the perspective that views all decision-making *as if* it were the explicit maximization of some objective function. To the extent that we reconstruct decisions in terms of that framework, we implicitly adopt the Newtonian conception of time. Only by paying attention to the actual content of the typical decision process can we determine the degree to which the activity is best explained in terms of real or Newtonian time.

## CONCLUSION

The differences between a Newtonian and real-time perspective strike at the very heart of economic analysis. In this chapter we have developed some of the more general implications of real time. The fundamental indeterminacy of economic processes and the inseparability of time and change are foremost among these. In the next chapter, we shall discuss more deeply the implications of our view of time for uncertainty and equilibrium. The traditional approaches to these issues will be shown to be inadequate. In chapters 6 and 7 we shall develop our real-time framework in the context of competitive processes and in some of the more important industrial organization and regulatory applications. Most of the remaining chapters in this book, then, can be seen as the development or elaboration of an alternative perspective on time.

## NOTE

1 One might view the formulation of a particular means–ends framework as the outcome of a maximization procedure on a higher level. This, however, merely pushes the question back one step. At some point the framework is formulated in a non-deterministic, entrepreneurial manner.

# 5

# Uncertainty in Equilibrium

> The existence of a problem of knowledge depends on the future being different from the past, while the possibility of the solution of the problem depends on the future being like the past. *Frank H. Knight (1921, p. 313)*

In this chapter we develop the implications of real time for the important ideas of uncertainty and equilibirum. As we have already seen, the "genuine uncertainty" of real time is of a more basic and thoroughgoing nature than that usually treated in neoclassical models. The most important features of genuine uncertainty are the inherent unlistability of all possible outcomes resulting from a course of action, and the complete endogeneity of the uncertainty. The first feature, discussed in the last chapter, is the basis of novelty or true surprise. This is in sharp contrast to the mere arrangement (or weighting) of known possibilities characteristic of neoclassical uncertainty. The second feature, analyzed in the current chapter, is the origin of an ongoing market process that itself produces changes to which the system must adapt. The state of complete adaptation or equilibrium, on the other hand, is pre-eminently a Newtonian concept. The absence of *any* tendency to change is incompatible with real time. Yet, as we shall see, some idea of equilibrium is important. Indeed, it would be difficult to imagine a viable economics without one. Thus, reconciliation between real time and equilibrium is necessary. A suitably reformulated equilibrium construct can be consistent with our real-time framework, and can also be the analytical source of the uncertainty and endogenous changes that pervade market processes. Real time, genuine uncertainty, and equilibrium all have important functions to perform in the analysis of an economic system. The detailed elaboration of this point is the task that we have set ourselves.

This chapter is divided into four sections. In the first, we examine both the endogeneity of uncertainty in real time and its incompatibility with standard notions of equilibrium. In the second section we analyze the anticipation of future events from the perspective of their typical and unique features. It will be shown that neoclassical economics deals with the typical and totally neglects the unique. The third section is a detailed examination of the equilibrium construct. The idea of exact equilibrium will be shown to be inadequate for understanding economic processes in real time. In its place, we advocate the idea of "pattern coordination." Finally, we explore the interrelation between equilibrium and optimality. Static suboptimality is there revealed to be an unhelpful concept. A useful welfare economics can only be based on a fully dynamic and non-deterministic perspective.

## GENUINE UNCERTAINTY

One of the most important features of genuine uncertainty is its endogenous and, consequently, ineradicable nature. In principle, activities directed toward anticipating the future or overcoming uncertainty in a world of real time cannot be completely successful. The famous Keynesian beauty contest (Keynes, 1964, p. 156) is an excellent illustration of this point. (We also make use of it in our discussion of the business cycle.) Since Keynes' illustration lacks an overall stable pattern of outcomes, the actual result is entirely time-dependent and, in this sense, completely unique. We use the term "genuine uncertainty" to refer not only to this aspect of prediction but, more generally, to the recognition that all attempts to characterize the future involve both unique and recurrent ("typical") features. Keynes' illustration emphasizes that aspect of genuine uncertainty that differentiates it from Newtonian or neoclassical uncertainty. This is the pure (Bergsonian) case of complete time dependency.

A hundred photographs are reproduced in a newspaper. Each contestant must choose the six prettiest or handsomest faces. The winner will be that contestant whose choices most closely approximate those of "average opinion." The goal of each contestant is therefore not to choose the six most attractive to him or her (opinion$_1$), or even to guess what average opinion believes to be the most attractive (opinion$_2$). Rather, the object must be to guess what average opinion believes that average opinion will choose (opinion$_3$). Thus, the goal is to guess opinion$_3$, which is, in turn, opinion$_4$. As we shall see, there is in principle no limit to the height of the levels of guessing and counterguessing. There is no *logically sufficient* reason to stop at any given point; all such stopping is, to a large extent, arbitrary or dervied from a convention. We have more to say on this last point in chapter 10.

The two features of Keynes' example that we shall explore in detail are its endogeneity and its inconsistency with static equilibrium.

## *Endogeneity*

Suppose there is an agency that collects and disseminates the guesses before they are actually entered in the contest (see the similar technique in Frydman, 1982). Now people know for sure what the average guesses of opinion$_3$ are at $t_1$. If every individual merely duplicates this opinion$_4$, then no one will win. The prize will be so diluted (let us assume) that it is not enough to offset the opportunity costs of engaging in the contest. Therefore, in an effort to improve his chances, each individual will revise his guesses. Consider that the individual could act in one of two ways: (1) he could choose those pictures the agency reveals as the average choice and receive a negligible payoff, or (2) he could deviate from those in the hope that others will do the same and he will approximate the new average choices. In the knowledge that at least some, if not all, will act in accordance with (2), all will, in fact, do so. Now, of course, the point is to outguess or outpredict the crowd on the nature of these revisions. Therefore, there is still uncertainty, despite the existence of the information-disseminating agency. Further information has not eliminated (or even, in this example, reduced) uncertainty but has merely transformed it to a higher level of counterguessing.[1] If the game is played round after round, people's opinions will continually change and there will be no natural end to the process.

There are two factors in Keynes' example responsible for its endogeneity. First, because we are dealing with a contest, it is obviously important to each contestant that he predict better than all the others. Thus, he has an incentive to gather such information as will give him an advantage or prevent others from gaining one. Second, because the individual is making predictions of predictions rather than of tastes, resource availability, and so forth, the relevant information will be what others are predicting. Therefore, knowledge gained over time by market participants will necessarily affect the objects of each agent's prediction. These considerations enable us to conclude that the very activity designed to cope with uncertainty (i.e., the acquisition of knowledge) is responsible for its continued existence. As soon as one level of uncertainty is eliminated, another level is necessarily created to replace it.

At any *point* in time, the uncertainty of this example can be seen in purely Newtonian terms. Every individual might be viewed as having a probability distribution over the possible guesses of average opinion. If we were to stop here, this would be no different than the uncertainty about tomorrow's weather or the outcome of some conventional game of chance. On the other hand, the important aspects of the example are only evident in the passage of time. From that perspective it becomes clear that we do not have the interaction of stable elements (like the isolated points of Newtonian time). The interaction itself ceaselessly changes those elements. As knowledge is allowed to increase, uncertainty is not eliminated but transformed.

### *Inconsistency with Equilibrium*

Purely time-dependent uncertainty is completely inconsistent with static equilibrium. In our example of this uncertainty there is no configuration of the "data" that is without a tendency to change. As long as time is allowed to pass, knowledge will grow and there will be endogenously produced change.[2] Accordingly, it is not possible for the system to settle down to an equilibrium, whether of the exact or stochastic variety. Individuals always have a private incentive to overcome remaining uncertainty. As we have seen, however, the collective result of the actions undertaken on the basis of this incentive is to transform, rather than eliminate, uncertainty.

In a recent article Roman Frydman (1982) applies Keynes' beauty contest to a model that examines the possibility of convergence to rational expectations equilibrium. Not surprisingly,

Frydman finds that under no plausible set of assumptions can we characterize a learning process that leads to an equilibrium. Such a process would have to involve forming expectations about the expectations of others (O'Driscoll, 1979, p. 162; cf. Rizzo, 1979, p. 11). Frydman's point, like ours, is that there is a form of uncertainty that cannot be eradicated by further knowledge. This is the time-dependent aspect of genuine uncertainty.

The critical contrast is therefore not, as some have suggested, between measurable and unmeasurable uncertainty (Knight, 1971), or even between subjective and objective interpretations of probability (Savage, 1977). It is instead between purely time-dependent and Newtonian forms of uncertainty. The former, as we have seen, is endogenously created and thus inconsistent with equilibrium, while the latter is essentially static and thus consistent with stochastic models of equilibrium. Neoclassical tools for handling uncertainty have been developed in the context of these models and consequently are adapted solely to the Newtonian perspective. To the extent that economists wish to construct models embodying time-dependent uncertainty, it is clear that new analytical tools will have to be developed.[3]

An important implication of time-dependent uncertainty is that exchanges will not take place at equilibrium prices. If the economic system endogenously produces disruptive forces, then we can no longer abstract from the problems of false trading. Instead of focusing our attention on the configuration of equilibrium exchanges or even the process of adjustment toward an equilibrium, the emphasis will shift to the pattern of disequilibrium exchanges. The "Austrian" business cycle theory is an example of systematic disequilibrium trading that results in a particular pattern of discoordinative behavior. This shall be examined in our chapter on money. Other attempts to study "disequilibrium patterns" have been reviewed by E. R. Weintraub (1979, pp. 141–54). The importance of these models lies in making the informational needs of agents quite specific. Since these needs cannot be fully satisfied by false prices, our attention is naturally shifted to the institutional framework and its role in promoting (or inhibiting) the coordination of plans. Nonprice conveyance of information is a necessary foundation for the process of monetary exchanges through time. We shall have more to say on this matter in the chapters on competition and money.

## GENUINE UNCERTAINTY: TYPICALITY AND UNIQUENESS

The purely time-dependent form of uncertainty discussed in the previous section must be an incomplete characterization of the way in which individuals anticipate the future. If the future were completely unpredictable in all respects, then planning and acting would be impossible. While complete stability and predictability are incompatible with time, their total absence is incompatible with action (Shackle, 1969, pp. 3–7). A stable framework within which it is possible to project consequences is a logical prerequisite for purposefulness. The solution to this paradox of uncertainty lies in the recognition of typical and unique aspects of future events. Genuine uncertainty is characterized by both relatively time-independent and time-dependent features in the flow of events. The crucial difficulty with neoclassical economics is its exclusive preoccupation with the former.

### *Typification*

Typification is the activity that enables us to grapple with an unknown future. It is the process of "extracting what stability and regularity there is in the flow of reality" (Bergson, 1946, p. 111). Stable features are called types (Schutz and Luckmann, 1973, pp. 229–41). The stability of types is not to be identified solely with those aspects of events that actually *have* been repeated in case after case. Rather, stability refers to those aspects that are repeatable, in the sense that they are not affected by the mere passage of time. Consider, for example, the prediction that there will be a police patrol tonight. This amounts to a pattern or type prediction because we are quite able to conceive of a patrol as persisting in some unchanged overall pattern through time. The precise route they will take, what they will find, how they will react to a bank robbery, and so on constitute the (relatively) unique or time-dependent features of an event. Even these can be further broken down into their typical and unique aspects. The exact form that any prediction takes is thus obviously dependent on the practical interests and conceptual framework of the predictor.

Typical aspects of events can be anticipated in one or two ways: either with certainty, or probabilistically. From the certainty perspective, the predictor simply asserts that there will be a police patrol. In the probabilistic perspective, on the other hand, the predictor associates with a whole set of mutually exclusive typical events a series of weights. Thus, the probability of a police patrol may be 0.4, that of a gang brawl 0.2 and that of a delivery of illegal narcotics 0.4. The typicality of the future events is no different in the second than in the first case; what is different is the way in which they are anticipated. Probabilistic anticipation is the "loose," as contrasted to rigid, determinism discussed in chapter 2. Nevertheless, even loose determinism is fundamentally static in at least two respects. First, there is a stationarity of the alternative events through time. This, after all, is the meaning of typicality. Open-endedness in the characterization of the alternatives is not possible. Second, techniques such as modification of probabilities based on Bayes' Theorem permit only deterministic changes. Given the occurrence of a certain subsequent typical event, there is only one way the probability weights can be altered.

The extraction of types or patterns is made possible by factors that affect both the state of the environment and individual interaction. In the first category, the possibility of typification rests on the stability of physical laws, that is, on the relative determinism of the world on the macro-(Newtonian) level. On this, of course, we can add nothing to the existing scientific literature. In the second category, there are the mutually reinforcing and stabilizing effects of rules of thumb and certain kinds of creative activity. Rules of thumb are adopted by agents when the computational demands of maximization are excessive (Hey, 1981, pp. 252–3), or when the recognition of time-dependent uncertainty makes the informational demands of maximization impossible (Loasby, 1976, p. 217). In the latter situation the probability distributions required by agents for maximization of expected utility are seen as incomplete descriptions of the relevant uncertainty. In either event, when agents follow rules of thumb their behavior is more predictable. Under a wide variety of situations the same rule will be applied.

Furthermore, creative entrepreneurship, spurred on by profit opportunities, strives to make coordination of plans possible. By shouldering uncertainty (Knight, 1971), or by attempting to foresee the future more accurately, entrepreneurs reduce the effective amount of uncertainty facing others (Kirzner, 1982). This does not mean that entrepreneurial activity does not create some uncertainty of its own. It simple means that, relative to a world of no entrepreneurship, the changes that exogenously impinge on a system are less disruptive. Because of entrepreneurship there is more stability and regularity in the flow of events.

### *Uniqueness*

The unique features of events are the non-repeatable aspects or, in other words, the specific time-dependent variants of a stable pattern. Non-repeatability emerges from an event's temporal "place value" (Schutz and Luckmann, 1973, p. 240), that is, from its order in the flow of events. From the experience of any given event we derive certain interpretatively relevant conceptual structures that modify any subsequent experience (Schutz and Luckmann, 1973, p. 240). Thus, any attempt to anticipate the unique aspects of an event changes their place value at least because the anticipation itself must now affect the eventual experience. This is endogeneity of genuine uncertainty about which we have been talking. Consideration of a future event's unique features also emphasizes the basic open-endedness of anticipation in real time. We anticipate events as to their typical features but we cannot fill in the "details" beforehand.

In contrast, neoclassical economics evades the distinction between uniqueness and typicality. Those aspects of events are conflated when each possible situation or outcome is "condensed" into a single scalar quantity. From this perspective we delude ourselves into thinking that we have fully characterized the event and thus eliminated the open-endedness of the future. In reality, we have only characterized a single typical feature of the event in question and ignored everything else.

Since events can never be predicted precisely but only predicted as to types, there are three important circumstances under which the individual's interpretative–predictive scheme can change. First, when the typical event is anticipated with certainty, it still may not occur: a police patrol need not materialize. If it does not, the individual will obviously revise his view of what is stable in the environment. This is similar to what is generally meant by the refutation of a theory: when a predicted typical event does not occur, the theory undergoes change. Second, when typical events are anticipated probabilistically any outcome may induce revisions in the agent's framework. This depends on whether the actual outcome causes the agent to believe that the underlying probability distribution is different than he had originally thought.

Finally, even when the typical event does occur, or when the occurrence of a given typical event out of a set of possibilities does not itself cause the perceived underlying probability distribution to change, the agent may be led to revise his scheme. The unique aspects of events (or, more exactly, what appeared unique relative to the initial framework) provide further "data points" for its improvement.[4] Since types are, by definition, the relatively stable elements in the flow of time, they will change only slowly. In other words, the interpretative framework and the types derived from it will change so gradually as to maintain their stability *relative* to the changes in the unique elements. Ultimately, however, a new framework necessarily arises out of the old. The bifurcation of our anticipatory vision into unique as well as typical features means that even correct prediction carries with it an endogenous source of eventual change. This source is the inevitable filling in of the "details" as events actually occur. As long as there are open-ended anticipations there will always, in the course of time, be at least gradual change in the frameworks from which they are derived.

## EQUILIBRIUM

In the last two sections we discussed the implications of real time for the characterization of uncertainty. We saw that, in a world of time and genuine uncertainty, there is ceaseless endogenous change. In this and subsequent sections we shall direct our attention to the seemingly contradictory idea of equilibrium. Equilibrium has traditionally been centered on the absence of endogenous change. It has been conceived as the state of affairs produced after all endogenous forces have fully worked themselves out. From this perspective, time and equilibrium are surely incompatible (Shackle, 1972, pp. 253–4). It would be a mistake, however, to insist that equilibrium entails the absence of any and all tendencies to change. The uncertainty framework developed in this book can be incorporated into an equilibrium construct in such a way as to allow for unpredictable change. As we shall see, an appropriately revised idea of equilibrium need not be inconsistent with real time.

### *Equilibrium as Exact Coordination*

Austrians generally follow Hayek (1937a,) in thinking of equilibrium in terms of the compatibility of individual plans. Thus, if A intends to buy *x* units of a good at \$*y* per unit, then B (or some group of B's) must intend to sell *x* at \$*y*. This is a situation of *ex ante* coordination. If equilibrium is to prevail, however, the intentions of the various parties must be based on the same set of expectations regarding the external data. A may plan to buy umbrellas tomorrow on the expectation that it will rain, while B may plan to sell umbrellas on the expectation that it will not. Under these circumstances, the plans of the relevant parties cannot in principle be carried out. There is no single state of the world in which both A and B will actually implement their plans. Accordingly, the state of *ex ante* coordination is not enough for equilibrium; there must also be no *logical* impossibility standing in the way of the actual consumation of intentions.

Hayekian equilibrium can be partial or general, and can prevail over the various "runs" of Marshallian time. The degree to which equilibrium requires the homogeneity of expectations can be seen by contrasting the long run with Hicksian temporary equilibrium. In the former, all individuals must base their plans on the same expectations over the indefinite future. Thus, there must be complete expectational homogeneity. In temporary equilibrium, on the other hand, plans to buy and sell may be based on conflicting expectations with respect to the farther future. In fact, the existence of purely speculative markets *requires* the divergence of expectations (Lachmann, 1978, p. 5). Bulls plan to buy on the expectation that the price will rise, and bears plan to sell on the expectation that it will fall.

Nevertheless, the attainment of temporary coordination requires that the intentions of buyers and sellers be based on the same expectations *with respect to the trading day*. Suppose individuals make their plans at the beginning of the day and implement them by the end of the day. The ability of all parties to carry out their plans requires that, for example, expectations with respect to the time of sale be homogeneous. Expectational heterogeneity with respect to the more distant future will not frustrate this temporary coordination. Hayekian equilibrium therefore must entail homogeneous expectations with respect to the time period within which equilibrium prevails. Outside of that period, however, expectations can, and sometimes must, be divergent.

The homogeneity of expectations does not imply that they will turn out to be correct. Coordinative equilibrium is fundamentally a subjectivist construct and does not require consistency with the objective external data. If the expectations on which both parties base their intentions prove to be incorrect, then we say that the data have changed. Indeed "change" in a subjectivist framework can only be defined relative to the state of expectations (Hayek, 1973a, p. 40). Equilibrium is thus perfectly consistent with error. Error, once discovered, will however cause the equilibrium position to change.

The consistency of Hayekian equilibrium with error provides the foundation for a wider appreciation of its subjectivist character. The importance of expectations means that equilibrium cannot be defined without reference to the interpretative–predictive schemes held by individuals. When these change so does the equilibrium. Furthermore, the objective possibilities, stressed by neoclassical economics as a codeterminant of equilibrium, are often not a binding constraint. In a world of divided knowledge, there is no single objective state of technique that governs the entire system. What the *individual* has learned is the constraint, and not all individuals will have learned the same things. Far from being an objective "pull" on the system, equilibrium makes sense only in the context of the presumed knowledge and expectations of economic agents. Equilibrium need not be a holdover from objectivist Ricardian economics. Instead, it can be seen as a particular relationship among a myriad individual minds.

### *Inadequacy of Exact Coordination*

Hayek's avowed intention in developing his concept of equilibrium as the consistency of individual plans was to marry time and equilibrium (Hayek, 1937a, p. 37). Since plans are forward-looking, he reasoned that plan coordination must entail time. Unfortunately, he did not fully understand the distinction between the Newtonian and real-time constructs. Hayekian equilibrium incorporated only Newtonian time. Nevertheless, Hayek and the other Austrians did realize that equilibrium is not a directly operational construct and that the real world was never in equilibrium. They saw, however, at least two empirical uses for the concept of exact equilibrium.

One was that it constitutes a research agenda; that is, it points to those factors worthy of further consideration. The other was a more sweeping claim: by reference to the construct, it was believed that we could predict the direction of real-world changes. In the following subsections we shall analyze these two views. Our examination of the purported uses of exact equilibrium will reveal its ultimate inadequacy.

*Research agenda* Mises developed what he called an *argumentum a contrario* (1966, p. 250). According to this, the equilibrium construct can be used as a foil against which to compare actual market situations. Thus, if conditions a, b and c together imply a certain equilibrium, then the absence of that equilibrium would imply that at least one of these conditions does not hold. Economic analysis then focuses on the forces responsible for this situation. Consequently, from Mises' perspective, the exact equilibrium construct merely provides us with a clue as to why certain results do not obtain. Hence, it is capable of only negative prediction of states of affairs. It does not elucidate the actual processes by which those states may be achieved. It points us in the direction of those countervailing forces that are responsible for the actual outcome being different from the equilibrium outcome. Thus, exact equilibrium elucidates not the actual processes themselves but only the reason they do not produce a certain result. Hence it is fundamentally capable of only negative prediction.

Mises, however, claimed too much. This method does not permit us to offer a logically sufficient explanation for the "failure" of actual processes. For this to be the case, the conditions of equilibrium would have to be necessary conditions, whereas, in fact, they are merely sufficient conditions (Hausman, 1981, p. 152). The absence of sufficient conditions does not imply the absence of the result predicted by the equilibrium construct (e.g., Pareto optimality). Only the absence of all possible sets of sufficient conditions (the conjunction of which is a necessary condition) would imply this. Therefore, the foil method provides only part of the total explanation for the observed phenomena. Such partial explanations are also consistent with outcomes other than those observed, because sometimes the other sufficient conditions will be present and sometimes they will be absent. Hence an element of *indeterminism* is introduced into the explanatory process.

*Direction of change* In contrast to Mises, Hayek argued that equilibrium could be useful in making positive predictions. Indeed he contended that "the statement of the conditions under which individual plans will be compatible is . . . implicitly a statement of what *will* happen if they are not compatible" (Hayek, 1941, p. 23; emphasis added). If all other prices are at their equilibrium levels and the price of apples is too high, relative to the price of oranges, to equate supply and demand, then the equilibrium construct tells us that the price of apples will fall. Hayek immediately recognized that, when there are many deviations from equilibrium, the "correct" change will depend on what is assumed to happen in the other markets (1941, p. 23, n. 1). In general, this will make predicting the direction of change an extremely complex matter.

The prediction of the direction of real-world changes is actually a form of pattern prediction. We are saying that a result of the type predicted by the construct will happen. If, as in our previous example, the price of apples were too high, a predicted fall is compatible with a whole host of actual changes. The only thing that unifies these changes is that they are all consistent with the type "fall-in-price." Therefore, for all practical or applied purposes we have departed from the exact conception of equilibrium. Equilibrium is now a direction rather than a point. This departure, however, has proceeded purely informally and is akin to merely "accidental" observational error.

As we have seen, both the research agenda and direction-of-change interpretations of the exact equilibrium construct take account of its imperfect applicability. But is this enough? Should we maintain an essentially timeless equilibrium and view indeterminism as merely a feature of the model's application? Or must we incorporate the indeterminism arising from real time and genuine uncertainty into the construct itself? If we are interested in using the idea of equilibrium to model or elucidate processes in real time, then consigning indeterminism merely to the realm of application is not sufficient. It is impermissible to model such a process as culminating in an exact equilibrium for two related reasons. First, recall the Popper–Schick proofs of the impossibility of agents predicting their own behavior (chapter 2). If agents are uncertain about what they will do in the future, then they will never make plans that are exactly coordinated with those of others. Commitments will then be of a general variety rather than pinpointed to the precise future behavior of others (even assuming that the latter could be predicted).

Second, Oskar Morgenstern demonstrated that the assumption of perfect foresight, a defining characteristic of exact equilibrium, is inconsistent with any equilibrating *process*. He showed that, when one individual's plan is dependent on that of another, perfect foresight will produce "an endless chain of reciprocally conjectural reactions and counter-reactions" (Morgenstern, 1935, p. 174). This was illustrated in the famous Holmes–Moriarity story that is worth quoting in full:

> Sherlock Holmes, pursued by his opponent, Moriarity, leaves London for Dover. The train stops at a station on the way, and he alights there rather than travelling on to Dover. He has seen Moriarity at the railway station, recognizes that he is very clever and expects that Moriarity will take a faster special train in order to catch him in Dover. Holmes' anticipation turns out to be correct. But what if Moriarity had been still more clever, had estimated Holmes' mental abilities and had foreseen his actions accordingly? Then, obviously, he would have travelled to the intermediate station. Holmes, again, would have had to calculate that and he himself would have decided to go on to Dover. Whereupon, Moriarity would again have "reacted" differently. Because of so much thinking they might not have been able to act at all or the intellectually weaker of the two would have surrendered in the Victoria Station, since the whole flight would have become unnecessary. (Morgenstern, 1935, pp. 173–4)

The equilibrium in this illustration would be a stable set of plans that might result in Holmes escaping or in his being captured. That aspect of the solution is unimportant (to us); what is important would be the absence of any tendency for the plans of the individuals to change. In equilibrium their plans would be coordinated in the sense that each is optimal given what the other individual is in fact planning. The moral of the Holmes–Moriarity story, however, is that perfect knowledge of each other's plans makes attaining such an equilibrium impossible. Neither individual will be satisfied with any tentatively adopted plan and so coordination cannot be achieved.[5] Despite allegedly perfect foresight –

or, rather, precisely because of it – the genuine uncertainty of the Keynesian beauty contest has reasserted itself.

Therefore, imperfect foresight is a necessary, although not sufficient, condition for a process to result in an equilibrium. This equilibrium cannot, however, be a position of exact co-ordination. A process in which there must be errors cannot, except by chance, culminate in an errorless equilibrium. Hence, if we are to retain the notion of equilibrium, we must incorporate the reality of error into the construct itself.

### *Pattern Coordination*

The inadequacy of exact Hayekian equilibrium for the analysis of processes in real time means that we are faced with two alternatives: either (1) revise the equilibrium construct so as to incorporate time and uncertainty, or (2) abandon equilibrium altogether. Since Austrians have never believed that the state of plan coordination is a direct description of the real world, the issue is not one of "realism"; instead, it is the usefulness of the idea as a tool of analysis.

In the broadest sense, equilibrium is inextricably linked to the causal mode of reasoning. An equilibrium is merely a state of affairs in which the exogenous disturbing forces or changes have completely worked themselves out (Machlup, 1958, p. 48). As a pure construct, it is thus a mental laboratory in which various causes can be isolated from one another and their effects fully traced. Therefore, we believe that *some* concept of equilibrium is an indispensable ingredient in all economic explanations.

The only feasible alternative is to revise our notion of equilibrium by taking account of time and uncertainty. This process has been started in the work of those neoclassical economists who utilize the idea of a stochastic equilibrium. We propose, however, a different construct: pattern coordination. This makes use of both the original Hayekian "compatibility of plans" and the distinction between typical and unique aspects of future events. The plans of individuals are in a pattern equilibrium if they are coordinated with respect to their typical features, even if their unique aspects fail to mesh.

Consider, as an illustration, Professors A and B, who teach in the same department and who plan to discuss their forthcoming jointly authored book. Their plans are coordinated with respect to the typical features of their activities if, for example, each expects the other to be in his office on the day he actually plans to be there. Since neither has decided his position on the book's central concern beforehand, the contents of their discussions can be seen as the unique feature. What they will say depends on the "insights" that will arise only in the course of conversation. These insights are surely time-dependent. The plans of A and B are coordinated, therefore, in the sense that each will come into the office on the proper day and at the proper time, but they are not coordinated in the sense that each has planned what to say to the other. There is an open-endedness to their plans that allows for spontaneity or novelty. This is a pattern coordination.

There is also a looser form of pattern coordination, which we can call "stochastic pattern coordination." In this case, the typical features of activities are probabilistically coordinated. Thus, in the above illustration, both A and B may "envisage" a probability distribution over the days of the week of the other coming into the office. They each decide when to come based on this probability distribution. Sometimes the typical aspect of their activities will mesh in the exact sense and sometimes they will not. Overall, however, each individual is doing the best he can under the circumstances and so an equilibrium has been attained. The exact contents of the discussions, when they do occur, remain time-dependent. Therefore, this aspect of each individual's plans is not subject to stochastic characterization and must be truly open-ended.

In a manner characteristic of Newtonian time constructs, the conception of exact equilibrium conflates plans with activities. The looser idea, which we have called pattern coordination, involves the coordination of plans but not of actual activities. Plans made in a world of real time, as we have seen, must be open-ended. They embody the typical features of prospective actions and events, while the details are "filled in" as actions and events come to pass. Thus, coordination can exist with respect to plans or the typical features of planned activities, but not with respect to the actual activities themselves. The latter are a complex of typical and unique features and are not stable in real time.

A broadened or wider view of causality underlies the use of pattern coordination as a tool of process analysis. In the exact conception of equilibrium, tracing out the full effects of a change means showing how that change brings about a precise result. In the pattern view, on the other hand, we show the "full" effects of a disturbance when we follow it out to a certain class of results. In this sense, the causal analysis is less "full" or complete than in the exact case. This very incompleteness, however, constitutes a major advantage of pattern coordination. Real time and genuine uncertainty are not, by construction, eliminated from the analysis.

Equilibrium, in our new, less rigid sense, does not entail the complete absence of all tendencies to change. As we have seen, some features are stable while others continue to vary. The relatively stable types or patterns are, in the short run, affected only by exogenous shocks to the system. In other words, something more than the mere passage of time is needed to induce pattern reorganization. The unique aspects of events, however, are time-dependent and hence change from within the system. These kinds of changes are what constitute the *endogenous* market process.[6] In that process market participants acquire non-theoretical "knowledge of the particular circumstances of time and place" (Hayek, 1945, p. 521) as the future comes into existence. Although such knowledge cannot be anticipated in either an exact or a probabilistic sense, the essence of entrepreneurship is to attempt to "see" these developments in advance. Because this aspect of the future is, by definition, time-dependent, no logically sufficient basis can be given for any particular prediction. Therefore, the entrepreneurial predictions will appear to be creative or intuitive rather than strict implications of a model. The goal of the economist, therefore, must be to render entrepreneurial prediction and its derivative behavior "intelligible." As we have seen in chapter 2, this means that the conceptual scheme attributed to the relevant mind construct must show how the predicted behavior is more likely given the scheme than otherwise.

The analysis of an individual dealing with unique features of future events must involve a non-distributional measure of uncertainty. We cannot distribute unity over a fixed set of possibilities and expect to capture the essential indeterminism or open-endedness of the future. Shackle (1969, pp. 67–85, 117–69) has developed a framework ("potential surprise") designed to cope with this aspect of expectation. We shall not here try to restate his position or the criticisms that have been offered (Shackle, 1969, pp. 86–108, 170–9). It is sufficient, however, to note that neither subjectivists nor anyone else has fully developed a formalism to deal with this problem. This is one of the most critical tasks that remain to be completed in order fully to implement a subjectivist research program.

There are, to be sure, certain similarities between our concept of pattern coordination and neoclassical stochastic equilibrium. Nevertheless, there is a fundamental distinction. The crux lies in the recognition of uniqueness. In a stochastic pattern equilibrium the typical features are probabilistically coordinated as in the conventional stochastic equilibrium. However, the neoclassical analysis ignores time dependency. In so doing, it reduces all ideas of uncertainty and inexact equilibrium to pure Newtonian constructs.

The usefulness of a non-deterministic conception of equilibrium lies in our ability to use it to model adjustments in a manner that does not foreordain their outcomes. As we shall see in the next chapter, the competitive process is a *discovery procedure* and thus, in principle, its results cannot be predicted. On the other hand, it is important to be able to say something about the major features of market processes. The idea of pattern coordination allows us to have it both ways: we can discuss adjustments in general (pattern) terms while recognizing the essential creativeness of market activities.

## EQUILIBRIUM AND OPTIMALITY

### *Knowledge Requirement for Equilibrium*

Unlike the general competitive equilibrium of Arrow and Debreu, a Hayekian equilibrium, in either its exact or its pattern form, is not necessarily Pareto-optimal. Participants in any given exchange are not assumed to possess all of the knowledge in the system or, especially, the knowledge of the observer. The knowledge requirement for plan coordination is simply that expectations be correct in the sense that nothing agents are "bound" to learn in the execution of their plans will falsify those expectations (Hayek, 1937a, p. 55). In effect, this means that equilibrium requires the absence of the type of endogenous learning that would upset initial (exact or pattern) plans. There ought to be nothing in the original configuration of data that will bring about their undoing. What individuals are bound to learn in any given situation depends, of course, on what the model-builder puts into his construction. This, in turn, depends on the empirical appropriateness of his assumptions about learning. Presumably, if an individual plans to erect a skyscraper he will inevitably learn whether the ground underneath will support such a heavy structure. Moreover, we may require him to learn what other individuals will reveal or do in the course of executing his plans. Market activity, for example, may cause the price of certain types of labor and materials to rise before the skyscraper is completed. This could result in the project being left unfinished. Only if such information is correctly anticipated at the beginning of the period can there be plan coordination.

### *Irrelevance of Suboptimality in Static Equilibrium Models*

A number of neoclassical economists have recognized that meaningful welfare economics cannot be based on Pareto optimality as the standard of evaluation. Suboptimality relative to knowledge possessed by an omniscient observer is completely irrelevant. In the absence of a feasible alternative institution that could remedy the problem, we have merely demonstrated that the world is imperfect (Demsetz, 1969). This, of course, will always be the case. Suboptimality relative to information possessed by some "isolated" individual in the system is also irrelevant in the absence of a tendency to dissemination. Dissemination may be impossible owing to the costs of acquiring information. If it is argued that optimality-producing information can, *in some way*, be provided to the system, there is an obvious puzzle. It is inexplicable, in a static context, that such information has not *already* been provided or is not already being provided at the optimal rate. Static models effectively abolish time and succession. All that eventually "will" happen happens now. Therefore, what started out as a suboptimal state of affairs is now revealed to have been an optimum all along. Standard equilibria are optimal with respect to the knowledge that the relevant agents do have. In other words, people make the best use of what they know (the "efficient markets" hypothesis). But this is trivial from a normative perspective: optimality here means nothing more or less than equilibrium. Pursuit of this line of reasoning would lead to the crude Panglossian tautology that has plagued the work of some economists (e.g. Stigler, 1982).

Only something exogenous to the model can account for the system's suboptimality. This is equivalent to saying that static maximizing models cannot explain (rationalize) suboptimality;

they can merely postulate it. Either an equilibrium is suboptimal in an irrelevant and unexplained sense, or it is optimal in an explained but trivial sense. Static welfare economics thus self-destructs. As long as there are logically sufficient reasons for a given imperfect state of knowledge, we obviously cannot say that there could be less ignorance. The pre-existing conditions (e.g., costs and benefits of search) rigorously imply that state of knowledge. Consequently, we must loosen the link between causes and results in order to say that things *could* be better or that more knowledge *could* prevail. As we have seen, a conceptual framework that takes time seriously will introduce such indeterminism in the structure of models.

Thus, from the dynamic perspective developed in this book, there can be some role for welfare economics. Since knowledge would then be changing, we obviously could not evaluate a system by the efficiency of its allocations relative to some fixed body of knowledge. Instead, the only possible standard would be the degree to which various processes and systems generate knowledge or make discoveries. The competitive market, viewed as an engine of discovery, is the topic of the next chapter. In that chapter, we deal with welfare analysis in a dynamic theory.

## NOTES

1 This is not to deny that the uncertainty could be overcome for an individual if the agency were to reveal the guesses only to that individual. If no one else knew this, then there would be no incentive for anyone except the lucky person to change his guesses. This, however, would mean that we were back in a Newtonian world.
2 For purposes of the model, time will stop if the agency called an end to its activities and people were required to make their final guesses.
3 G. L. S. Shackle has made an important start in this direction. See especially Shackle (1969).
4 Although the framework may have predicted "well" in the past, it could have done better. In addition, circumstances may have changed and so the framework must also change in order to do equally well in the future.
5 Another example of the phenomenon was provided by G. B. Richardson (1960). Assume, initially, that in one industry there is an "initially" expected rate of return higher than the normal rate. Assume further that all market participants have perfect foresight of this and that all the other conventional assumptions of the competitive model have been satis-

fied. If each potential entrant must take into account the behavior of others because they can produce competitive supply, there will be either an indefinite expansion of output or no expansion at all. If everyone foresees a supernormal return, then an indefinitely large number of firms will enter at the same time and the actual rate of return will be indefinitely lower than the "initially" expected return. But if people are very clever they will foresee this and not enter. If, however, no one enters, then the rate will again fail to be bid down to the equilibrium level. In neither case, then, is the assumption of perfect foresight compatible with a tendency toward equilibrium. This is not a mere cobweb-like situation but rather a problem of logical circularity. Each potential entrant must make his decisions on the basis of what others decide. Perfect knowledge of what they intend to do, however, paralyzes the ability of each to make any decisions at all. Also cf. Frydman, O'Driscoll, and Schotter (1982).

6 There is an "exogenous market process" only in the sense of a market reaction to exogenous shocks. Although the process may be initiated by something outside the system, the adjustment process itself is endogenous.

# Part II

# Applications

# 6

# Competition and Discovery

> The theory of perfect competition is unscientific because, by assuming a world of perfect knowledge in which firms cannot interact to change their economic environments, such a theory imposes pompous preconditions on our subject matter: competitors are so constrained in the behavior in which they can engage . . . . we are precluded from understanding economic reality or developing a testable theory. *Burton H. Klein (1977, p. 71)*

## INTRODUCTION

### *A Parable on Competition*

Consider a sports game for which spectators and participants agree that the rules are fair. The judges of individual sports events profess, however, to know beforehand what the outcome of individual contests should be. Failure of the sports events to produce the predicted outcome results in condemnation of them by these judges. Judicial nullification sometimes involves substituting the preferred or predicted winner for the actual winner of the contest. Sometimes, however, the judges require that the sports event be replayed over and over again, until the "correct" outcome is produced. Plays are called back, races rerun, and contests repeated, not because of untoward conduct or fouls committed by participants, but solely because the "wrong" outcome results. If, contrary to judicial expectations, a particular participant or team persists in winning, that person or team is handicapped or perhaps even forbidden from playing in the future. The judges assert that they are enforcing rules, but the evidence that rules have been broken is inferred from the fact that other than the predicted winner came out first in the game.

Some creative judges produce theories about what unfair activity *must* be going on to produce the unwanted results. However, these theories generally involve hypothetical actions not observed by anyone. Observable behavior that is blamed for bad outcomes cannot be distinguished by participants or spectators from approved behavior.

Clearly, no such sports contest exists. The enforcement of such rules would make a mockery of playing the game or running the race. Almost everyone recognizes that the winner of a sports event cannot be defined apart from who finishes first or scores the most points. "Winning" means nothing but playing fairly and coming in first. "Playing fairly" is defined before the fact in terms of observable behavior during the contest, and not, of course, in terms of after-the-fact outcomes. Teams or individuals scoring highly are not penalized for doing so, and certainly are not implicated in cheating merely because they frequently win by large margins. There is no sports foul of "excess points."

Indeed, sports contests are played precisely because we cannot and do not know before the event who is the better player or team. Prior expectations of winners and losers are frequently falsified. To know the outcome with certainty would be to render the playing of the game unintelligible. To rig the results after the fact would be to perpetrate an injustice on players and spectators alike.

We claim that this procedure, which would be rejected out of hand for sports competition – or any other kind of competitive "race" in life, including that for most scientific analysis – is precisely that adopted by the vast majority of economists in thinking about competition. What would be an obvious paradox is suppressed by redefining "competition" to mean nearly the opposite of the behavior and phenomena it obstensibly denotes.

In this chapter, we argue that economic competition has more in common with other competitive activities in life than it has with economists' standard conceptualization of economic competition. Competition is most fruitfully viewed as a process rather than a state of affairs. Viewing competition in static terms causes numerous analytical problems, some of which we highlight in this chapter. Among other things, static competition theory ignores the fact that only if there is a rivalrous, competitive process will the desirable normative properties of competition tend to be produced. For instance, statutory monopolies are objectionable not only because they produce a *given* product at higher pieces, but also because they fail to produce the range and quality of products preferred by consumers.

More generally, we argue that the theory of perfect competition denies the very reality it purports to study, is a poor predictive theory, and is untenable in normative analysis. As well as offering a critique of current approaches, we present our own approach. We try to be concrete and offer examples, for we believe that only by offering numerous examples can we suggest just how unsatisfactory the dominant theory of competition is. Moreover, in many cases we view these problems as exemplary of the future research agenda of a process theory of competition.

## *Perfect Competition*

It is well-known that in economic theory "competition" means the opposite of its meaning either in ordinary language or in commonsense economic discussions of competition. This ironic use of "competition" is seen as a virtue rather than a vice. Theorists argue that perfect competition teaches us about important relationships among economic variables in competitive equilibrium and about certain normative properties of equilibrium. Before examining these professed benefits, we shall look at what is lost by using the theory.

Perfect competition is a theory of states, not of processes; it tells us nothing about the adjustment from one competitive equilibrium state to another. In fact, if we consider what we know from general economic theory, we must be pessimistic about the system's ability to move from one hypothetical equilibrium state to another. Equilibrium positions are not path-independent. False trading, for example, produces wealth effects, which in turn generate a new implied equilibrium, different from the original one.

Not only does theory tell us nothing about adjustment processes, but, when taken seriously, it implies that there ought to be no process of adjustment at all (see chapter 3 above, pp. 54–5). Once a new equilibrium is known, agents move to it immediately.

Competition in fact is a continuous process and not a set of conditions. As Hayek (1948, p. 94) observed of competition, its "essential characteristics are assumed away by the assumptions underlying static analysis." The received theory of competition is comparative static, focusing on beginning and end points. Economic agents are interested in neither the beginning nor end points, but in coping with never-ending adjustments. The theory of perfect competition analyzes the state of affairs or equilibrium conditions that would exist if all competitive activity ceased. *It is not an approximation but the negation of that activity.*

All theories abstract from part of reality. Theorists must determine in each case the appropriate degree of abstraction. What is essential and permanent to the phenomena ought to be part of the analysis. It would, for example, be a pretty poor economic theory that abstracted from scarcity. All genuinely economic, as opposed to purely computational, problems arise, however, because of the passage of time and concomitant changes in knowledge and the data. Economics must analyze the process of adaption to change as surely as it analyzes scarcity. Under some conditions, this adaptive process is competitive. We need, therefore, a theory of the competitive process. Neoclassical economics contains no such theory.

The orthodox theory of competition postulates a situation in which a large number of buyers and sellers of a homogeneous good transact in an environment of free entry, parametric pricing, and perfect knowledge. We have already added our own criticisms of perfect knowledge to those of numerous other authors. Here we would emphasize that the problem of incomplete knowledge and the necessity of adaptation exist only to the extent that the data change unexpectedly. "Economic problems arise always and only in consequence of change. So long as things continue as before, or at least as they were expected to, there arise no new problems requiring a decision, no need to form a new plan" (Hayek, 1945, p. 523).

The existence of scarcity necessitates agents' making a set of choices – a plan. In a static world of scarcity, however, each individual would need to form only one plan per lifetime. Plan revision occurs not because goods are scarce but because of changes in the environment, or in the individual agent himself.[1] If the static model were a close approximation of reality, we would have exhausted our subject long ago. There is just so much that can be said about the Pure Logic of Choice in an unchanging world. Yet in the theory of competition, which ought to be pre-eminently a theory of change, the static model of pure competition reigns supreme.

For example, contrast a process view of product heterogeneity to the orthodox one. Neoclassical economic theory treats product differentiation as an equilibrium phenomenon, the outgrowth of consistent plans between consumers and producers. Yet product differentiation may also be the outcome of a process in which entrepreneurs try to mesh their plans with those of consumers. Because of changing conditions (including but not limited to changes in consumer tastes), producers are not sure what buyers want. By a process of trial and error, producers change nonprice variables in an attempt to discover how best to serve consumer wants. This producer-generated trial and error process is likely also to generate consumer experimentation with heterogeneous offerings. The observable result, which is not part of anyone's explicit intention, is "product differentiation." The attempt to discover by trial and error the actual set of consumer tastes is bound to produce greater diversity in product offerings. Uncertainty and a high degree of competition, not market power and imperfect competition, produce this result. Heterogeneous expectations and tastes characterize the process.

The treatment of product heterogeneity is an instance of a more general issue. Concepts and problems whose existence derives from change and the passage of time are often analyzed in static terms. The positive analysis is deficient, and will almost inevitably mislead the analyst in policy application. We say more about this issue in what follows.

## THE DISCOVERY OF OPPORTUNITIES

### *Equilibrium*

In our analysis of competition, plan coordination is the norm. As we have seen, the plan coordination concept was the outcome of Hayek's early attempt to reformulate equilibrium analysis for a multi-person economy in time. The Pure Logic of Choice is abstract and deductive. The degree to which an economy actually tends toward complete plan coordination ("equilibrium") determines the applicability of equilibrium models to real-world economies. For Hayek (1937a, pp. 43–4), the analysis of equilibrating tendencies constituted the "empirical element" in economics.

The focus on forces tending to equilibrium explains the concern with entrepreneurship in modern Austrian work, since the entrepreneur is the active coordinating agent in market economies.

Prices are signals or indicators, but not unfailing guides to economizers. Institutions provide a background for decision-making, and these set practical limits to the divergence of expectations. Nonetheless, it is entrepreneurs who are alert to opportunities, and, indeed, whose creativity is the very source of many of these opportunities.[2] In static equilibrium, there can be no profit opportunities. But only by acting on their hunches and forecasts, so as to grasp profits, could entrepreneurs bring about a situation in which equilibrium is approached.

Hayek originally defined as an equilibrium a situation in which there is both *ex ante* plan consistency, and no information disruptive of plans that agents are bound to learn in the course of executing their plans. Exogenous disturbances might occur before these plans are executed, and upset the equilibrium. As long as agents did not themselves bring about these disturbances by the very execution of their plans, their plans were coordinated and consistent. Endogenous market forces would then tend to bring the system to the original equilibrium position.

In his work on entrepreneurship, Kirzner (1973) has consistently adhered to Hayek's early view. Yet by focusing on entrepreneurship, we can understand better the reasons that surely entered into Hayek's revised approach to competition, coordination, and equilibrium. The fundamental problem is that the "tendency to equilibrium" view does not take time seriously. The latter is, of course, as serious an internal criticism as one could levy against a subjectivist analysis.

### *Process*

Competition is a dynamic process, a process in time. Since, as we have seen, knowledge must change with the passage of time, individual agents will alter their plans as time passes. This changing of plans disrupts the plans of other agents. Conventional learning models are, however, "clockwork" models, whose most significant characteristics have been succinctly described by Littlechild:

> The agents are equipped with forecasting functions and decision functions to enable them to cope with uncertainty. Indeed, the agents *are* these functions. But though their specific forecasts and decisions may change over time in response to change in economic conditions, *the functions*

> *themselves remain the same*. The agents never learn to predict any better as a result of their experience. Nothing will ever occur for which they are not prepared, nor can they even initiate anything which is not preordained. They are clock-work Bayesians, wound up with prior distributions and sent on their way, to attain eventually, if circumstances permit, that everlasting peace in which they never need to move their posteriors. (Littlechild, 1977, pp. 7–8)

The theory problem is modeling competition as a continual process. One could formally model the economy as a clock-work mechanism, and then hypothesize a never-ending stream of exogenous shocks wrought by entrepreneurs outside the system. In such a model, the passage of time would not be accompanied by learning. To prevent the system from "winding down," one would need to bring in the entrepreneur as a *deus ex machina.* Schumpeter chose this latter course in his *Theory of Economic Development* (1934). The circular flow is then the natural state of the economy, in to which it settles unless disturbed by disruptive entrepreneurs. The Schumpeterian gambit maintains the Newtonian conception of time and places the entrepreneur outside the system. Yet surely neither entrepreneurship nor learning ought to be completely exogenous (i.e., unexplained) in a process analysis, even if one accepts that there are exogenous components to both.

In "Competition as a Discovery Procedure," Hayek (1978), explicitly integrated true learning (i.e., changes in the learning functions themselves) into a process theory. He brought the entrepreneur in from the shadows and made him part of the economic system. In so doing, Hayek offered a genuinely novel view of the function of competitive institutions. He treated a competitive market as a spontaneously evolved set of institutions and customs facilitating information acquisition. To simplify only slightly, nearly everything assumed to be data in orthodox constructions is the object of a trial and error process in Hayek's approach. As Hayek put it,

> Competition is valuable *only* because, and so far as, its results are unpredictable and on the whole different from those which anyone has, or could have, deliberately arrived at. Further, . . . the generally beneficial effects of competition

> must include disappointing or defeating some particular expectations or intentions. (Hayek, 1978, p. 180)

Hayek's view embodies endogenous learning and entrepreneurship. Moreover, it captures that essential element of competition that is absent from alternative economic conceptualizations: the element of surprise or the unexpected. It thereby meets the criterion suggested in our sports contest example; at least some of the time, the outcome of a competitive struggle must be other than what we expect.

## KNOWLEDGE AND COMPETITION

There are five general characteristics of knowledge with which a Hayekian view of competition is concerned. Knowledge is (1) private, (2) empirical, (3) often tacit, (4) not all gained through price signals, and (5) often the source of surprise. Each of these characteristics is important, and together they distinguish a process from a static conception of competition.

### *Private Knowledge*

A large and significant part of advanced economic theory explicitly or implicitly rejects the privacy of knowledge. The strong version of the Efficient Market hypothesis explicitly denies that *any* knowledge remains private, and not just part of the data of the system. With relatively few exceptions,[3] Rational Expectations theorists fashion models as though information available to anyone is available to all. While it certainly would be an exaggeration to suggest that privacy of knowledge is generally accepted, there is nonetheless some recognition of this issue in other areas of theory.

In the literature on localized information,[4] some knowledge is private and not datum. Privacy models can be used to analyze numerous issues, including the ability of individuals to exploit the knowledge on the market. We consider this literature to be salutary, and we have no disagreement with it as far as it goes. Our problem with the direction it has taken comes out in the following discussion of the other characteristics of knowledge.

### *Empirical Knowledge*

The knowledge sought by economic agents is empirical in the following sense. They are primarily seeking "knowledge of the particular circumstances of time and place" (Hayek, 1945, p. 52). When acquired, this knowledge does not consist of abstract scientific propositions, which form the basis of logical deductions to certain conclusions. Empirical knowledge consists of information of temporary and fleeting significance, which may be factual (i.e., profitable) only so long as others do not also know it. Almost any profit opportunity fits this characterization.

The value of incomplete information partly depends on the processor of the information. Each actor must exercise judgment about information and its place in his overall plan. What an agent ought to do cannot be determined by an outside observer possessed of different information, judgments, tastes, and plans. There is, consequently, no uniquely rational or "correct" course of action, as may be the case when dealing with a scientific–deductive problem. This latter point requires emphasis, given economists' inclination to pronounce on "the rational" course of action in numerous situations.

In a situation of *given* means and *given* ends, there may be only one course of action that will maximize the relevant objective function. This would be true by virtue of our construction of the problem. We may choose to label this course of action "rational." We can deduce *the* "rational" or "correct" action only because we have converted an empirical or trial and error learning problem into a logical or deductive problem. This conversion is acceptable if and only if all required information is available simultaneously to the decision-maker. Only in this case could one logically deduce an optimal course of action. It is misleading to conceive of decision-making, which involves trial and error discovery of incomplete information, as though it were a scientific problem, about which agents "theorized." Hayek stated the point clearly and concisely:

> Implication is a logical relationship *which can be meaningfully asserted only of propositions simultaneously present to one and the same mind* . . . . Only to a mind to which all these facts were simultaneously known would the answer

> necessarily follow from the facts given to it. The practical problem, however, arises precisely because the facts are never given to a single mind, and because, in consequence, it is necessary that in the solution of the problem knowledge should be used that is dispersed among many people. (Hayek, 1945, p. 530)

### *Tacit Knowledge*

The non-deductive or non-scientific quality of much economic knowledge is obviously related to its privateness. Both are also related to the tacit quality of much economically important knowledge. In all areas of human endeavour, individuals employ knowledge that either they are not aware they possess or they cannot characterize precisely enough to communicate to others. In philosopher Gilbert Ryle's terminology, they "know how" to do something but do not "know that" so and so is true of what they do (Ryle, 1949).

Scientific progress occurs as the stock of interpersonal and communicable knowledge increases. In this regard, however, scientific knowledge and progress are poor models of economic knowledge and progress (Sowell, 1980, pp. 8–11). Thus, tacit knowledge may take the form of a skill or may be embodied in a custom or unarticulated rule of behavior. Bicycling and swimming are two examples. Relatively few accomplished at either activity understand the principles involved, or are even adept at teaching others how to ride or swim. Bicyclists and swimmers know *how* but not *that*. They may very well be fit subjects for imitation. Apprenticeship, not a reference work or university short course, is the learning model. Michael Polanyi illustrated the theoretical point with reference to swimming:

> The decisive factor by which the swimmer keeps himself afloat is the manner by which he regulates his respiration; he keeps his buoyancy at an increased level by refraining from emptying his lungs when breathing out and by inflating them more than usual when breathing in; yet this is not generally known to swimmers. (Polanyi, 1962, p. 49)

Two important implications follow from the above considerations. First, discovering tacit knowledge involves time-consuming processes that may never be successful. Other market participants may not be able to discover the source or reasons for an entrepreneur's success. His profits may accordingly persist for a substantial length of time. Second, some of what individuals do and why they do it cannot be successfully communicated or explained to third parties. Third-party observers ought not to expect agents to be able to rationalize their conduct. We develop some of the further implications of this for public policy on competition and monopoly.

Since much information is tacit and cannot be communicated, *even in equilibrium*, not everyone will know everything. Economic systems do not move toward a situation in which information is fully disseminated, at least not explicitly. Some knowledge will remain private.

### *Nonprice Signals*

When it comes to the role of prices in allocating resources, Hayek's message seems to have been learned almost too well. The proposition that "the price system [is] a mechanism for communicating information" (Hayek, 1945, p. 526) plays an especially important role in the localized information literature. But the context in which Hayek presented the idea has been forgotten. The proposition has been transformed into the entirely different one that "nothing but" price signals communicate information on markets. Its corollary is that, unless price signals accurately reflect equilibrium scarcity values, we cannot or ought not rely on them.

A world in which prices were always at their general equilibrium level would be a world in which prices were not needed. To understand this point, consider the function of the Walrasian auctioneer. He centralizes information and insures that individuals do not act on disequilibrium data. Equilibrium prices are generated via the *tâtonnement* process. No real time passes and no false trading occurs. Though nominally in time, the Walrasian world is really static. The most interesting feature, however, is the centralization of information. Formal economic theory provides no argument for decentralization. Based on general equilibrium theory, perfect competition theory is more applicable to centralized than to decentralized economies. Static models of centralized information render real competition superfluous and literally wasteful. In this world, we can forget prices and just have the central processor of information issue production orders instead. The prices of general equilibrium theory do not provide information of the type we have been discussing. These prices are simply statements of equilibrium rates of trade-off.

What of the idea that prices guide behavior? First, prices are useful guides or signals because, and insofar as, they reveal discrepancies, previous maladjustments, and errors. It surely misses the point to ask if they are now "correct." Prices reveal what people want relatively more urgently now, and in the future, not what they would want in a hypothetical and unattainable equilibrium. No known system accomplishes the latter, and it is pointless if not misleading to make this a normative reference point.

Second, prices and markets function as part of a social system, not in isolation. A social system generates many kinds of signals and rules besides prices. Unless all these other guides are superfluous, it is erroneous to suggest that prices alone are sufficient guides. A theory of passive response to prices and only to prices is not a theory of human action, but a physics of automatons.

Nonprice constraints are as much part of a decentralized economy as are the prices they help to generate. These constraints are reference frameworks and orientation points, in terms of which actors form expectations. Prices are formed on markets composed of contracts, rules, and customs, which are part of the constraints and basis for observed behavior.[5]

The tendency in the industrial organization and applied price theory literature is to view nonprice constraints as either extraneous or suspicious intrusions on "competition." We are arguing to the contrary, namely that these constraints are often necessary accompaniments to markets. For example, it is strictly impossible to imagine a "price system" devoid of contracts and property rights. Yet much of the focus of the applied literature involves casting suspicion on all nonprice constraints on behavior (e.g. resale price maintenance). There is a presumption against them, and agents must justify their existence. We think this attitude follows from the presumption that prices "ought to" allocate resources, because they do so in perfectly competitive models. Not prices but people allocate resources, and flesh and blood human actors depend on all these nonprice variables in their decision-making.

Third, to varying degrees agents are endowed with entrepreneurial ability. Entrepreneurs do not merely respond to, but also create, change. They *outguess* market prices when these prices do not seem consistent (Rothbard, 1970, II, pp. 464–9). Whether we call this entrepreneurship a capacity to find out "particular circumstances" (Hayek, 1945, p. 52) or "alertness" (Kirzner, 1973, pp. 65–9), it is a *sine qua non* of a market economy. Yet this "driving force" of market economies is absent from models of perfect competition. Schumpeterians and Austrians have tried to fill this gap with theories of entrepreneurship.

### *Surprise*

Competitive market processes must produce results surprising (at least in part) to market participants *and* observers. Any interactive social process in real time produces unintended and hence unforeseen results. This will be true if for no other reason than the conflicting goals of diverse members of society. Whenever there is goal conflict, there must be a social mechanism to reconcile these conflicts. The mechanism may involve peaceful or non-peaceful reconciliation. It may entail either private or collective action. If private, it may involve market or non-market approaches. Regardless of the mechanism, some agents must experience disappointment and revise their plans. This plan revision must involve their making choices other than the ones they had originally wanted to make.

The outcomes of social processes are unintended for three interrelated reasons. First, there is the need to reconcile conflicting plans. Second, there are always unintended by-products to individual actions in a society. Acting individuals inevitably produce results that were, in Adam Smith's phraseology, "no part of their intention." This realization is surely the basis for *any* social theory and is, in any case, the core principle of modern economics (Buchanan, 1976; O'Driscoll, 1977). Any economically interesting analysis of attempts to engineer *ex ante* economic and social outcomes necessarily involves specifying unintended consequences of human action. For instance, the results of imposing below-market rental prices on housing units is an example of the principle involved. The intended outcome (plentiful and cheap housing) is the *given* for the problem; the *analysis* entails deducing the unintended outcome (expensive and depleted housing stock). What is true of economic theory is likewise true of sound sociological and political analysis. Each discipline studies the unintended consequences of human action.[6]

Third, actions are not merely "additive." As the number of

buyers and sellers of a good increases, this may result in not merely more production and trade, but also a more highly developed market for the good. For instance, if an increasing number of traders seek liquidity and try to economize on holding inventories of real goods, they may succeed not only in achieving their goals but in facilitating the emergence of a medium of exchange (Menger, 1892). As Marx emphasized, quantitative changes evolve into qualitative differences.

The unintended consequences of human action must often be as surprising to the theorists as they are to market participants. Similarity of problems renders pattern prediction feasible (as in the rent control case). Yet the seeming precision of such predictions masks basic theoretical ambiguity. A myriad of outcomes is possible. Will the controls be enforced or not enforced? Evaded (how?) or not evaded? Will the government eventually subsidize enough construction to meet the excess demand (Sweden) or not (the USA and UK)? The attempt to predict precisely the unintended by-products of human action would involve, *inter alia*, a predictive theory of human institutions. Nothing short of discovering the "laws of history" would make this endeavour possible. Past efforts in this area have been conspicuous failures. Our only prediction of the future is that this record will continue unchanged.

The final element of surprise concerns expectations formation. We have more to say on "objectivist" theories, such as rational expectations, in the chapter on money (chapter 9). Here we simply observe that a subjectivist approach emphasizes the diversity of expectations. This diversity is a function both of the diversity of human beings and of the effects of change and the passage of time. Pre-reconciliation of plans and forecasting of the future would necessitate each individual's predicting the mental states and choices of large numbers of unknown people, whose decisions affect his environment and his choices. Theories that entail or assume this ability violate the basic requirements of a subjectivist and methodologically individualistic analysis. They fail to take differences among individuals seriously. The theories proceed "as if" there were only one decision-maker. These theories produce unintelligible results when applied to decentralized economies. Yet, to recapitulate, the modern theory of competition assumes centralized information (in the auctioneer), and (usually) uniformity of expectations. It would thus be only a slight exaggeration to say that neoclassical economics has produced an elegant static theory of centralized resource allocation, but no theory of competition in a decentralized economy.

## PROCESS THEORIES AND NORMATIVE ECONOMICS

A theory of competition as a process will necessarily be at odds with static theories of competition. These latter equate competition with the attainment of certain conditions, the existence of certain market structures, and the presence of stereotypical behavior (e.g. price-taking) by transactors. If markets fail to replicate these conditions or to produce certain results (e.g., $P = MC$), then this is taken as imperfection of competition. This conception underlies the proclivity, illustrated in our parable, to condemn actual market outcomes.

If competition serves a social purpose, it must produce something that we could not have in its absence. To the degree that competition does what we could have done equally cheaply in its absence, it is wasteful. Competition in fact leads to the discovery of opportunities that would otherwise go unnoticed. It thus generates a spontaneous discovery process, the exact course of which is unpredictable. This process includes, *inter alia*, both the discovery of hitherto unsatisfied wants and the products to satisfy those wants, and the invention of lower-cost methods of satisfying preferences. It also encompasses the creation of new economic forms, customs, and structures.

None of this suggests, of course, that competition does not also fulfill its traditional functions of creating incentives to keep one's prices and costs in line with other producers. Even in this case, however, the discovery process plays a crucial role. Costs are not a well-defined given; they change as productive techniques vary. Even in highly competitive industries that best fit the model of pure competition, such as agriculture, different production techniques exist literally side by side. The differences are sometimes dramatic, as in tending of vineyards and production of wine. They exist also, however, in activities as prosaic as the growing of feed corn. If we move to industries of heterogeneous goods, then the relevant price is no longer a given, and ascertaining its profit-maximizing level is part of the competitive discovery process. It is not, then, what competition does to fulfill our expectations that recommends it: it is what competition does that we would not have expected it to do that recommends it.

Normative analysis of competition must differ in process and static theories of competition. In its positive analysis, process theory analyzes the competitive discovery procedure inherent in the coordination of plans. Accordingly, process economists focus on the capacity of social systems to discover and innovate. Contrast the emphasis on change and discovery with the approach of standard welfare economics. Choices are pre-reconciled under known conditions, which generate predictable outcomes. As Kaldor (1934, p. 147) pointed out, "the formation of prices must *precede* the process of exchange and not be the result of it." In effect, the outcomes of trade must be known by agents before the trades are consummated. Further, the analyst–observer knows the outcome in the guise of well-known equalities at the margin.

Emphasis on the unintended consequences of human actions leads to another decisive difference between process and neo-classical normative analyses. Standard optimality criteria are foreign to a process approach. Optimality criteria are static rather than dynamic, and judge performance or outcomes rather than processes or operation. They presume that social processes ought to produce outcomes that can be specified in advance. This argument is taken up in more detail in the next chapter. Here we will just observe that there is no straightforward way of applying standard optimality concepts to institutions or processes. To know whether an institution or process is optimal, we would need to know the very information whose discovery is the object of that process or the operation of that institution. Once again, if we could independently ascertain the information, the institution or process in question would be superfluous.

Even casual inspection of the literature reveals a systematic conflation between general equilibrium theory and classical arguments in favor of free competition or *laissez-faire*. Consider the following argument of Kornai:

> The modern equilibrium theory is nothing else than a mathematically exact formulation of Smith's "invisible hand" which harmonizes the interest of egoistic individuals in an optimal manner. At the time of Smith, . . . this description of the functioning of a capitalist economy was not unrealistic (though not exact either). More than a hundred years were

> required for Smith's intuition to be expressed in a faultlessly exact form; by the time it was achieved, it became utterly anachronistic. (Kornai, 1971, p. 349)

Or compare Hahn:

> When the claim is made – and the claim is as old as Adam Smith – that a myriad of self-seeking agents left to themselves will lead to a coherent and efficient disposition of economic resources, Arrow and Debreu show what the world would have to look like if the claim is to be true. In doing this they provide the most potent avenue of falsification of the claims. (Hahn, 1973, p. 324)[7]

In fact, Smith's defense of competition involves a theory of unplanned or spontaneous order. This tradition, in which Smith forms a middle link between the scholastics and natural law theorists on the one hand and modern theorists like Mises and Hayek on the other, is an alternative to modern general equilibrium theory and not an early or crude anticipation of it. A theory of evolved orders is not a theory of optimality or efficiency, precisely because it is a process and not an end-state theory. Social efficiency or global optimality concepts must be foreign to process theories. *Individuals* economize and, in this sense, attempt to allocate their own resources efficiently. There is no social choice process, however, in which society chooses so as to maximize "social utility." Outside of a static context and absent the stringent assumptions of general competitive theory, it cannot be demonstrated that the pursuit of individual optimality results in a well-defined social optimum (*unless* all that is meant by the latter is the process of individual optimization). As a corollary, however, one cannot apply static welfare criteria to demonstrate that there is suboptimality.

It is simply anachronistic to attribute modern welfare concepts to eighteenth- or even to most nineteenth-century writers. No such concepts existed then. Many modern interpreters apparently believe that Smith *et al.* "must" have been groping toward modern welfare analysis, but lacked the necessary training in calculus to articulate their views. Nonetheless, careful reading of *The Wealth of Nations* provides little support for the thesis that Smith was a crude neoclassical welfare theorist.

First, Smith wrote of advancing (not maximizing) the material well-being (not utility) of the common man (not society as a whole). He thus frequently advocated uncompensated property rights transfers, as when he recommended removing monopolistic trading privileges for the benefit of consumers and to the detriment of the monopolists.

Second, Smith relied heavily (though not exclusively) on arguments in terms of rights and liberty. For example, he argued that:

> The property which every man has in his own labor, as it is the original foundation of all other property, so it is the most sacred and inviolable. The patrimony of a poor man lies in the strength and dexterity of his hand; and to hinder him from employing this strength and dexterity in what manner he thinks proper without injury to his neighbour, is a plain violation of this most sacred property. It is a manifest encroachment upon the first liberty both of the workman, and those who might be disposed to employ him. (Smith, 1937, pp. 121–2)

Smith's argument is stereotypical of the classical arguments for free and competitive markets. Competition would permit individuals to achieve those goals most important to them. For Smith, this would lead to the maximal attainable gain for most, *given* side constraints of which individual liberty was the most important. He did not suggest that the result of this would conform to any particular, preconceived outcome of non-individualist welfare criteria.

Arguments in terms of liberty formed important parts of the classical liberal case for competition. Liberty was valued both in its own right and for instrumental reasons. Paralleling the common law, liberal political economy justified outcomes, at least in part, because they resulted from a system of voluntary trade and political freedom.[8] The *modus vivendi* of a process of free exchange and production created a presumption in its favor. Only if this process were operative would we know what individuals valued most. In other words, the classical liberal argument for free exchange and competition – an argument inextricably intertwined with the classical political–economic case for competition – is a process argument. It is also a fundamentally different argument than modern ones in terms of optimality criteria and social utility maximization.

Our major point is not doctrine-historical but substantive. Any dynamic analysis of competition must have criteria alternative to those of static welfare theory. It would be strictly inconsistent to fall back on static welfare theory in assessing markets. Whatever can be claimed on their behalf must depend on the alternative criteria. Elements of a normative analysis are presented in the next section.

## DYNAMIC EQUILIBRIUM

Theorists have traditionally utilized exact or deterministic equilibrium concepts. Indeterminism and unpredictability show up in fitting or applying the concept and analysis to concrete problems. By emphasizing the unpredictability and indeterminateness of social process, we are not raising a new problem so much as proposing a new solution. As Coddington (1975, p. 156) has said, "When it comes to being put to some use, the static method abandons its own formalization anyway. The choice then becomes less dramatic: between abandoning formalization openly or abandoning it in a surreptitious way." We have argued above that our alternative approach would permit theorists to incorporate time and change in a meaningful way in models.

The passage of time makes it inevitable that some expectations will not be met, some plans not fulfilled. Some disappointment of expectations and a degree of frustration in implementing plans are inevitable in any social system. No set of policies or institutions can insulate us from the effects of time's passing. The relevant question is how different institutions and policies affect individuals' adaptations to unexpected outcomes.

Once we abandon the static framework, our theoretical and policy focus changes. For instance, owners of existing entitlements always prefer policies that insulate them insofar as possible from the undesirable effects of a changing environment. These preferences may sometimes by justified by a static analysis (e.g., by a favorable "equity–efficiency" trade-off). These claims automatically carry diminished weight in a nonstatic framework. Policies protecting existing entitlements inhibit adaptation of agents to past and future changes. To the extent that this happens, the probability that a market participant chosen at random will be able to fulfill his plans diminishes. Even those protected owners of current entitlements will find adaptation in the future more, not less, difficult because of their seeking current protection. Thus, "sick" industries become sicker not better as they are protected more thoroughly.[9]

As we saw in the previous chapter, exact coordination of individuals' activities is not only practically impossible but also conceptually self-contradictory. Acting takes place in real time, and, as time passes, agents learn and alter their behavior. Complete coordination of activities thus cannot be a state toward which social systems are moving. Its possible, however, to postulate a tendency toward *pattern coordination* (a true dynamic equilibrium). This depends, *inter alia*, on the degree to which typical features persist with the passage of time. If, on the contrary, there were *no* typical features, then we could not speak of a tendency to equilibrium in any sense of the term.

Pattern coordination consists of coordination among the typical but not the unique aspects of individual behavior. In this context, two variants of a normative criterion suggest themselves. The first variant ranks different pattern equilibria, while the second deals with properties of the transition process from one equilibrium to another.

With respect to the first case, it is important to realize that any given instance of concrete behavior can be described in a myriad of ways. Many patterns of typical features can in principle be identified in a set of actions. The same vector of actions can thus comprise numerous pattern equilibria. Some are, however, "better" from agents' perspectives than others. To refer to the illustration of the previous chapter, Professor B may identify several patterns of his co-author's (Professor A's) behavior. The realization that A comes into the office on Mondays and Wednesdays may be a more useful insight than the fact that he carries his briefcase whenever he comes into the office. Some pattern equilibria enable agents to coordinate their activities more effectively than others. To repeat, no form of pattern coordination will permit exact coordination of activities because there will always be unique features of events and actions. Our criterion of evaluation must, therefore, relate to the degree of coordination consistent with the *endogenous* change within the system and thus with the existence of real time.

With respect to the second case, the criterion is essentially the same. Suppose that the system is exogenously shocked, so that the typical features of agents' behavior change. In the movement from one pattern equilibrium to another, some attempts at coordination will be frustrated. The actions of A may be predicated on the no-longer-typical features of B's behavior (and vice versa). Nonetheless, we can still assess the performance of an economic system on the basis of its adjustment to change. Here the criterion is the relative amount of coordination consistent with the system's *exogenous* change.

More concretely, we can attempt to base our judgments of various policies on the likelihood that a given change will result in a randomly chosen individual's fulfilling his plans (Hayek, 1978, pp. 183–4). This criterion has two interrelated features. First, some social systems or policies adapt to changes with greater or lesser plan frustration. Second, other systems completely or partially block adaptation to change, thus also resulting in plan frustration.

We illustrate our point by referring again to the example of rent control. First, we argue for plan coordination as the preferable equilibrium concept. Second, we explain why a market process approach requires adopting the concept of pattern rather than that of exact coordination.

The economically crucial effect of setting rents below market levels is surely *not* that they create a market excess demand for housing. The crucial and more general effect of these controls involves their effect on plan coordination and market signalling of relative scarcity values. If a public housing authority were created to supply the requisite housing units, then any excess demand would be temporary. Yet frustration and discoordination of plans would persist. We will show this first by considering the standard case of no public housing, and then by considering the case in which excess demand is supplied governmentally.

After effective controls are imposed, housing services will be *temporarily* in excess demand. Lessors and lessees cannot make their plans mesh. Over time, however, the housing stock will deteriorate until housing services supplied satisfy observed demand at the controlled rental prices. Even with market excess demand eliminated, plans continue to be frustrated, however, for renters cannot bid higher prices for the higher-quality units that they prefer.[10]

Now we consider the case in which a public housing authority supplies the unsatisfied demand at controlled prices. Market excess demand is eliminated in the long run, and plans are apparently fulfilled. In reality, however, plan frustration (but no market excess demand) appears in other sectors and under other guises. Taxpayers must shoulder part of the housing cost of entitlement-holding tenants. Net taxpayers (i.e., those paying more in taxes than the value of subsidized housing received) must now curtail their planned consumption of other goods. Moreover, satisfaction of renters' preferences will be more apparent than real. Renters will be satisfied with their existing housing stock only because they are unable to implement other plans, such as moving to more desirable areas. Entrepreneurs wishing to respond to price signals in nonhousing markets (e.g., in manufacturing) and workers wishing to take advantage of higher wages will be frustrated in their attempts to move to more desirable cities or regions by the inflexibility of the housing market. Eventually, these planned moves will be cancelled and the best will be made of the current location. There is frustration and lack of coordination, but the market excess demand is eliminated. The state housing authority will perceive that it has "solved" the problem. Instead, it has *added* to the discoordination of plans. This can be seen by considering why a region would be attractive to firms and workers.

Consumers' preferences would be better satisfied by immigration of firms and individuals into the hypothetically more desirable region. Without this immigration, wants that could be satisfied will go unfulfilled. Plans cannot be executed. The mechanism that would normally facilitate adaptations – rising rental prices in growing regions – is rendered inoperative by the controls. There is probably no government with sufficient command over resources to supply excess housing demand of a *mobile* population (the source of inflexibility in the housing stock alluded to above). Even if public housing authorities were able to draw on the necessary funds, no effective system of signalling and incentives exists to inform managers of the relative importance of different housing demands. The very reason for the housing authority, the rent controls, has eliminated market-generated signals (i.e., flexible price changes).[11]

Thus far we have been arguing the case for adopting plan coordination as the equilibrium concept. We now will explain the reasons for adopting a process approach and pattern coordination concept. The rent control case is vastly more complex than even we have made it thus far. Textbook analysis is misleading in a number of respects. For example, the New York City housing market has not yet fully adapted to a system of rent controls first put in place during World War II. This situation certainly does not stem from the housing stock's failure to deteriorate sufficiently! Rather, controls generate a process of response, where each stage generates changes in the environment that cause further responses. In turn, market participants' responses produce further political responses. Public choice theorists would (correctly) assure us that the political changes are endogenous to the system. This endogeneity can be best captured in a model of rent control incorporating a dynamic conception of time.

Each control breeds evasions of the control. Each evasion produces further changes in the market environment and additional adaptations. In the political arena, those evasions produce demands for new controls, some of which are supplied. There is literally no end to this process so long as there are calculating entrepreneurs, economic and political, who can profit from existing opportunities. There simply is no static equilibrium to which anything will settle down. The rent control case is a prime example of how a process may never cease or stabilize. If we were to predict the future course of events in the New York City housing market, we could predict only possible patterns. The only sure prediction is that the details will be upset endogenously.

For any applied problem, theorists can and do cut off the analysis at a point at which they have reduced the unexplained phenomena to second-order effects. It is misleading, however, to suggest that they have identified an equilibrium, in the sense of a complete state of rest. They have just delimited an analytically convenient place to end one chapter of a story. What is a second-order effect often becomes a first-order problem subsequently. For instance, no analysis of the economics of converting rental units to cooperative apartments (a legal form that is economically similar to condominium ownership) would be complete if it did not relate the process to the long-standing system of rent controls in New York City. Yet such conversions belonged to the category of second-order effects until comparatively recently.

Our process view is fully consonant with cutting-off analysis in accord with the problem at hand (writing "chapters" of analysis). *By not employing an exact or deterministic equilibrium concept, however, we enhance the chance that related and dependent events will be seen as such, rather than as the product of unrelated exogenous shocks* (such as the case of cooperative apartment conversion and rent controls). This is one major advantage, as we see it, of abandoning the search for determinateness at the conceptual rather than at the application stage.

We agree that a *fruitful* equilibrium concept is necessary for developing a systematic analysis. As we saw in the last chapter, equilibrium analysis is a type of causal reasoning. Causal reasoning about process in time differs from static analysis, however, and the equilibrium concept must change accordingly. Maximal possible plan coordination is the most straightforward adaptation of the plan coordination concept to dynamic problems. Like any other normative economic criterion, this one leaves some issues unresolved. For instance, one could increase the likelihood that some plans would be fulfilled by decreasing the likelihood that others will be fulfilled. Likewise, one would presumably wish to minimize the chance that some plans, such as those of a would-be murderer, would be implemented. This is to recognize that the basic questions of right and wrong, of the justice of entitlements, and of the role of the private and governmental sectors must be resolved *before* economic reasoning can be used in policy analysis. If this fact is made more obvious by adopting the criterion of maximal plan coordination, so much the better.

Our claim here is that a well thought out economic analysis can contribute to public policy discussions. As in the rent control example, economic analysis may serve largely to clarify fact patterns for policy-makers. Indeed, the rent control case is a paradigmatic example of Arrow's observation (1968, p. 376) that "the notion that through the workings of an entire system effects may be very different from, and even opposed to, intentions is surely the most important intellectual contribution that economic thought has made to the general understanding of social processes." More than any other modern school, Austrian subjectivists have consistently applied this insight to social processes. One's attention is drawn to the unintended effects of human actions by systematically analyzing these as part of a process in time. Economic models in which agents foresee all events (even in a probabilistic sense) render unintelligible any concept of unintended consequences of human action. Insofar as models postulate perfect foresight, they obscure "the most important" contribution of the economic way of thinking.

We have argued that neoclassical economic theory misconceives the problems when it abstracts from the passage of real time, a tendency that has been particularly harmful in the theory of competition. In the next section, we develop our point further. We focus on the technique of assuming that agents engage in continuous utility maximization. We suggest that they cannot do this in a world of uncertainty and changing knowledge. Not only is the requisite knowledge for continuous utility maximization absent, but the techniques and institutions people actually use to cope with uncertainty are seriously misunderstood if continuous utility maximization is assumed. We argue that agents follow rules and use institutions as a substitute for continuously choosing at the margin. These rules and institutions are not themselves entirely the product of rational choice. We then briefly relate our argument to some recent work on the theory of the firm.

## RULES VERSUS CONTINUOUS UTILITY MAXIMIZATION

Neoclassical attempts to explain rules in the widest sense, including customs, law, and other institutionally embodied complexes of rules, are marred by consistent misdiagnosis. A single error characterizes much recent work on such varied topics as the theory of the firm, the efficiency of legal rules, and rules versus authority in monetary policy. In no other area does a subjectivist process approach yield such different conclusions from orthodox models and shed so much light on an important topic.

Any model that explains social rules solely in terms of maximizing behavior fundamentally misconstrues the phenomena. Men follow a rule when they respond in the same way to perceptions of a recurrent pattern. They thereby exhibit regularity of behavior in typical situations. Rule-following behavior is the product, however, not of knowledge or omniscience but of ignorance. This is certainly true for the large class of social rules, examined here, which are the product of a process of evolution rather than maximization.

Superficially, it might appear that continuous utility maximization would also result in a pattern of decisions similar to rule-following behavior. Nevertheless, the opposite is the case. What makes an event "typical" is that it shares certain abstract properties with other events of this type. Nonetheless, events of a type or class differ in details, often significantly. If, in fact, individuals were to know enough to discriminate among events of a class, then they would not follow rules or adopt consistent decision patterns in dealing with these events. Rule-following agents decide on the basis of the abstract properties of members of a class. When an agent knows enough about the details or particulars of a case, and of the differential effects of alternative decisions, then he decides not according to rules but on a "case-by-case" basis (or on "the merits of the case"). Case-by-case decisions involve treating similar cases differently, while rule-guided decisions involve treating similar cases identically.

The Rule of Law is perhaps the best illustration of our point. Stated simply, the rule requires judicial decision-makers to treat cases of the same class the same way (Leoni, 1961, pp. 59–76). In adhering to a concept of the Rule of Law, judges are under no illusion that cases are all the same in every detail. Nor would most legal commentators deny that, in some sense, there may be a net social gain from occasionally relaxing a rule. The practical problem is that, while we know that there are probably cases in which (for instance) it would be better not to punish the guilty, we can never know concretely which cases conform to this hypothetical situation. What jurists and legal commentators have discovered is that in the preponderance of cases justice is served by consistent application of relevant rules. And similarly for rules generally.

Rules evolve and are adopted because they work, whether these be rules of justice or of procedure within a firm. In the case of evolved rules of conduct or behavior, people obeying the rule often do not know why they work. In many cases, they may not even be aware that they are following a rule. Rule-following behavior precedes knowledge of this behavior. Understanding this behavior and being able to articulate or rationalize the rule is an even later development.

To be able to articulate why rules work presupposes more knowledge about the processes governed by rules than rule followers often can or do have. Justice is much more difficult to articulate than it is to practice. Were individuals to know enough to rationalize a rule, they would generally know enough to abandon it. If, for example, we had a scientific explanation (theory) of what a successful monetary rule accomplishes, we could in principle dispense with the rule. Indeed, monetarists emphasize this point in defending their money-stock rule. It is *ignorance* of the lag structure that necessitates adoption of a monetary rule.

The aforementioned character of rules derives from their being evolved. Without doing violence to the phenomena, we cannot conceive of evolved rules and institutions as the product of a maximization process. We reject maximization models here for two interrelated reasons. First, agents arrive at patterns of action through a trial and error process. Successful procedures are adopted and unsuccessful ones are rejected. More precisely, those agents who do not adopt successful rules cannot adapt to the relevant environment. In a market situation, this would mean losses and eventual forced withdrawal from the unsuccessful activity. Individuals stumble upon rules unconsciously, and, to repeat, are often unaware that they have done so. Not only do rules involve tacit knowledge, but their adoption is also often tacit. Maximization models cannot incorporate this insights. Hayek stated the issue concisely:

> Man acted before he thought and did not understand before he acted. What we call understanding is in the last resort simply his capacity to respond to his environment with a pattern of actions that help him to persist. Such is the modicum of truth in behaviorism and pragmatism, doctrines which, however, have so crudely oversimplified the determining relationships as to become more obstacles than helps to their appreciation. (Hayek, 1973, p. 18)[12]

Our second reason for rejecting maximizing models as explanations of evolved rules relates to the optimality of these rules. The outcomes of evolutionary processes will not generally be optimal in any nontrivial sense of the term. There is no "rule set" from which we draw. Evolved rules are not the product of choices over known alternative rules. Rule-governed behavior is the *unintended* outcome of trial and error procedures. As in biological evolution, starting along one evolutionary path closes off options. In a trial and error procedure, knowledge of alternatives is often gained only as they are tried. The "choosing" of a rule is consequently done without knowledge of alternative rules. Indeed, adopting one rule diminishes the likelihood that the adopter will learn about the alternatives. To adopt a rule is to regularize behavior, and to abandon further trial and error activities along certain lines. "Workable" not "optimal" is the appropriate modifier for evolved rules.[13]

If our analysis is correct, then the question of the "efficiency" of economic, political, and legal rules must be reconsidered.[14] Such rules represent the framework within which rational or maximizing behavior takes place. The adoption of such frameworks is itself not always the product of a maximizing procedure. It is, then, not so much an error as a misnomer to talk of the "efficiency" of political, legal, and market rules and of rule-based institutions. Given these rules, we may analyze the efficiency of choices. But the rules themselves are adopted, at least in part, by an *a-rational* process. To suppose that, for instance, the legal framework is the product of rational choice only pushes back the question of the framework within which *that* choice was made. One would eventually be led into an infinite regress, a problem avoided by adopting an evolutionary approach to rules and institutions.

"Economic imperialism" is widely interpreted as the application of continuous utility maximization models to all human problems. If carried through, this approach will yield not knowledge but the pretence of knowledge. By claiming more for the theory of maximizing behavior than it can deliver, economists will only put their theory into disrepute in those situations for which it is well suited. In pointing this out, we are only suggesting that economists take their own protestations seriously. Economics analyzes marginal adjustments. We surely can explain the effects of changes in constraints on institutions at the margin; this, however, is not sufficient to generate a complete social theory of institutions. Likewise, we may feel confident of the effects of economic factors on voting; this does not, however, imply that economics yields a deterministic theory of voting.

## THE THEORY OF THE FIRM

In this chapter, we have outlined a subjectivist theory of competition. We highlighted a few topics on which subjectivism casts new light. We also attempted to indicate how concretely a subjectivist analysis might differ from standard formulations. At this point, we would like to focus on a subject of significant interest to economists in recent years: the theory of the firm. Surprisingly, there is no subjectivist or Austrian theory of the firm. This is true even though the subjectivist approach is particularly appropriate for analyzing firms as evolved social institutions. The absence of a subjectivist theory of the firm is even more remarkable, since Coase's (1937) article has a subjectivist flavor.

The theory of the firm encompasses the question of both why firms exist and how they behave given that they exist. With respect to the first question, the situation as first described by Coase (1937) still represents the classic statement of the problem:

> An economist thinks of the economic system as being co-ordinated by the price mechanism and society becomes not an organization but an organism. The economic system "works itself." This does not mean that there is no planning by individuals. These exercise foresight and choose between alternatives. This is necessarily so if there is to be order in the system. But this theory assumes that the direction of resources is dependent directly on the price mechanism. Indeed, it is often considered to be an objection to economic planning that it merely tries to do what is already done by the price mechanism. (Coase, 1937, p. 387)

The *existence* of firms represents a paradox for formal economic theory because it represents "nonprice planning." This paradox derives from the exclusive reliance of the theory on prices to allocate resources, a reliance we criticized above. In Coase's analysis, individuals compare the costs of using the price system to the costs of nonprice planning. Firms represent nonprice market institutions within which decisions are made and resources allocated. On the market, there is an "optimum" amount of this nonprice planning (Coase, 1937, p. 389n.). The limit to vertical integration is set by the calculational chaos that may infect non-price planning. If, for instance, the market for an input were to disappear entirely through vertical integration, then all firms using the input would be caught in an economic calculation problem. There would be no market to yield transfer prices within the firm. The firms could no longer calculate profits and losses in this line of activity (Rothbard, 1970, II, pp. 554–60).

We have long found Coase's approach to the existence of firms congenial. It incorporates the essential conclusion of the economic calculation debate. That is, calculation of profits and losses is impossible without competitive markets for inputs. Gains from hierarchial organizations can be captured only so long as they do not completely eliminate factor markets. Coase's approach is an excellent static conceptualization of the problem.[15]

The Coasean solution does not, however, address the question of firm behaviour in response to change. Neoclassical production deals with this issue but does so in "Newtonian time." Subjectivists cannot be comfortable with the theory, but they have not offered a substitute approach. We believe, however, that Richard Nelson and Sidney Winter (1982) have given us the elements of a dynamic theory of the firm. In effect, they apply a Hayekian theory of rules and evolved market institutions to firm behavior. Their explicit debt is to Schumpeter, but to exactly those parts of the Schumpeterian system that have most in common with the work of Menger and Hayek.

Nelson and Winter view firms as generated by an evolutionary process. Existing firms can be best explained by reference to prior adaptations of the environment. This adaptation is revealed as rule-following behavior, or "routines" in their terminology. Routines characterizing firm behavior correspond to genes in biology. A firm's routine largely but not completely determines its behavior, as well as its ability to cope with environmental change. Thus, firms adapt to the environment in different ways. The way in which they adapt may determine their survival characteristics for future environmental changes. If a firm's routine is inappropriate to a changing environment, and the firm does not hit on a new routine quickly enough, it will be "selected out," i.e., may suffer losses and disappear.[16]

We read Nelson and Winter as avoiding the pitfall of taking the evolutionary analogy too literally. Entrepreneurs can consciously alter their firms' routine, as can human and some nonhuman species. There is also a Lamarckian element in their story; acquired characteristics are inheritable.

An important advantage of Nelson and Winter's approach is the ease with which the entrepreneur is integrated into the analysis. Indeed, the entrepreneur is absolutely indispensable to their story. He is a force for change but is not the product of *ad hoc* theorizing. He disturbs firms' routines by changing the environment. In turn, conscious entrepreneurial adaptation to a changing environment is sometimes the only way a firm, locked into a now inappropriate routine, may survive. Entrepreneurial innovation may result eventually in a new routine, an adaptation to the new environment. Nelson and Winter focus their analysis on innovation, invention, and the upsetting of firm routines.

Clearly, much more work needs to be done on a subjectivist or Austrian theory of firm behavior. Any theory along these lines must take seriously the Menger/Hayek distinction between designed and undesigned social institutions. Certainly, firm owners attempt to maximize their profits through the vehicle of their firms. The pattern of firm survival and the character of surviving firms is not simply the result, however, of conscious planning and rational profit maximization. The industrial landscape reflects both the results of conscious planning and the unintended consequences of entrepreneurial interaction in the marketplace. (Firms do not, for instance, normally plan their own demise.) We find an evolutionary approach like Nelson and Winter's to be attractive because it allows for both planning and profit maximization, and unplanned consequences. Entrepreneurs can, to some extent, influence their environment and affect the fortunes of their firms. But firms are ultimately either "selected" or not. Evolutionary forces in the environment reflect the unplanned consequences of others' actions (both purchasers of a firm's products and competitive firms).

Though consciously an essay in Schumpeterian economics, Nelson and Winter's work may have the unintended consequences of providing a building block for a subjectivist theory of the firm. In any case, their work exemplifies the sharp contrast between neoclassical theory and one incorporating the effects of the passage of time. Their contribution is a first step toward an alternative theory of the firm. More generally, it offers an approach to modeling institutional change.

## APPENDIX: STOCHASTIC EQUILIBRIUM

In modeling learning, change, error, and expectations, theorists increasingly employ the concept of a stochastic equilibrium. In such models, there is an underlying stochastic process generating the data. Expectations of rational agents will tend to the mathematically expected value. "Learning" involves updating of priors until the subjective probability distribution conforms to this objective probability distribution. Apparent forecast error is optimal. Since information is costly to acquire, it does not pay agents to acquire more information about the underlying stochastic process. There is variance in the outcomes, but experienced errors in forecasts will not lead agents to revise their optimal forecasts or to alter their behavior.

Some of our misgivings with this approach were stated above in reference to Hahn's "learning functions." In the dynamic or pattern equilibrium that we have articulated, there is genuine learning. The competitive market process is a never-ending learning process. In an explicitly evolutionary theory this learning is captured in the process of adaptation and innovation. There is no learning in a stationary stochastic equilibrium (Hahn, 1973, pp. 18–20; Littlechild, 1977, pp. 6–8).

Similarly, "imperfections" in the market process do not necessarily arise from participants' choosing an "optimal level" of error. The errors on which we are focusing *arise from the very attempt to arrive at individual adjustment to the environment.* They are unintended and unplanned consequences of individuals' actions and interactions. These market errors or imperfections may take the form of "too much" product heterogeneity, as firms try to discover and satisfy consumer tastes. The errors may also show up as poorly invested capital (chapters 8–9). In our theory, agents will be dissatisfied with outcomes, will revise expectations, and will alter their behavior in the face of error. Error is part of the very market process itself, part of the stimulus to further adjustments. In general equilibrium models, none of this should occur, since all observed error is "optimal." At the descriptive level, we think our framework provides a better understanding of a wide range of phenomena, from the behavior of firms on competitive markets to agents' desperate attempts to cope with "ragged (uneven) inflation." At the normative level, our approach and that of neoclassical economics frequently generate diametrically opposed policy prescriptions. We examine some of these in the next chapter.

As noted above, neoclassical models to which we are referring postulate an underlying objective stochastic process. This assumption is very helpful if one is studying Brownian motion, the decay of radioactive particles, and, to a lesser extent, the weather. Social science surely must also take account of how physical processes affect human decisions. But there is no given, underlying process to which individuals must conform. In an open system, the process itself is largely the product of individuals' tastes, aspirations, and expectations. They help make this "objective" process whatever it is. It is not something entirely apart from human beings, but is partly of their creation. In forming expectations, they are not guessing about the collision of heavenly bodies. They are forming expectations about other individuals forming expectations about them, and so forth, as in the classic Keynesian beauty-contest example. Every shift in their expectations changes others' expectations, thereby changing the data. There may be no unique, objective value to which expectations "ought to" conform. Sometimes there may be such an "objective" value, as in the cycle of weather and crop failures; other times there may not be, as in certain aspects of inflationary expectations.

As in a number of other areas, we are not claiming that there are no applications of stochastic equilibrium in economics. Our objection is to the implied assumption that it is the one, uniquely correct way of understanding informational issues, even if the approach does violence to the phenomena itself. For instance, in their effort to explain learning, neoclassical economists are one step short of "proving" that there is no error in the world. Before falling with them into this abyss, we may want to step back and consider alternatives.

## NOTES

1 "*Man wants liberty to become the man he wants to become*. He does so precisely because he does not know what man he will want to become in time. Let us remove once and for all the instrumental defense of liberty, the only one that can possibly be derived directly from orthodox economic analysis. Man does not want liberty in order to maximize his utility, or that of the society of which he is a part. *He wants liberty to become the man he wants to become*" (Buchanan, 1979, p. 112).

2 Kirzner (1973, 1979) emphasizes entrepreneurial discovery of existing opportunities. Shackle (1979) emphasizes entrepreneurial creativity; entrepreneurial actions themselves make the profit opportunities.

3 Lucas (1975) is one conspicuous exception.

4 Hurwicz (1973) provides a useful bibliography up to the early 1970s. Recent work includes Grossman (1976, 1977) and Grossman and Stiglitz (1976), which also contain partial bibliographies. See also O'Driscoll (1981).

5 The importance of contractual and nonprice constraints in competitive markets arose in *Chicago Board of Trade v. United States,* 246 U.S. 231 (1918). Apparently the court did not understand that price restraints could, at least in principle, foster competition. We would have to examine this case more carefully to make a definitive judgment. But it does seem to represent an example of our point here. See the interesting discussion in Bork (1978, pp. 41–7).

6 Menger (1963, p. 146) perceived the basic question of all social sciences as: "How can it be that the institutions which serve the common welfare and are extremely significant for its development can come into being without a common will directed towards establishing them? Marx's conception of social science was, of course, similar to Menger's.

7 We submit that Hahn is logically in error in this argument. Arrow and Debreu have given us *sufficient* conditions for the attainment of competitive equilibrium. Hahn's argument would be strictly correct only if the Arrow-Debreu conditions were *necessary* (see the discussion in chapter 5).

8 Cf. Epstein (1982, p. 55) on the common-law system's concern with private property, individual liberty, and corrective justice: "The initial ethical premise of the system is that possession is the root of title, or that taking possession of an unowned thing is prima facie evidence of individual ownership, as lawyers say, in a fee. The rule is stated as a presumption that can be rebutted only by a person whose earlier possession gives rise to a higher title." Justice depends, then, on the process producing ownership, and not on presumed benefits of the pattern of ownership of property.

9 Two examples come to mind. Milk price supports (and agricultural price supports generally) have not solved or alleviated farm problems, but have perpetuated and even exacerbated them. Current problems of US steel producers have a history going back to nineteenth-century protective tariffs. Each round of protection creates more dependency on existing and future protection.

10 Here and in what follows, one could recast our analysis in terms of "notional" excess demands. We have no desire to quibble over words. Our substantive point would remain: *even when there is no effective excess demand, plans may be frustrated.* This point is recognized in macroeconomics; see Clower (1965).

11 A more complete property rights analysis could demonstrate that managers of the housing authority would not be as likely to respond to market signals as would entrepreneurs who could appropriate the profits of correct decisions. Our case is not entirely hypothetical. We understand that the extensive and longstanding system of rent controls has inhibited regional growth and mobility in Great Britain.

12 Friedman has argued that "natural selection" explanations and continuous

utility maximization explanations are complements rather than substitutes. Thus, successful firms are selected by the market. But as theorists we can suppose that it is "as if" firms are conscious profit maximizers (Friedman, 1953). Langlois effectively refutes Friedman's position. He argues that it is dubious methodologically, and, building on Sidney Winter's work, points out that profit-maximizers who are best adapted to an equilibrium state may be selected out during the equilibration process. Survivors might then not be true "optimizers" (Langlois, 1982a, pp. 19–22).

13 Our anthropomorphic language presents a barrier in discussing evolutionary processes. In speaking of "adopting" a rule, we do not wish to imply conscious choice by the adopter: quite the contrary.

14 Such a reconsideration was started in a special volume of the *Journal of Legal Studies,* to which both of us contributed (March 1980).

15 None of what we have said here is intended as an implicit criticism of Alchian and Demsetz's theory of the firm (1972), which we view as dealing with one aspect of the firm. This aspect is not of particular concern to us here.

16 A distinction between the maximizing and evolutionary approaches can be illustrated in this case. If there is a "correct" adaptation to the new environment, rationality and profit maximization are invoked to ensure that the firm *will* survive. The evolutionary approach supposes no such thing. For instance, a firm may not survive environmental change even were it true that an infinitely long search would insure its survival and even prosperity. The evolutionary approach thus implicitly incorporates the passage of real time, which in this case incorporates cash and other relevant constraints. Trial and error discovery takes time, and firms may run out of resources before they discover a profitable response to change. Optimization models do not incorporate real time. Thus constraints such as liquidity constraints, which operate in real time, are ignored. See note 12 (above).

# 7

# The Political Economy of Competition and Monopoly

The "order" of the market emerges *only* from the *process* of voluntary exchange among participating individuals. The "order" is, itself, defined as the outcome of the *process* that generates it. The "it," the allocation-distribution result, does not, and cannot, exist independently of the trading process. Absent this process, there is and can be no "order."
*James M. Buchanan (1982b, p. 5)*

## COMPETITION: STATIC AND DYNAMIC

In the previous chapter, we analyzed the sources and effects of unexpected change on behavior. Regardless of recent attention paid to particular issues or problems of dynamic competition (e.g., advertising), economic theorists still employ static analysis of competition and monopoly. Our critique is directed less to the fruitful positive analysis of competition and monopoly developed in recent years, and more toward conventional normative analysis. We find congenial much of the recent positive analysis of regulation, antitrust, and competitive practices. This work includes, *inter alia*, the "Chicago School of Antitrust" (Posner, 1979), the UCLA–Chicago tradition in industrial organization, and the "New Institutionalism." Indeed, some of our own work belongs in these areas.

Even in this recent work, however, the normative analysis is less appealing that the positive economics. Normative analysis remains essentially static, even when the positive analysis is dynamic. Normative implications are drawn on the presupposition that the market process quickly achieves a pre-existing or predetermined equilibrium position (Reder, 1982, pp. 11–13). There is a postulated ontological order, dictated by tastes, opportunities, etc., toward which markets converge rapidly. In the epigraph for this chapter, Professor Buchanan criticized this presupposition. The view criticized there embodies the fallacy of conceptual realism: the belief that mental constructs and purely hypothetical states have an existence in reality.

There are generally many possible orders or equilibria, depending on the operative institutional processes. Different processes and institutional arrangements are not merely better or worse mechanisms for arriving at the *same* given end points. Rather, different institutions and attendant processes generate different orders. No one of these needs to be the "correct," "true," or "optimal" order or outcome. There is no institutional or process-independent order, such as is suggested by relating equilibrium positions to tastes, endowments, and transformation possibilities (i.e., "data"). That is, there is no order defined apart from the process generating it.

There are, however, systematic relationships between outcomes and processes producing them (Sowell, 1980, pp. 98–100 and passim). "Systematic" does not mean deterministic. Particular features or aspects of social outcomes may be attainable by a number of processes. Policies influencing one outcome or feature will not, however, leave other things constant. Nor do they leave the process itself unaffected.

Systematic criticism of outcomes logically involves criticism of the process producing those outcomes. Similarly, approval of a process producing an order entails approval of the resultant order. For instance, one cannot consistently approve of markets as allocational mechanisms, while objecting to distributional results. In objecting to market outcomes, one is in reality objecting to market processes. In upholding a different allocational–distributional outcome, one is implicitly upholding a different social process. Conversely, sanctioning a social process or mechanism, like the market, logically entails approval of the outcomes (Rawls, 1963, p. 102). "Social choice" involves simultaneous choice of means and affirmation of ends or outcomes.

## UNCERTAINTY AND MARKETS

We have argued that economic problems arise only in consequence of unexpected change, i.e., change relative to expectations. In characterizing a disturbance as "unexpected," we focus precisely on those events for which no probability distribution can be meaningfully postulated. Richard Langlois has recently clarified the issue in question by distinguishing between structural and parametric knowledge. In neoclassical economics, "uncertainty" refers to situations in which agents know the structure of the problem but are unsure of the exact value of one or more parameters. As Arrow phrased it,

> Uncertainty means that we do not have a complete description of the world which we fully believe to be true. Instead, we consider the world to be in one or another of a range of states. Each state of the world is a description which is complete for all relevant purposes. Our uncertainty consists in not knowing which state is the true one. (Arrow, 1974, p. 33–4)

As Langlois has observed:

> The agent is implicitly presumed to have an exhaustive list of possible actions and states of the world and, equally importantly, a mean/ends framework relating the actions and states of the world to his utility. We might say that the agent has certain knowledge of the structure of the problem he faces or, to put it another way, that he has perfect *structural* knowledge. Imperfections in that agent's knowledge extend only to specific parameters of the problem. . . . He may have imperfect *parametric* knowledge, but never imperfect structural knowledge; he may acquire parametric information, but never structural information. (Langlois, 1984, p. 29)

In our terminology, the agent may know typical features but simply be unable to list all possible unique features (cf. Loasby, 1976, p. 9). He faces an open-ended problem for one of two reasons. First, he may have no relevant experience on the basis of which he could calculate probabilities of outcomes. This situation is characteristic of unique features. Second, the possibilities and their likelihood are not independent of his actions and those of other agents. We have previously emphasized the fact that economic "data" are not objective, in the sense of being independent of human volition and action. Unless one believes in the strictest form of philosophical determinism, this insures a realm of true uncertainty in human affairs. The imperfection in knowledge is structural and not merely parametric.

As argued in the last chapter, behavioral regularity results not from continuous utility maximization but from rule-following. Rule-following behavior reflects, in turn, a high degree of genuine uncertainty, not certainty. Continuous utility maximization under uncertainty would produce unpredictable results. These results are contrary to conventional wisdom, but this wisdom is not the product of systematic analysis. In a recent article, Ronald Heiner (1983) subjected the conventional wisdom to systematic analysis and sided with the position being articulated here. He observed that:

> In the special case of no uncertainty, the behavior of perfectly informed, fully optimizing agents responding with complete flexibility to every perturbation in their environment would not produce easily recognizable patterns, but rather would be extremely difficult to predict. Thus, it is in the limits to maximizing behavior that we will find the origin of predictable behavior. (Heiner, 1983, p. 561)

Decision-makers face the greatest risk of loss (and gain) when forced to adopt new behavioral rules. The adoption of new rules is a discrete, time-consuming learning process, which not all agents complete successfully. We offer the following example to illustrate our point. Good economic theory predicted the general (typical) effects of deregulating air fares: *Ceteris paribus*, real airline tariffs would fall; better resource allocation would result. Careful analysis would also have predicted an industry shake-out. Cartel prices produce excess capacity. With deregulation, excess capacity would predictably be employed providing services that cover incremental but not full costs. In the long run, excess capacity would be removed. Real air fares would rise again, though to a level below the old regulated price. In simple diagrammatic terms $P_c$ was the cartel price, $P_m$ the market or competitive price, and $P_e$ the temporarily depressed price reflecting excess capacity (see figure 2).

Airlines have had great difficulty in coping with the transition from a regulated to a competitive environment, in part because most of it took place during one of the most severe of postwar

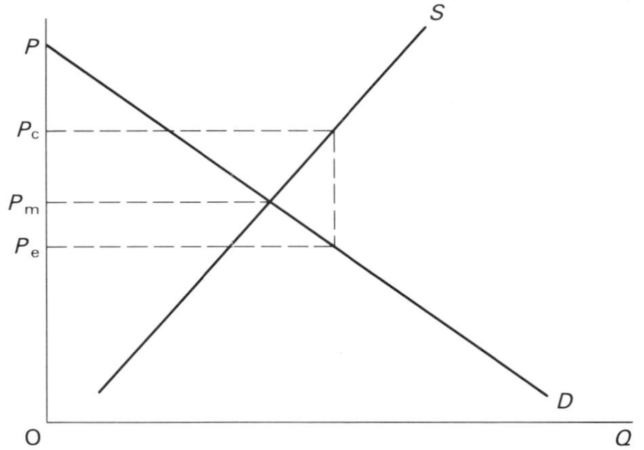


Figure 2

recessions. It is also true however that, for all intents and purposes, airlines had always been regulated. Behavioral rules were geared to survival in a regulated cartel environment. Being the first transportation industry to be deregulated, the airlines had nothing to imitate. The actual experience under deregulation proved surprising to many observers, supporters and opponents of deregulation alike. Among other things, opponents feared the demise of services to small communities. This fear was effectively translated into protection for such services. Deregulation proponents argued that any loss of services would be a price worth paying for improved resource allocation. Few questioned, however, that small community services would not be viable. There was little experience with the economics of such service in a deregulated environment.[1] Critics and supporters of deregulation alike were proved wrong, as small operators picked up and sometimes expanded small community services heretofore provided by major carriers. "Commuter" lines are the fastest growing segment of the industry.

At the onset of deregulation, it was generally believed that carriers could maximize profits by flying widebody aircraft with high-density seating on well traveled routes (such as New York–Los Angeles). Based on accumulated knowledge and experience in the industry, there was every reason to expect this to be a successful strategy. Yet, the very carriers adopting this strategy (e.g., United Airlines) fared relatively poorly. On the other hand, Piedmont, a regional carrier, is among the most profitable airlines. Its strategy consists of connecting medium-sized cities on routes of 300–600 miles, utilizing smaller jet aircraft.[2]

Airline deregulation illustrates an important implication of the evolutionary theory of the firm. Environmental change renders much accumulated knowledge obsolete. Airlines are now engaged in a trail and error process of discovering the adapting to a new environment. For instance, United Airlines, which had abandoned short "feeder-routes" in favor of longer "high-density" routes, is now reversing strategy. And it is imitating low-cost interlopers with its cut-rate "Friendship Express" service.[3]

The modern evolutionary theory of the firm must, however, be distinguished from nineteenth-century views of evolution. These emphasized gradualism of evolutionary change, summarized in Marshall's dictum (borrowed from Darwin): *Natura non facit saltum.* For gradual changes, much of our analysis might seem inapplicable or exaggerated. Modern biology now recognizes, however, that evolutionary change is often sudden if not catastrophic. Biologists, who borrowed the concept of evolution from eighteenth-century political economy, have now progressed beyond their social science brethren.

Consider the neoclassical production function. In a world of real time, conventional characterizations of the production function are misleading: "The production possibility set is a description of the state of the firm's knowledge about the possibilities of transforming commodities" (Arrow and Hahn, 1971, p. 53). This is an inadequate representation of what firms know at any given moment. As time passes, technology changes. Firms acquire information about "segments" of various different production functions. They thus know more than could be provided by learning about any one opportunity set. Yet they know less than is suggested by static analysis. They experience only limited ranges of any particular production function, never the complete production set (Nelson and Winter, 1982, pp. 59–65).

We illustrate the practical import of this by considering the effects of a disturbance or innovation. Firms will not move costlessly and immediately to the profit-maximizing point on the relevant production function. In the ensuing selection process, some firms will be eliminated. Some of the losers may be firms that, if they had survived, would have been low-cost producers (above, pp. 128–9). If all such change were anticipated, it would be pointless and misleading to talk about "disturbances," much less to analyze the adjustment process. Firms would anticipate and already would have adopted optimally to the change. Indeed, neoclassical economic theory has difficulty explaining why firms (i.e., asset-owning organizations), as opposed to lines of commerce, would ever disappear. In anticipating environmental change, firms would shed unprofitable lines of commerce and enter new ones. Personal computers would be the product of firms formerly engaged in making quill pens. In this world swift application of Occam's Razor would eliminate evolutionary analysis in favor of the hypothesis of continuous utility maximization. Neoclassical theorists are perhaps inclined to reject evolutionary theorizing precisely because it appears superfluous. And it is superfluous in a world of zero information costs. If one does not assume zero information costs, however, then the conclusions of the evolutionary approach cannot be ignored.

Long-run assumptions suffuse standard analyses. Even when economists ostensibly employ short-run analysis, they implicitly assume away informational problems. Transactors are viewed as adapting perfectly and costlessly to postulated disturbances. Standard analytical tools and procedures impose these assumptions on problems. Indeed, our critique is directed less at what is stated formally and openly in textbook and applied analysis, and more at what is implicit and hidden.

We offer a vivid illustration of a piece of positive analysis that surreptitiously employs a long-run equilibrium assumption to deal with a short-run adjustment problem. In that analysis, Professor Stigler "tested" the proposition that firms generally produce under conditions of constant cost (Stigler, 1966, pp. 141–4). He did this by investigating firms' responses to changing demand conditions (see figure 3). Confronted by falling demand for their products, firms with constant costs over a wide range ($MC_A$) would respond by shutting down. Firms with rising costs over a wide range ($MC_B$) would cut back output but continue operating. Stigler found that output restrictions by existing firms dominated plant closings. He accordingly concluded that $MC_B$ better approximates industrial cost conditions than $MC_A$.

What Stigler actually did was conduct a multiple test of: (1) cost conditions, (2) price-taking behavior, and (3) equilibrium conditions. He implicitly assumed that competitive firms facing constant long-run costs would also face constant short-run costs,

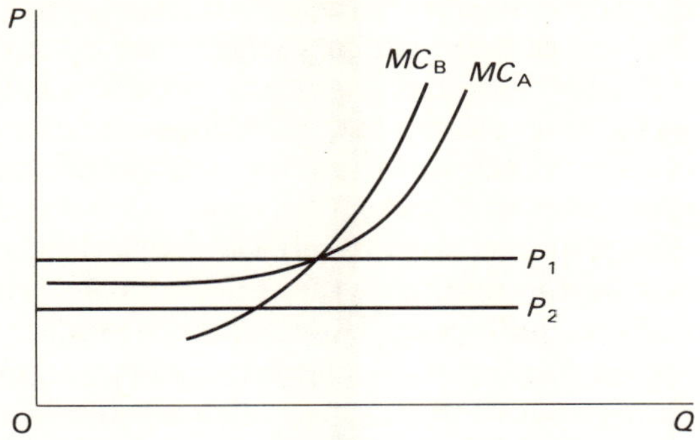


Figure 3

as well as be price-takers outside of long-run equilibrium. Arrow (1959) has demonstrated the implausibility of the second and third conditions. Without bringing in most of the considerations already discussed, we could adduce an explanation more plausible than Stigler's. Let us first stipulate that in fact cutbacks predominate over shutdowns. We assume, however, that, *à la* Arrow, firms confront downward-sloping demand curves in the short run. We can then explain the empirical results, even in situations in which marginal costs were constant across all runs. Our hypothesis is accordingly more robust than Stigler's, since it applies to situations of both constant and increasing costs. Further, we can illuminate why even competitive firms might keep prices constant in the face of falling demand (a phenomenon not without examples). This latter would occur, for instance, in the case of linear demand curves and constant costs, if demand changed equiproportionately at every price.

Perfect-adaptation models are implausible, yet economists adhere to them. Often, they do so because the alternative appears to be theoretical nihilism. Since nihilism is not the alternative, it is time to re-examine an essentially untenable position.

## OPTIMAL POLICY

Standard welfare economics deduces a set of conditions that must be satisfied in order for there to be optimal resource allocation

(Baumol, 1965, pp. 356ff.). Stated most generally, these conditions demand equality at the margin of social benefits and costs. This approach is applied to such issues as externalities, monopolies, and tariffs. Under idealized conditions, markets yield an optimal allocation of resources. If the unfettered operation of markets produces a divergence between social benefits and costs, be it in the form of externality, monopolistic output restriction, or whatever, this is attributed to "market failure."

The theory of economic policy prescribes three main approaches to dealing with market failure: taxation, regulation, and antitrust. There is usually a choice between two of these general approaches. For instance, antitrust policy is largely inapplicable to externality problems. Similarly, though a few observers have proposed using tax policy to influence monopolists, policy-makers generally weigh choices between regulation and antitrust for monopoly problems.

For most major questions, there is a large literature on choice of policy instruments. There is also typically a substantial literature on various methods of implementing a particular policy, e.g. taxation. Within and among alternatives, the criteria applied to policy choices are those of general equilibrium welfare theory. Policy judgments are typically made on the basis of presumed differences in informational requirements and transactions costs. This literature frequently begs important questions and exaggerates the differences among the three policy approaches. We argue our position by reference to two concrete examples: control of pollution, and control of monopoly.

### *Pollution*

Ronald Coase (1960) challenged the Pigovian policy of using taxes and subsidies to control pollution, arguing that taxation of externalities would not generally result in optimal resource allocation. He criticized reasoning that presumes producers of externalities cause costly interactions and ought automatically to be taxed. "Victims" of pollution may in practice be least-cost avoiders of harm. In setting a tax at an apparently optimal level, authorities may thus effect an uneconomic use of resources. Coase focused here on the information requirements for implementing optimal policy. He suggested that preferred solutions generally arise when parties negotiate among themselves to rearrange property titles. If high transactions costs preclude negotiations, Coase suggested carefully drafted liability rules as a solution. These rules ought to take account of comparative costs of avoiding harm, as well as presumptions regarding the identities of the highest-valued users of resources. Coase further argued that cases of apparent market failure were often the effects of statutory exemptions from standard liability rules. His article spawned the modern property-rights approach to externalities and to legal questions generally.

Proponents of the Pigovian tradition were slow in responding effectively to the Coasean challenge. Baumol's (1972) reply was, however, an articulate case for the classic taxation alternative. It is, moveover, explicit about informational assumptions that are usually implicit, thereby revealing problems inherent in all theories of optimal taxation. The following quotation succinctly states the case:

> Despite the validity in principle of the tax-subsidy approach of the Pigouvian tradition, in practice it suffers from serious difficulties. For we do not know how to to estimate the magnitude of the social costs, the data needed to implement the Pigouvian tax-subsidy proposals. For example, a very substantial proportion of the cost of the pollution is psychic; and even if we knew how to evaluate the psychic cost of some one individual we seem to have little hope of dealing with effects so widely diffused through the population.
>
> This would not be very serious if one could hope to learn by experience. One might try any plausible set of taxes and subsidies and then attempt, by a set of trial and error steps, to approach the desired magnitude. Unfortunately, convergence toward the desired solution by an iterative procedure of this sort requires some sort of measure of the improvement (if any) that has been achieved at each step so that the next trial step can be adjusted accordingly. But we do not know the optimal combination of outputs, so we simply have no way of judging whether a given change in the trial tax values will then have moved matters in the right direction.
>
> These difficulties are compounded by another characteristic of externalities which has already been mentioned – the likelihood that in the presence of externalities there will be a multiplicity of local maxima. . . . Consequently, even if an

> iterative process were possible, it might only drive us toward a local maximum, and may thus fail to take advantage of the really significant opportunities to improve economic welfare. (Baumol, 1972, p. 316)

Theories of optimal taxation ignore the fact that information necessary for their implementation will always be missing. Cost is subjective, and forward-looking. As such, cost is not a directly observable magnitude. There is, further, no calculational mechanism with which to measure gains and losses from alternative levels of taxation. Finally, to extend Baumol's argument, the data of the problem are not constant. This alone negates any iterative solution. During a time-consuming iterative process, data change. An iterative taxation system has neither a calculational mechanism, nor the entrepreneurship driving market behavior.

Baumol adduced an argument almost isomorphic to the more general argument against nonprice resource allocation. Mises and Hayek first stated this more general argument as a critique of "socialist," i.e. nonprice, resource allocation. Absent a system of markets, especially factor markets, transactors are unable systematically to calculate benefits and costs of various actions or production plans. The initial socialist response or "solution" was to set price and marginal cost equal. But this response is an evasion of, not a solution to, the informational and calculational dilemma posed by Mises and Hayek. How could a central planner ascertain the subjective cost or marginal value of an action to millions of citizens? It is true, of course, that *if* marginal cost and consumer preferences are institutionally independent, and *if* information about these is costlessly available, then marginal cost pricing is equivalent to the competitive "solution." The Mises–Hayek critique questioned these assumptions, not the conclusion of the valid but unsound socialist argument. In fact, it was the Austrians, particularly Wieser, who had long before demonstrated the logical validity of that argument.

The next socialist solution was to suggest an iterative process for allocating resources. Arbitrary prices would be set and then adjusted in response to observed excess demands. Hayek replied that, without real markets for factors, profits and losses would be impossible to calculate. In a socialist economy, there would be no factor owners to weigh (internalize) the risks and rewards of alternative production plans. The absence of private property rights in capital (if not in other factors) is the essential characteristic of socialism. Accordingly, there would be no competitive bidding process producing offers to internalize. Further, without title to residual claims, socialist managers of resources would lack incentives to act entrepreneurially in discovering opportunities.

The force of these arguments is measurably increased when one recalls that Mises and Hayek always presumed that significant changes in data typify all economies. Though they had by then abandoned the goal of abolishing markets, the advocates of socialism ignored the informational issues and assumed static conditions in their response. Somehow, however, texts repeat the myth that Mises and Hayek were "answered" (cf. Reder, 1982, p. 4).

In the Mises–Hayek analysis, socialism is intervention carried out systematically in all markets. It substitutes nonprice and nonmarket allocation for pricing and market institutions. Particularistic intervention at the micro-level is socialism writ small. To paraphrase Robertson, market interventions generate islands of calculational chaos in a sea of markets. It is a misnomer to speak of "calculating" the benefits and costs of intervention, when the evident effect of such intervention is interference with the market's calculational procedures. Consider the use of taxes to influence output levels (as opposed simply to raising revenue). Taxes are often viewed as substitutes for intervention by regulation or other means; yet the two alternatives are more similar than not.

If a tax rate is to be optimal, policy-makers must know the optimal level of the taxed activity (e.g., discharging effluents into a river). If that were known, however, a regulatory system prescribing this level of activity would seem neither inferior nor more costly than the tax alternative. The *informational* requirements of taxation and regulatory approaches are formally identical, a point made evident in the Baumol quotation above. And the informational requirements for optimal regulation are simply those for optimal nonprice resource allocation. There can be no theory of optimal regulatory (taxing) behavior until there is a theory of nonprice resource allocation that actually addresses the original Mises–Hayek argument.

Taxation of an activity is often proffered as a "market" approach, which substitutes for a regulatory or interventionist approach. Economists mislead themselves and their readers, however, by speaking of "tax prices." The only shared features that taxes have with prices is their dimensionality. Taxes do not result from a market process, nor do they reflect allocational decisions of resource owners. Taxes affect prices but are not themselves market prices measuring an economic trade-off at the margin. In other words, taxation is a method of intervening, not an alternative to intervention or nonmarket allocation. Absence of markets and improperly specified property rights do generate economic problems. The very absence of relevant markets, however, implies the absence of any ability to acquire the very information needed to correct the problem. If markets are not providing signals to transactors on all costs of an action, policy-makers will also lack this information. Moreover, even were they to possess the required information, political decision-makers face different incentives than do entrepreneurs.

Let us hasten to point out what we are *not* saying. By itself, the foregoing is neither an argument for unfettered markets, nor a criticism of any kind of intervention. (Indeed, the foregoing is strictly positive analysis.) We would, however, criticize any argument that a cost-benefit calculus can be applied to such intervention. We ourselves are sympathetic, for instance, to judicial rectification of tortious acts performed by polluters. But our support of judicial remedy rests on a belief in principles of corrective justice. We would not pretend that social utility is being maximized by the use of common-law remedies. We would be quite pleased, however, if the victim were made whole. Pursuit of the latter strikes us as a worthy enough goal even if it falls short of an artificial welfare ideal that is, in any case, unattainable in principle.

## *Antitrust*

For a variety of perceived economic problems, antitrust policy represents an alternative to a classic regulatory solution. For instance, as deregulation of the transportation sector has occurred, Congress has removed the antitrust immunity of firms engaged in surface and air transportation. The discipline exerted by the antitrust statutes has been substituted for that of the regulatory process. Many economists would favor this procedure generally, because, within a framework of rules, it seems to leave outcomes to market processes. While many individual antitrust policies, such as resale price maintenance and prohibitions on vertical mergers, have been criticized, there is substantial agreement among economists on the need for a policy on horizontal mergers and collusion.

This support for antitrust cuts across the political spectrum, although proponents of market solutions must be ambivalent toward the use of antitrust laws. Antitrust may be a preferred substitute for activist regulation, but it is still an intervention. Antitrust policy diminishes or eliminates the market value of asset titles, and circumscribes private property rights. The tension between support of a market-oriented policy and advocacy of antitrust is heightened by the realization that antitrust law has little basis at common law.[4] It is not the development of reorganized legal principles, like the law of torts and contract, so much as an application of administrative law. Epstein (1982) has recently argued that antitrust policy is broadly inconsistent with common-law doctrine and principles of corrective justice.

Our concern in this section, however, is with the economics of public policy toward monopoly. We associate any problems with standard economic analysis rather than with defects in legal reasoning or the political process, though the latter two factors are also undoubtedly sources of difficulties. We focus on informational issues suppressed or ignored in standard formulations, issues that infinitely complicate the process of utilizing economic analysis in antitrust policy. We suggest that the informational requirements for antitrust policy are closer to those for a regulatory approach than is generally recognized. These requirements are qualitatively the same as for other forms of nonmarket resource allocation.

Competitive values or allocations do not exist "out there," independently ascertainable apart from actual market results. Competitive prices and cost can be consistently defined only as the outcomes of competitive processes. There are not competitive results unless there is competition. As Buchanan reminds us, the "order" produced by competition "is, itself, defined as the outcome of the process that generates it . . . . The allocational–distributional result does not, and cannot, exist independently of the trading process." Without competition, there is no reference point to which comparisons with real-world results can be made. In absence of competitive markets, economic theory cannot tell us what is optimal. Still less can theory yield detailed predictions of what firms would have done under competitive conditions. Antitrust economics assumes, however, that policy-makers can do just this – or, at least, it assumes that they can move us in the correction direction. Yet even the latter is doubtful.

There are a few abstract distinctions that can be posited about the outcomes of monopolistic as compared with competitive markets. *Ceteris paribus*, monopolists produce less at a higher price. This is true, however, virtually by definition. In a static framework, the theory is pellucidly clear and deterministic. Problems arise, however, when it is applied to actual market arrangements. We refer to the familiar diagram representing monopolistic equilibrium (figure 4).

As is illustrated in the figure, a monopolist is treated as knowing or being capable of discovering competitive equilibrium. The monopolists chooses, however, to maximize profits by producing at $Q_m$ instead of $Q_c$. He faces the same production possibilities, demand, etc., as would exist in a competitive environment. Regulatory or antitrust can move the market from $(P_m, Q_m)$ to $(P_c, Q_c)$. If, however, we relax the assumptions of standard theory, these policy conclusions appear much less certain. Indeed, outside of long-run equilibrium, it is not clear that we can distinguish conceptually between the behavior of competitors and monopolists.

As Arrow (1959) first made clear, the characteristics associated with perfect competition would only eventuate in long-run static equilibrium. In "Toward a Theory of Price Adjustment," Arrow (1959, p. 42) presented "the theoretical analysis of the decisions

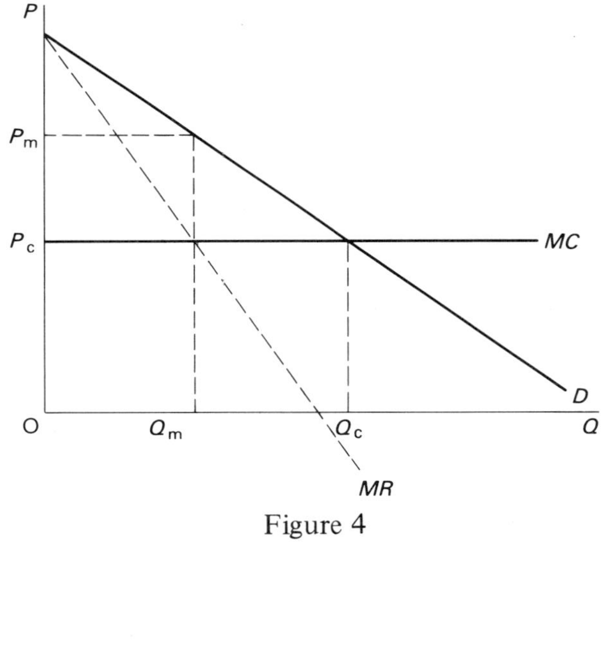


Figure 4

as to price." We do not normally associate pricing decisions with competitors, because neoclassical theory treats prices parametrically in competitive models. As Arrow (p. 46) noted, however, in disequilibrium there is no reason to believe that Jevon's Law of One Price would apply. He associated disequilibrium with an imbalance between supply and demand. If, for instance, demand exceeds supply at a disequilibrium price, then, so long as production is time-consuming, entrepreneurs will discover that they can raise their prices without losing all their customers to competitors. In other words, each entrepreneur will realize that he is in the position of a profit-maximizing monopolist. By a trial and error process, the entrepreneur seeks out the price–quantity combination that maximizes the profit of his competitive firm. In this disequilibrium process, competitive firms confront downward-sloping demand curves.

Arrow chose to model a dynamic process using a static model: that for a neoclassical monopolist. We rejected this ploy because it captures one feature of the competitive process – the search for a profit-maximizing price – at the cost of losing sight of all the other features characterizing competition. As we argued in previous chapters, the attribution of "equilibrium" to reality (as opposed to a model) is an egregious example of the fallacy of misplaced concreteness. The *world* is never "in equilibrium." In chapter 6 (pp. 113–14), we suggested that the appropriate response is to abandon formalism and static assumptions at the stage of modeling the system (rather than in applying the model). Professor Arrow adopted the alternative strategy. In this instance, his more conventional approach does highlight one salient point. If the conditions of perfectly competitive theory are not met – and they never can be fulfilled in reality – then formal economic theory cannot distinguish between the behavior of a monopolist and that of a competitor. It is not simply that the theories of competition and monopoly are difficult to apply to the complex fact-patterns of antitrust cases: rather, the theories are analytically indistinguishable.

Arrow compressed the competitive and monopolistic cases into one by arguing that competitors will often confront the same pricing problem as monopolists. Elsewhere, O'Driscoll (1982) argued that monopolistic markets are more like competitive markets than is true in neoclassical models. If all costs are properly measured, than a monopolist will price equal to cost at the margin.

This is true even though he confronts a less than infinitely elastic demand curve.

Regardless of which tack one takes (Arrow's or O'Driscoll's), the analysis undermines the sharp distinction between monopoly and competition characteristic of formal neoclassical theory. This is not to suggest that the two market types cannot be sharply distinguished. In the next section, we present an alternative approach to a theory of monopoly. Neoclassical economics does not, however, provide this distinction.

Not only does antitrust policy lack the sound theoretical foundations it claims for itself, but, as a practical matter, the informational requirements needed to implement it will never be attainable. It is true, of course, that policy-makers do not look at the relationship between price and marginal cost in antitrust cases. Marginal cost is unobservable, a fact apparent even in non-subjectivist formulations of cost theory. Rather, policy-makers look at other characteristics that they believe distinguish competition and monopoly. Not surprisingly, we question this procedure.

Put simply, no one knows what a competitive market would look like in the absense of competition. This is surely the essential lesson of a process view of competition. The point is driven home by considering again the course of one episode or instance of deregulation: the airline industry. One of the most striking results of de-monopolizing the airline industry is the *greater* degree of product heterogeneity and the *larger* dispersion of fares. Neither result would be predicted by neoclassical theory. Each result is fully consistent with a process view. Indeed, the greater diversity of product offerings is a prediction of a process theory of competition, as we indicated in chapter 6.

As regulations have been relaxed, airlines have increased the diversity of their services. Cut-rate (less than full-fare coach) service has certainly increased. Imitating low-cost interlopers, traditional trunk carriers have introduced "no-frills" transportations; for instance, United Airlines has reconfigured jets with lighter-weight seats so that more can be fitted on each plane. But the range of services and classes has also increased, fine-tuning output to the diversity of consumer preferences. The introduction of business class is one example of satisfying the diversity of consumer preferences.

Interloper airlines are frequently responsible not only for the low-cost service, but also for the greater diversity of offerings.

This reflects their greater orientation toward marketing. Newcomers know only a relatively competitive environment. Existing trunk carriers had adapted to a regulated environment with well specified monopoly rights. The trunk carriers were superb at public relations and weak on marketing. In regulated environments, firms are concerned overwhelmingly with explaining or justifying existing industry practices. Competitive firms are prone to upset shopworn practices. In the process, they develop other skills.

Airline deregulation has revealed accumulated inefficiencies in the regulated environment. New carriers not only have lower factor costs (labor and capital), but also use absolutely less of almost all factors. Greater flexibility in utilizing labor permits firms to have a smaller labor pool. For instance, New York Air utilizes workers interchangeably (e.g., reservation clerks and stewardesses). Likewise, 30 minutes used to be a quick turnaround time for aircraft: now, Southwest Airlines (a Texas based carrier that was never regulated) can unload and refill a plane in 10 minutes.

Consideration of the effects of airline deregulation reveals that monopolized (or cartelized) markets differ from competitive ones in several, not just one, dimension. There are systematic differences besides pricing disparities between the two. Monopolists tend to produce the wrong goods from the perspective of consumers. There is lack of diversity and, as we suggest below, a tendency to lower-quality goods in monopolized markets compared with a competitive environment. These effects receive short shift in neoclassical analysis, because of the stringent assumptions of these models. In the latter, and the good is a given and cost conditions are data. Price is the only dimension in which monopoly can differ from competition. This does not merely reflect simplifying assumptions, but goes to the heart of the static conception of competition. Prices are statements of rates of trade-off among commodities, rather than reflecting discrepancies among individuals' plans and the existence of profit opportunities.[5] Further, price is the only market-signaling mechanism. This leaves price the only control variable, and relative scarcity values the only endogenously produced information. Tastes, for instance, are and must be exogenous.

The multifaceted effects of monopoly were understood by classical political economists (cf. Smith, 1937, pp. 147; 575–6; 595–6). Their insights on nonprice effects of monopoly were lost as neoclassical economic theory was formalized, to survive only in what Nelson and Winter (1982, p. 46) have described as the "appreciative" theory of competitive adaptation that we teach to undergraduates. This informal theory of price bears little relation to formal theory.

In a process analysis of competition, firms must, *inter alia*, discover consumer preferences. Competition provides incentives to undertake the search, incentives largely lacking with monopoly.[6] In presenting our own approach to monopoly, we clarify and sharpen this analytic point. First, however, we consider the case of telecommunication policy.

American Telephone and Telegraph Company (AT&T) long beguiled observers with its apparent efficiency, innovation, and orientation to consumer preferences. It seemed to be a monopoly that worked. In reality, deregulation has revealed deficiencies in all three respects. In analyzing AT&T, economists failed to adopt a systematic opportunity-cost approach. The question should never have been AT&T's performance relative to the US Post Office, or to foreign telephone service. The question is, and should have been, AT&T's performance relative to that of firms in a deregulated environment.

Deregulation came first to the office telephone market. Western Electric (AT&T's manufacturing subsidiary) rapidly lost its share of the market to competitors because of inferior technology. As the home equipment market opened up, a similar process began taking place. Indeed, a great deal of equipment now sold in Bell System retail stores was not made by Western Electric.

AT&T's use of capital resources is extravagant compared with its competitors. For instance, MCI's microwave towers are smaller and cost considerably less than AT&T's. Recent closings of Western Electric plants apparently signal recognition of technological backwardness. Engineers and scientists may find it difficult to think of AT&T as technologically behind the times. AT&T is well known for its basic research. Economists, however, ought not to be perplexed. Beneficence in support of pure research is irrelevant: ability to bring technology to the bottom line is what counts. Deregulation in telecommunications is repeating a familiar pattern. Existing firms, heretofore possessing statutory monopolies, must catch up with interlopers.

We have argued that the effects of monopoly are more complex than a price–cost divergence. Some costs tend to be higher, others lower. Output characteristics are not as well attuned to consumer preferences as on competitive markets. We have suggested that these differences can be related systematically to the different property rights possessed by monopolists and competitors. In the final section, we develop some of our theoretical points in greater depth. We also consider some policy options.

## PROPERTY RIGHTS THEORY OF MONOPOLY

In this final section, we make explicit our conceptualization of the differences between monopoly and competition. In so doing, we present elements of a theory of monopoly. There is obviously more than one way to distinguish among market types. In fact, O'Driscoll (1982) presents two distinct conceptualizations of monopoly that are consistent with an overall subjectivist analysis. We believe that the one approach offered here is both fruitful and consistent with recent developments in other areas of economics.

We define monopoly as an enforceable property right in a product or market share. A monopoly right can encompass a great deal of economic activity or apply to a wide geographic area; or it can be narrow in scope and circumscribed geographically. When monopolists holding market shares or operating jointly in a territory or market cooperate, we call this situation a "cartel." Cartels are shared monopolies. There is thus no separate oligopoly theory.

Monopolistic and competitive markets are characterized by different property rights structures. Variations in rights structures generate relevant incentive effects. Competitive firms do not engage in rivalrous activities because they have a preference or predisposition to compete. Rather, they face constraints compelling rivalrous behavior merely to maintain, much less to expand, existing market shares or profits. This analytic approach is consistent with the emphasis on property rights that has evolved in other economic areas (e.g., in externality theory and in the analysis of exploitable resources).

A competitive firm has no *ex ante* property right in a share of the market or a portion of market demand. Each period, it must expend resources to re-acquire market share, sales, profits, etc. Other firms are in the same position. Actions leading to previous success can be imitated, reducing their expected payoff. This stimulates expenditure of resources to find ways to do as well or better than before. It is this process, only sketched here, that we describe as "rivalry." It occurs because of the structure of property rights.

Competitive firms have no property rights or titles to a market share, and certainly none to profits. In a market with free entry and no restriction on competitive practices (e.g., no advertising bans), past market shares yield no *ex ante* guarantee of future market performance. Observed market shares are *ex post* outcomes. Absent a secure property right, they tell us little about future market shares.

Firms owning secure property rights to market shares would be foolish to expend resources in the same manner as competitive firms. For instance, a monopolist will do less of the kind of innovation stimulated by competition. Instead, he will devote resources to innovating in public and governmental relations. These expenditures help secure his property right, though producing little or nothing of value to customers. This is a kind of inefficiency that until recently has escaped the notice of conventional monopoly theory. It exemplifies the kind of specific costs incurred by monopolists.[7] There are other costs incurred by competitive firms but not by monopolists. Many of these are expenditures made necessary by the actions of rivals. They are exemplified by advertising and marketing costs that are spared a monopolist. Some critics of competition characterize them as waste. Other issues aside, we see that the alternative is not necessarily less but different costs incurred. Costs incurred in the competitive process, however, produce some expected payoffs for consumers.

Let us return to airline deregulation to illustrate the latter point. Regulated trunk carriers invested in excess capacity under CAB regulation. Because they faced supra-market rates, they flew too many flights and utilized larger than necessary aircraft. This investment was profit-maximizing, but wasteful from the perspective of consumers. Excess capacity enabled airlines to capture peak-load traffic, generating monopoly returns. Aircraft were full or nearly so only a relatively small portion of the time. During those periods, revenues were far above costs. In normal times, capacity was underutilized. Losses incurred during normal periods were less than monopoly returns in peak periods. With lower competitive fares, firms cannot afford this procedure. In the new competitive environment, airlines better apportion their resources to average demand. Peak-load pricing substitutes for excess capacity.

To an outside observer, it is "obvious" that resources were being wasted under CAB regulation. And there was inefficiency from the consumers' perspective, the only one that should matter in market analysis. For the monopolist, however, the utilization of capital was profitable. Property rights analysis focuses on the source of the perverse effects of private profit maximization. These effects derive from the monopoly right itself, which insulates the producer from competitive pressures.

One could tell our story somewhat differently by characterizing airlines' behavior as rational responses to regulatory actions. In the end, this would be the same story. Regulation is not adventitious, but is the mechanism by which a monopoly right is enforced if not secured. Without regulation, the right is unenforceable and thus economically irrelevant. Property rights analysis focuses on issues like the specification and enforcement of legal entitlements or rights. This approach raises the question of how a right is acquired and enforced. Standard neoclassical analysis is weakest on this issue. Even property rights theorists have failed to extend their analysis systematically to monopoly theory. Yet the questions raised in this literature have special importance to the monopoly question. Especially in the transportation area, regulatory commissions were the relevant enforcement mechanism of monopoly rights.

There is good reason for subjectivists and process theorists to adopt a property rights theory of monopoly. This can be best understood by recalling the introductory discussion in this chapter. We related outcomes to the processes generating them. Institutions play a crucial role in shaping social processes. Changes in fundamental institutions will generate different economic processes, and thus different outcomes. We view property rights as a fundamental institution, partly determining the nature of economic processes. Property rights analysis focuses on the structural environment of economic processes. Langlois has gone so far as to characterize modern process theory as the "New Institutional Economics," though with an important caveat:

> The problem with the Historical School and many of the early Institutionalists is that they wanted an economics with institutions but without theory; the problem with many neoclassicists is that they want economic theory without institutions; what we should really want is both institutions

> and theory – not only pure economic theory informed by the existence of specific institutions, but also an economic theory *of* institutions. (Langlois, 1982a, pp. 16–17)

We have not attempted to articulate a theory of institutions. We have, however, emphasized the importance of specifying the property rights and relevant legal rules in any economic theory of competition and monopoly. Failure to do so leads to incomplete and erroneous analysis. To illustrate this latter point, we consider the central issue of neoclassical monopoly theory – the entry question.

Monopoly yields a net revenue, yet by assumption no entry occurs. Monopoly rent, and the associated "deadweight loss," are unexploited profit opportunities. These ought not to persist; their existence ought to lead to their own demise.

Neoclassical monopoly theory postulates but does not explain the existence of monopoly. It leaves the entry problem unresolved. Traditional entry barrier arguments have lost their appeal in the face of criticism (Demsetz, 1982). Some even believe that they are all but abandoned (Posner, 1979). In any case, like many other authors, we are unconvinced by traditional entry barrier models. Generally, the models suffer from one of two failings (or both). Either they identify a real scarcity as a "barrier" (e.g., advertising or capital costs), or they identify a cost already incurred by existing producers as barriers to new entrants (e.g., start-up costs). Information and capital costs reflect real scarcities. If potential entrants cannot afford to incur the full costs of competing, then this merely indicates that entry is not profitable and ought not occur. Start-up costs reflect a particular kind of information costs. Among other things, new firms typically must operate at a loss, even with negative cash flow, for an initial period. This requires making an initial investment, no different in principle from all other capital expenditures. An initial outgo in early periods is compensated by returns in later periods. At root, treatment of a subset of capital or information costs as suspect or unnecessary reflects a belief that these costs are not, or ought not to be, real. We know of no way of conjuring away either these costs or the informational factors that they reflect. In any case, positive analysis must take perceived costs as they exist.

For reasons not entirely clear, economists are impatient about the existence of profits but view with equanimity models postulating the persistence of monopoly returns. In positive and normative analysis, entrepreneurial profits are merely "short-run" phenomena; the analysis quickly moves to the long run. Modern theories of efficient markets and rational expectations explicitly treat profits as random events of transient duration. Profits cannot exist for more than one period, since this would permit agents to respond and obtain, in effect, something for nothing – a return over cost. At the same time, neoclassical monopoly theory postulates the existence of supra-normal returns period after period. (The "period" in the industrial organization literature is certainly a year in duration.)

Profits represent no conundrum for a process view of economics. Changing economic conditions are continuously generating new profit opportunities (and eliminating old ones). Asymmetric information is an integral part of subjectivist analysis. The "man on the spot," the specialist, has superior information. He can exploit or profit from this superior information. Over time, others will discover the information. If he has not already fully exploited the the profit opportunity, it will be competed away. Adam Smith's view of the link between specialized knowledge ("trade secrets") and profit was basically sound: "Secrets of this kind. . .can seldom be long kept; and the extraordinary profit can last very little longer than they are kept" (Smith, 1937, p. 60). What must be added to Smith's observation is the recognition that markets continuously present entrepreneurs with new menus of profit opportunities, even though each opportunity eventually disappears.

In the absence of a secure property title, persistent monopoly gains ought to be as troublesome to neoclassical economists as they are to process theorists. Not only the monopolists' gain, but also the associated "deadweight loss" represent unexploited profit opportunities (O'Driscoll, 1982, pp. 199–204). These potential gains are not the result of temporary disequilibrium, asymmetric information, or any other information problem. Monopolies are obvious features of the economic landscape, their gains revealed for all to see. They ought to represent especially ripe targets for entrepreneurial action. Gains from invading a monopolist's turf are inherently less speculative than ordinary profit opportunities. Profit maximization by monopolists almost invariably creates relatively secure profit opportunities for interlopers. If, for instance, the monopolist price discriminates, then this very pricing policy guarantees arbitrage profits. If the monopolist has a uniform pricing and service policy, then there are typically high-valued customers who would prefer a superior service at a higher price. In the latter case, the interloper "skims the cream" off the top of the business.

As with nineteenth-century railroad monopolies, the two situations can go hand in hand. The railroads engaged in value-of-service ratemaking but tended to provide roughly uniform service to all shippers. With the rise of motorized trucking, railroads first lost the high-valued customers. Trucks offered more flexible service, which better met the scheduling demands of shippers placing a relatively high value on timely delivery. Moreover, trucking is inherently less prone to damage shipments, because of such problems as coupler-slack in rail transportation. In the end, railroads were left with low-valued business, like hauling shipments of bulk commodities and agricultural produce. Yet sunk investments and common-carrier responsibilities left them with overhead costs not recoverable from revenue generated by remaining business. Losses on passenger service added to this problem in many cases. Only the recent deregulation of railroad rates has halted the 60-year decline of rail freight transportation.

Monopoly gains simply cannot persist in the face of determined profit-seeking entrepreneurs. If a monopoly position is to be maintained, the monopolist must possess a secure title to, or property right in, a share of the market. Only the state can secure such titles and grant such property rights. Applied economic analysis of monopoly should, accordingly, identify and explicate the legal or governmental source of that monopoly as its first order of business. This position does not derive from a tautological definition of monopoly as a right or privilege granted by a governmental unit: it is, rather, a conclusion of economic analysis.

The property rights approach ennuciated here is basically the view of monopoly at common law, as restated by Blackstone (1803, p. 159) when he described monopoly as "a license or privilege allowed by the king for the sole buying and selling, making, working or using of any thing whatsoever; whereby the subject in general is restrained from that liberty of manufacturing or trading which he had before." The common-law view was absorbed into American law, being clearly stated in the *Charles River Bridge* case.[8] The court there defined monopoly as "the withdrawal of that which is a common right from the community and vesting it in one or more individuals, to the exclusion of all others." The story of how the common-law conception of monopoly was transformed into the modern statutory conception is an intriguing one, which, however, goes far beyond the subject of this chapter (but see Bork, 1978, pp. 15–49; and O'Driscoll, 1982). Our point here is theoretical: Monopoly rents can persist only if legally protected. From the perspective of a property rights theory, neither antitrust nor regulation is an appropriate vehicle for controlling monopolies. Regulation and perhaps antitrust policy are sources of monopoly power. Deregulation and repeal of legal protections are the appropriate responses. Surface and air transportation are not special cases, but are paradigmatic examples of monopoly in practice.

There is no question that distinctions between ordinary private property rights, which are necessary for decentralized economic organization, and monopoly rights are often fine ones. Patents and copyrights are tough cases. Traditional arguments in their favor are well known. Though we are suspicious of some of these, we are by no means prepared to argue here forcefully and universally against either patents or copyrights. From a property rights perspective, however, the time is ripe for reconsidering the case for both patents and copyrights. Since Sir Arnold Plant's critique of patents, there has been comparatively little attention paid by property rights theorists to the subject (but see Littlechild, 1979, pp. 42–3; and Rothbard, 1970, pp. 652–60). The use of video cassette recorders has raised law and economics issues in copyright law, which invite reconsideration of its basic premises.

Relative to neoclassical formulations, property rights theory is more appreciative of the economic usefulness and significance of contractual restrictions and "restraints" on market participants. The theory emphasizes that economic activity can occur only in an institutional and legal setting. The process of contracting and legally binding oneself is a prelude to almost any economic relationship. A market economy is a complex web of vertical and horizontal restraints without which economic activity would be impossible. These contractual relationships, which constrain some activities, do not inhibit but rather make possible competition (as a process). In almost any purchase of an existing business, for instance, the buyer will want some assurance that the seller will not immediately re-enter the market as a competitor. The seller is not injured by permitting such contracts, but is helped: he can obtain a higher price for his business. To the degree that resources are thereby moved to a high-valued user, consumers are also helped. Yet, after the fact, the seller of the business is restricted and consumers are seemingly denied a potential competitor. Such contracts are taken to be restrictions on competition. Yet these and other contractual restraints generally make possible the formation and recombining of assets and resources that is the driving force behind competition and economic progress. Indeed, to the extent that individuals are attracted to a market by the realization that they can easily sell their enterprise, these restraints foster competition. There is no trade-off between values. Contractual freedom is a necessary condition to obtain the value of competition.

Where we would draw the line, and where we think it must be drawn, is between contractual and third-party imposed restraints. Questions of political rights aside, third-party restraints have significantly different effects than those agreed upon contractually by the relevant parties. Consider again the issue of the sale of a firm. The potential buyer will offer up to the present value of expected returns from acquiring the firm. The potential seller will weigh the value of the offer against the expected losses suffered by agreeing to a restriction on his future conduct. If the current owner of the firm (the potential seller) evaluates the offer as being worth more than the present value of these losses, his decision reflects a judgment about the value of his services in that industry. He is worth more outside the industry than in it. His customers are not being deprived of the services of a superior competitor. At least, that is the best judgment of the seller himself at the time of the deal. We can think of no reason why sellers' expectations would be systematically biased in this regard.

Third-party restraints cannot be presumed to be efficient from the perspective of any of the participants. They have not been voluntarily entered into by the affected parties. Assuming that anyone benefits, all others save the third party lose (in an *ex ante* sense) from the restrictions imposed by third parties. If effective, third-party restrictions on entry thwart resource owners from competing with protected firms. A monopoly grant prevents efficient competitors from offering their product on an equal footing.

We recognize that in a limited sense there is "competition" to be the monopolist, or to share monopoly power in a cartel. We believe that more confusion is sown than knowledge acquired, however, by describing political favor-seeking as a competitive process. There is no reason to believe that superior entrepreneurs in the *economic marketplace* will win out in the political arena. There is good reason to believe the opposite, as the skills required for political and economic success are quite different. (Hayek, 1944, chapter 9). Further, special pleaders are a biased sample of businessmen, tending to be those who have *failed* to achieve their goals in the marketplace (Kolko, 1967).

Finally, as a factual matter, existing producers tend to be given monopoly rights in "grandfather" clauses. This is particularly objectionable from a process perspective. A major benefit of open markets consists of allowing entrants (and existing firms) to innovate or to recombine factors in imaginative ways. It is precisely this process that is stifled by monopolistic restrictions. Over the long run, static welfare losses pale in significance compared with this dynamic effect. Of course, these losses are inherently not measurable, and will accordingly be underestimated in any kind of particularistic weighing of costs and benefits. We can, moreover, rely on would-be monopolists to account for all possible benefits of any legal restriction. Arguments for tariffs are a classic example of this process. We know what the domestic industrialists gain. We can only imagine what we will all lose as consumers. Whenever public policy debates are conducted on such cost–benefit calculations, the argument will be tilted in favor of the proposed restriction and against open markets.

In recent years, Hayek (1973, pp. 55–71) has emphasized that public policy discussions must, for this and other reasons, be conducted on grounds of principle and not expediency. This, of course, means that discussions must be based on sound theoretical arguments, economic and non-economic. We believe that a property rights theory of monopoly provides the economic part of these arguments by focusing on the systematic effects of alternative institutional regimes. For the same reason that individuals rely on rules in situations of general ignorance – the economy of information required – public policy discussions ought to focus more on comparative institutional analysis. Economics is simply not capable of providing the information needed to make case-by-case decisions, like that required in antitrust cases.

Regardless, then, of the soundness of our particular conceptualization of the monopoly question, we would argue for an institutional and property rights analysis of competition and monopoly. This shift in focus requires abandoning the institutionless analysis of neoclassical theory. In the last two chapters, we have offered a theoretical alternative to that theory.

## NOTES

1 The success of Allegheny Airlines (now US Air) in contracting out its commuter operations to smaller carriers should, in retrospect, have been accorded more attention by analysts. Allegheny's experience revealed the potential profitability of commuter operations. See Doty (1977).
2 On Piedmont's success, see Briggs (1981).
3 On United's strategy, see *Business Week* for April 13, 1981 (p. 49); August 17, 1981 (pp. 27–9); and October 19, 1981 (pp. 83–4). Also see *Aviation Week & Space Technology*, August 24, 1981 (p. 30).
4 See O'Driscoll (1982, pp. 191–3); and more generally, the discussion in Letwin (1965).
5 Once the assumption of equilibrium was dropped, Arrow (1959) had to delve into a series of interrelated theoretical issues. These included, *inter alia*, the meaning of competition, expectations, pricing strategy, and non-price sources of information. All of these arose for "an objectively competitive market" (Arrow, 1959, p. 46). None are standard issues in the theory of competition, though all are on the agenda of questions that we have argued should be analyzed in micro-theory. All these become critical theoretical issues once one abandons the assumption that prices are parametric. As Arrow (1959, p. 42) noted, "every relevant variable, except those classified as exogenous for the whole economic system, is the result of a decision on the part of some one individual unit of the economy." But as he concluded (p. 43), "Each individual participant in the economy is supposed to take prices as given and determine his choices as to purchases and sales accordingly; there is no one left over whose job it is to make a decision on price."
6 Competition to become or to replace an existing monopolist is no substitute for competition in an open market. The former involves striving to appropriate rents; resources expended in this process are expended solely to transfer income. Resources devoted to the pursuit of profits on competitive markets are expended at least in part to improve consumer satisfaction. In practice, of course, existing statutory monopolists are almost never dislodged by interlopers. Some franchised providers of cable TV services may be replaced in the coming years. Even were this to occur, it would not address the problems arising from the monopolistic provision of these services.

7 The literature on rent-seeking has given prominence to this and other issues in monopoly theory. Tullock (1967) and Posner (1975) helped initiate that literature. We would only suggest here that the rent-seeking literature fits better with a subjectivist analysis than with orthodox formulations.

8 II Peters 567.

# 8

# A Subjectivist Theory of a Capital-using Economy

> Beer barrels and blast furnaces, harbour installations and hotel-room furniture are not capital by virtue of their physical properties but by virtue of their economic functions. *Ludwig M. Lachmann (1956, p. vii)*

## INTRODUCTION

Conceiving of competition as a discovery procedure – as a set of institutions that facilitate the discovery of profit opportunities – draws our attention away from the comparison of alternative equilibrium states and toward the workings of market processes. The shift in focus from timeless equilibria to market processes having an explicit real-time dimension creates a special role for the theory of capital. Capital goods, after all, bear a certain temporal relationship to the consumption goods that they help to produce. Expectations (and changes in expectations) on the part of entrepreneurs about future supply and demand conditions for consumption goods have implications about current choices made and actions taken with respect to the corresponding capital goods. Equivalently, consumption activities that extend over time are reflected in the constellation of capital goods that exist at a particular point in time.

While the capital goods themselves are the concrete objects of valuation and exchange, the ultimate basis for their valuation and exchange is future consumption activity, which, in turn, serves as

This chapter was contributed by Roger W. Garrison, Assistant Professor of Economics at Auburn University.

the basis for production plans. Of course, the continually changing demands for consumer goods imply a continual revaluation of capital goods used in their production. Further changes in the valuation of particular goods result from the discovery of inconsistencies between the production plans of different entrepreneurs. And such discoveries are themselves the result of the market process that guides production towards the ultimate satisfaction of consumer demand. These are the ideas that subjectivist capital theory strives to elucidate and systematize. The theory maintains its subjectivist quality by highlighting the plans of entrepreneurs or other market participants (the *subjects* of the economic activity) rather than the capital goods themselves (the *objects* of their actions).

In alternative theories capital goods have, at best, a shadowy existence. General equilibrium theories of the neoclassical variety have relevance only when the analysis is confined to the allocation of resources at a particular point in time.[1] Attempts to extend the analysis to the problem of intertemporal allocation have been largely unsuccessful. Including the "date of availability" as part of the definition of each particular consumption good forces a time dimension into the general equilibrium model, but the analysis itself remains timeless.[2] The period of time that separates the application of inputs and the emergence of outputs is a period in which market conditions are not allowed to change either as a cause or as a consequence of such things as changing expectations about consumer demand or newly perceived plan inconsistencies. As was argued in chapter 4, the time dimension in such models is only a facade. Capital goods that may be created and used up during the production process play no role whatever in the analysis.

Classical models, at least on this count, exhibit more similarities than differences when compared with their neoclassical counterparts. Although an explicit period of production is built into the models patterned after classical theory, the collection of capital goods spanning this period is never brought into view. Classical models are completely specified in terms of the initial inputs and the ultimate outputs – which, in turn, become the inputs of the subsequent period. The basic structure of these models requires that the list of inputs and the list of outputs be qualitatively identical. Corn and iron, for instance, are used to produce greater quantities of corn and iron. (The quantitative difference between inputs and outputs, the surplus, becomes the primary focus of classical analysis.)

This vision of the "production of commodities by means of commodities" (Sraffa, 1960) has served as a basis for capital theory in spite of the fact that the vision admits of no distinct capital goods. Capital theory of this type is based on the premise that the time separating the input commodities and the output commodities is a satisfactory surrogate for capital. Insights about the nature of capital goods that come into (and go out of) existence during this time and about the relationships between different kinds of capital goods are simply out of reach.

Unquestionably, both classical and neoclassical theories provide useful perspectives for some purposes. But when the concern is about the market processes involving various kinds of capital goods in the hands of different entrepreneurs, these alternative theories are not in direct competition with the ideas presented in this chapter. If the objective were simply to draw attention to the commonality among all forms of capital, the Austrian, or subjectivist, view would be complementary to the alternative views. Time is the common denominator of capital goods – and the recognition of this fact is the common denominator of capital theories. But the exchanging of capital goods and the restructuring of production processes cannot be explained in terms of the *alikeness* of all capital. A satisfactory explanation must be in terms of the *differences* among capital goods – differences as perceived by the entrepreneurs who are engaged in these activities.

Entrepreneurs both influence and are influenced by the market processes that convert resources into consumption goods. The analysis of these processes is what constitutes capital theory in the subjectivist view. While such an analysis is a worthwhile objective in its own right, it also sets the stage for the analysis of monetary disturbances, which is the subject of the following chapter.

## THE DEVELOPMENT OF SUBJECTIVIST CAPITAL THEORY: AN OVERVIEW

The extent to which Austrian capital theory has had a distinct subjectivist flavor has waxed and waned from its beginnings to the present day. Clearly, Menger's treatment of the theory of capital in his *Principles* represented an extension of his subjective value theory as first developed to apply to consumption goods (Menger, 1981, pp. 80–7). This same capital theory lost much of its subjectivist flavor in the hands of Böhm-Bawerk (1959, vol. 2, pp. 77–118 and passim), whose attempt to formalize the theory and to express the rearrangements of capital goods quantitatively caused the Austrian insights to take on more of a classical (Ricardian) appearance. This obscured the essential subjectivist theme and needlessly exposed the ideas to criticism from a formalistic point of view.[3] History records the dissatisfaction with these developments on the part of Menger and other members of the Austrian school (Schumpeter, 1954, p. 847; Kirzner, 1976, p. 76; Streissler and Weber, 1973, pp. 231f.). Mises rejected the arithmetic approach offered by Böhm-Bawerk and recast the arguments in a subjectivist mold.[4] He went on to indicate, in very general terms, how this vision of a capital-using economy could serve as the basis for the analysis of monetary disturbances (Mises, 1953, pp. 339–66).

Mises' suggestive discussions led Hayek (1967a) to elaborate on the integration of capital theory and monetary theory and to devise some analytical tools that were capable of tracing the course of a monetary disturbance in terms of its effect on the markets for various kinds of capital goods. Although Hayek in 1935 had an appreciation for the essential subjectivist nature of capital theory, the task he had set for himself (in *Prices and Production*) required that he greatly simplify and even fictionalize the Austrian vision of the economy's production process. This was his means of solving an otherwise intractable problem. But as a result, the theory was once again to become a target for the formalists. The seemingly mechanistic sequence of price changes and resource movements – when divorced from their subjectivist underpinnings – did not tell an altogether convincing story.

Hayek's analytical efforts did provide a skeletal outline for subsequent analysis, which, according to his introductory remarks, were all they were intended to do. In a later effort, *The Pure Theory of Capital* (1941), he retraced his own steps in order to eliminate some of the fictitious and mechanistic aspects of the earlier outline. This book was to become the basis for a more comprehensive analysis of monetary disturbances. But neither he nor any of his followers were able (or willing) to rework the analysis of monetary disturbances in the light of this long and ponderous treatment of capital theory. Modern writers have tended to adopt the original Hayekian outline as their point of departure. Attempts to advance the theory have taken the form of generalizing from the specific sequence of price changes and resource movements identified by Hayek and refocusing the analysis on the expectations of entrepreneurs (see Hayek, 1939; O'Driscoll, 1979; Wagner, 1979; Lewin, 1982; and Garrison, 1984). These developments have had the effect of eliminating the mechanistic flavor of the theory and acknowledging once again the subjectivist insights first offered by Menger.

## THE MENGERIAN VISION

To formulate a subjectivist theory of a capital-using economy, we can begin by considering, from a subjectivist viewpoint, what Adam Smith called "that early and rude state of society which precedes both the accumulation of stock and the appropriation of land . . ." (Smith, 1937, p. 47). This, in fact, is precisely where Menger began with his own theory. Nature, left to its own devices, will yield up a certain kind and amount of consumption goods (Menger, 1981, pp. 73f.). Components of this "natural yield" take on the quality of goods to the extent – and only to the extent – that individuals (subjectively) value them. Such valuing is evidenced by individual acts of exchange and consumption. In this setting the consumption goods are the only objects of economic analysis. To say that the goods were "produced" by nature is to use the word "produced" in a strictly non-economic sense. It was the intention of neither the individuals nor nature that anything at all be produced. Notions such as the cost of production and the period of production simply have no meaning in the context of these natural processes having a fortuitous yield.

Smith sought to link the objects of consumption to a different sort of object, namely labor, so as to establish that there is a regular pattern in the natural order of things. The alternative task that Menger and later subjectivists set for themselves was somewhat different. The extension of value theory beyond its application to consumption does not consist of the identification of related *objects*. It deals instead with the perceptions and actions of the *subjects* who value the natural yield. Once individuals begin to perceive particular sequences in the course of "natural production," value is imputed to the earlier stages of the natural process in accordance with the value attached to the corresponding consumption goods. A sapling is valued for the fruit it will eventually yield;

fertile land is valued for the crops it will grow. This is Menger's Law.[5] Given the perceptions and expectations of individual actors, their actions involving objects in the earlier stages of natural processes, such as the guarding of especially high-yield land areas, can be understood in the same way as their actions involving consumption goods. So long as the vision is confined to the "early and rude state of society," it is tempting to refer to the objects of such actions as "natural capital." This concept provides a clear base from which to build the subjectivist theory of a capital-using economy.

The analysis takes on a new dimension as soon as allowance is made for the fact that individuals can do more than simply await nature's yield. By intervening in the natural processes, individuals can have an effect on the quantity and quality of the subsequent yield. Such acts of intervention may occur only in the late stages of the process – the act of pruning vines – or they may occur at earlier stages as well – the act of preparing the soil. The fabrication of instruments with which to prepare the soil would be a still earlier act of intervention. These acts of intervention constitute "production" in the economic sense of the word. The direct objects of these acts (pruned vines, prepared soil, fabricated instruments) constitute capital goods. To understand the objectives of the "producers" is to understand that the earlier a producer intervenes, the greater are the opportunities to tailor the production process to suit his own purposes. This provides an intuitive basis for the notion that the more "roundabout processes" tend to have a greater yield in value terms.

Introducing the concept of capital goods in this way suggests that further analysis should focus on both the value of various goods in relation to the consumption they help to produce and the temporal relationship between the capital and the consumption goods. That capital has a time as well as a value dimension is not unique to subjectivist theory,[6] but the particular way in which these two dimensions are introduced and developed is. The following sections go on to develop the intertemporal and relative price relationships among capital goods in a modern capital-using economy and to demonstrate their relevance to macroeconomic theorizing. The final section deals with prevalent misconceptions of the basic notions of "roundaboutness," the "period of production," and the "original factors of production," and with common criticisms of capital theories that make use of these notions.

## THE STRUCTURE OF PRODUCTION

When the analysis is pressed beyond the "early and rude state of society," the objects at which the actions of individuals are directed and the interrelationships between these actions grow in complexity, but the essential features of the analysis remain the same. Acts of production bear a fundamental relationship to the prospective acts of consumption that production makes possible. The value of the objects of productive activity is systematically related to both the prospective value of the corresponding goods and the time that separates the act of production and the subsequent act of consumption. In the analysis of a capital-using economy, the idea of interventions with a natural process at particular points in time is replaced with the idea of stages of production (Hayek, 1967a, pp. 37–47). A production process is conceived as a sequence of stages, and the capital goods that constitute a given stage are seen as having both a value and a time dimension. An accounting of the pattern and usage of capital goods throughout the entire economy in terms of these two dimensions defines the economy's "structure of production."

As developers of this Austrian vision have clearly recognized, there are two distinct but closely related ways in which to conceive of the economy's structure of production (see, for example, Böhm-Bawerk, 1959, vol. 2, p. 314; Hayek, 1967a, p. 40). It can be viewed as a sequence of productive acts that cause working capital, or "goods in process," to move through time from one stage of production to another until the final stage yields consumption goods. Alternatively, the structure can be seen as the pattern of productive activity taking place at a given point in time. The two conceptions are completely congruent only for the case of a perfectly synchronized economy – what Mises called the "imaginary state of the evenly rotating economy" (Mises, 1966, pp. 244–50). Apart from its serving as a device for abstracting from change, however, this perfect synchronization is of little interest. The pattern of productive activities is constantly being adjusted to changing conditions. Even so, there still exists a distinct relationship between the temporal and the atemporal perspective. A redirecting of productive activity at a particular point in time implies a corresponding alteration in the pattern of activity *over* time. The reallocation of capital goods, for instance, away from the later stages of production and into the earlier stages corresponds to a level of consumption that first falls during the period in which capital goods are being reallocated and then rises to a new height.

This correspondence holds perfectly only under the strict assumption that consumption plans and production plans are fully coordinated with one another over time. But to invoke such a strict assumption would be to mask the market process that fosters the less-than-perfect coordination that characterizes any market economy. In actuality, when market conditions change – that is, when there is a change in consumer demand, resource availability, or technology – the producer begins to react. Through the passage of time, he continues to react – in part to his changing perceptions of the new conditions, and in part to the earlier reactions of his own and other producers. This real-time market process constitutes the primary subject matter of Austrian analysis. The goal of such analysis, Austrian or otherwise, is to determine whether and how the market can transform the desired pattern of consumption in the future into a pattern of production in the present,[7] and to determine the extent to which coordination of the two patterns is fostered under different institutional arrangements and in the face of alternative government policies.

A common misunderstanding can be avoided, and the element of subjectivism can be re-emphasized, by pointing out that the notion of a "stage of production" is itself a subjective concept.[8] That is, it has meaning only in terms of the relationship (as perceived by producers) between the capital goods that make up a stage of production and the future consumption goods. A given stage does not correspond to a particular industry or even to a particular, objectively defined, collection of capital goods. A paper mill that supplies paper for the production of greeting cards and also for use by a blueprinter is operating simultaneously in two separate stages of production. The difficulty of concretizing the notion of stages of production does not render the notion meaningless or unhelpful: it only reminds us that there is no easy solution to the problem of intertemporal coordination. Conceiving of the production process in terms of (subjectively defined) stages of production does help to identify the specific nature of the coordination problem, and it points the way to a satisfactory solution to that problem.

That the problem of continually restructuring production activities so as to conform to changing demands is an *economic* problem stems from the fact that the capital goods that make up the various stages are heterogeneous in nature and are of various degrees of specificity.[9] If each capital good were perfectly specific with respect to its own production process, the problem of structuring (there could be no *re*structuring) these processes would be purely technological. Alternatively, if all capital goods were homogeneous in nature, the problem would cease to exist. In fact, the very notion of structuring and restructuring would cease to have meaning. The applicability of economic principles depends on the fact that many capital goods can be used in many different ways but with varying degrees of success. Recognizing this fact about capital requires very little perceptiveness, but understanding its implications for the analysis of a capital-using economy is the exception rather than the rule. Frank Knight (1934, pp. 257–86) conceived of the economy's production processes as consisting of a collection of highly specific and complementary capital goods. Don Patinkin (1965, pp. 199ff.) conceived of the economy's production processes as consisting of a single homogeneous good. Each of these conceptions was intended to simplify the theories in which they were employed. But neither was able to shed much light on the workings of a capital-using economy. To make either of these polar assumptions about the nature of capital (extreme specificity or extreme homogeneity) is to assume away the phenomena that the Austrian analysis is intended to elucidate.

Capital goods are related to one another, some as substitutes, some as complements. This fact would suggest that a theory of a capital-using economy must, at a bare minimum, allow for three distinctly different capital goods. (A two-good model of the capital sector could not allow for both substitutability and complementarity.) To allow for both intertemporal and a-temporal substitutability and for both intertemporal and a-temporal complementarity, the number of different capital goods must be multiplied. And allowing for *various degrees* of substitutability and complementarity requires still further multiplication. In its richest form, the capital theory introduced by Menger and developed by Böhm-Bawerk, Mises, and Hayek cannot adequately be modeled by a three-good capital sector or even by an *x*-good capital sector where *x* is some determinate number. The Austrian theory of capital is based instead on the concept of a complex structure of production made up of a wide assortment of capital goods. The rejection of determinate models of the capital sector is consistent with the rejection of input-output models of the economy in general. The insistence on allowing for a virtually infinite degree of complexity reflects the insights of Mises on the problem of economic calculation (Mises, 1966, pp. 200–31), and of Hayek on the use of knowledge in society (Hayek, 1945).

## THE RATE OF INTEREST IN A CAPITAL-USING ECONOMY

As indicated above, the anticipated value of future consumption goods and the present value of capital goods are related in a systematic way. If market participants were completely indifferent about time considerations – that is, if they had no "time preferences" – the equilibrium value of the (present) inputs of each production process would completely exhaust the value of the (future) output. The inputs, whether land, labor, or capital, would not be "productive" in the classical sense, which is to say that they would produce no "surplus value."

But market participants are not indifferent about time considerations: they do have time preferences. Whether it is taken as a logical imperative or a broad generalization, there is a systematic preference for "sooner" rather than "later"; the future is systematically discounted.[10] As a consequence, the sum of the equilibrium values of (present) inputs falls short of the anticipated value of (future) output by the extent of the time discount. In a classical model this value differential would be taken to indicate that the inputs are "productive." Austrian theorists have consistently rejected this inference. In their view the difference between the value of the inputs and the value of the output is fully attributed to the time preferences of market participants. A systematic discounting of the future is both necessary and sufficient to give rise to the market phenomena that superficially may be seen as value productivity.

In the Austrian literature the interest rate, broadly conceived, is synonymous with the rate of time discount implicit in the pattern of prices of capital goods and other inputs. Although the rate that prevails in the loan market is the most conspicuous manifestation of the rate of interest, the loan rate is not necessarily the most appropriate focus for analysis (Rothbard, 1970, pp. 321ff.). The conventional view that the interest rate is determined by supply and demand in the loanable-funds market is based on a narrow definition of the rate of interest – one that takes the interest rate and the loan rate to be synonymous. While it is true that the market process will cause the loan rate to be adjusted to the market rate of interest, broadly conceived, the determinants of the latter are not confined to the market for loanable funds.

The primary focus of the Austrian theory of capital and interest is the prices of individual capital goods and of other inputs. Actual prices, of course, will provide an imperfect reflection of the general market rate of time discount owing to the absence of complete intertemporal coordination. The demand price for any particular capital good will be determined by its discounted marginal value in the mind of the entrepreneur who is contemplating using the capital good in a particular way. Its value to him is likely to be reckoned largely in terms of the price he expects that entrepreneurs in the next stage of production will pay him for his immediate output. For example, the steel mill's demand price for iron ore depends upon the expected market price for sheet steel. The demand price for capital goods in the next stage is determined similarly. Ultimately, the demand price of any capital good is linked to the expected market value of the prospective consumption good. The supply price is determined by the next highest, similarly determined value.

The forces of supply and demand as embodied in the actions of individual entrepreneurs result in the establishment of a market price for each capital good. The combined effect of the discounting in the minds of the different entrepreneurs in each stage of the entire sequence of stages tends to reflect the general rate of time discount and the interval of time separating the particular capital good and the prospective consumption good. Thus, the idea of a structure of production together with the idea of competition as a discovery procedure combine to suggest how a capital-using market-oriented economy functions.

A macroeconomic view of this same market process reveals a new dimension to the coordination problem. The market's ability to solve this more global coordination problem – conventionally conceived as the problem of coordinating savings decisions with investment decisions – has always been the central issue in macroeconomics. Identifying the Austrian contribution to macroeconomics follows a more general discussion of variations in the economy's final output and their relationship to the structure of production.

## VARIATIONS IN THE FINAL OUTPUT OF THE PRODUCTION PROCESS

The issue of what causes the level of output in a smoothly functioning economy to vary over time is fundamental to macroeconomics. In fact, answering this question should be considered a prerequisite to addressing such macro-maladies as cyclical unemployment.[11] Unfortunately, this issue is typically relegated to a separate discussion on the subject of economic growth, and even then the variations considered are restricted to alternative (continuous) rates of growth. Austrian economists have traditionally rejected this dichotomization of macroeconomics and economic growth. Final output will vary over time in part because the production process is being adjusted normally in response to changes in market conditions and in part because that same process is experiencing a malfunction of some kind. For methodological soundness it is necessary to identify the possible and relevant sources of variation in a coordinated economy before considering the cause(s) of variations associated with a market malfunction. In more general terms, we must know how things could ever go right before we can ask what might possibly go wrong.[12]

Quite apart from the unwanted and disruptive fluctuations in the economy's output, a number of factors can be identified that will have a predictable influence on the nature and magnitude of that output. There is a nearly infinite number of possible preference changes that will eventually be reflected in the economy's final output. All but a few of such possible changes consist of increases or decreases in the demands for particular goods and services and are the proper concern of microeconomics. The remaining few possibilities consist of broadly defined preferences that, by their very nature, have systematic and economy-wide consequences. These preference changes, which are the proper concern of macroeconomics, bear an almost one-to-one relationship to the traditional macroeconomic aggregates of employment, money, and saving and investment. Changes in preferences directly related to the first two aggregates, which have served as the primary focus of analysis outside the Austrian school, will be discussed in sequence in the present section. The following section will focus on the one aspect of the process that has special relevance both inside and outside the Austrian school.

The level of final output may change because of a change in demand for leisure time or, what amounts to the same thing, a change in the supply of labor. If "leisure" were included in the accounting of final output, this preference change could best be analyzed with the usual microeconomic tools. The effect would be seen as the "production" of a larger (smaller) quantity of leisure time and a smaller (larger) quantity of other goods. But because the "production of leisure" is autistic in nature, it is rightly excluded from the *market's* final output. Hence, a change in the labor - leisure trade-off is seen as giving rise to a change in the *level* of final output. Further, an increase in the demand for leisure will have a systematic effect on the structure of production. Some production processes involve capital goods that are predominately complements to labor; others involve capital goods that are predominately substitutes for labor. A decrease in the supply of labor will decrease the demand for complementary capital and increase the demand for capital that serves as a labor substitute. Corresponding changes in the quantities of the different kinds of capital goods supplied and demanded will be brought about.

Conceiving each of the various production processes as a temporal sequence of stages complicates the effect of a change in the labor - leisure trade-off, but it does not affect its essential features. Some production processess may include some stages in which capital and labor are complements and other stages in which capital and labor are substitutes. While there may be no *a priori* basis on which to specify how the final output of such production processes will be affected by a change in the supply of labor, there is no reason to believe that the market process itself cannot adjust for the preference change.

The relationship between the labour–leisure trade-off and the level of final output has served as the focus for the writings of D. H. Robertson (1949), and was typical of pre-Keynesian British macroeconomics.[13] Robertson was concerned with the particulars of the market processes that translate changes in leisure preferences into changes in productive activities, and with the possibility that governmental policies, particularly banking policies, interfere in a systematic way with these market processes. There are many modern manifestations of this mode of analysis. Depicting the market process triggered by a monetary expansion in terms of the interplay between the short-run and the long-run Phillips curve is one of the clearest examples. Monetary factors create a distortion in the labor

–leisure trade-off – a distortion that is subsequently corrected by market forces. A second example, which is not so self-evident, is the "rational expectations" models. Logically, these models need not turn on the labour–leisure trade-off, but in most instances they do.[14] It should be recognized that much of modern macroeconomics is fundamentally Robertsonian in this respect.

In an alternative approach, the demand for money takes the place of the demand for leisure. As in the labor–leisure-based models, if real cash holdings were included in the accounting of final output – that is, if money were treated as a consumption good – the analysis would be microeconomic in form. An increase in liquidity preferences would give rise to an increase in the real quantity of money demanded and supplied and a decrease in the quantity of all other goods. (This general equilibrium proposition holds for money only in the case of a competitively produced commodity money. Under a fiat system administered by an angelic and omniscient central bank, the decrease in the production of non-monetary goods could be avoided.) But the uniqueness of the character of money argues for its exclusion from the accounting of final output. This recasts the analysis in terms of macroeconomics and raises the question of the relationship between changes in the demand for money and the *level* of final output.

In both classical and neoclassical analysis, changes in the demand for money have no long-run effect on the economy's output. But the market process that translates such changes into nominal price changes can be a long and troubled process, which can itself have a significant effect on the short-run level of output. Stating the relationship between money and output in these terms is a useful way of interpreting and assessing the contribution of John Maynard Keynes (see, for instance, Keynes, 1964, pp. 229–36). It also serves to draw a parallel between this approach and the approach adopted by Robertson. With the focus on the demand for money, the analysis takes the form of identifying the market process by which the economy adjusts to a change in liquidity preferences and of considering the possibility that government policies, particularly banking policies, may ameliorate or exacerbate the problems inherent in this adjustment process.

Modern macroeconomics has virtually ignored the relationship between changes in liquidity preferences and alterations in the multi-stage production process as conceived by the Austrian school. But the classic article on the effects of inflation by Kessel and

Alchian (1962) suggests how a change in the demand for (or the supply of) money can systematically alter the collection of capital goods that make up the structure of production. Once again, the analysis parallels Robertson's analysis of the effects of changes in the demand for leisure. Kessel and Alchian (1962, p. 534) argue, in effect, that transactions balances and short-lived capital goods are complements, whereas transactions balances and long-lived capital goods are substitutes. Thus, a decrease in the demand for real cash holdings, whether exogenous or the effect of inflationary expectations, would be accompanied by a decrease in the demand for short-lived capital goods and an increase in the demand for long-lived capital goods. The resulting relative-price changes would bring about a systematic restructuring of the economy's production process. The fact that both short-lived and long-lived capital goods are employed in varying degrees in each of the temporally sequenced stages of production complicates the effect of a change in the demand for money, but does not alter the principle that governs the restructuring of the production process.

The relationship between the demand for money and the structure of production identified by Kessel and Alchian deserves attention, even though the effect of the life of capital goods on the demand for transactions balances has not been clearly established. The existence of long-lived capital goods that change hands a number of times blurs the distinction on which the relationship rests. Conversely, the choice within a single firm between the production and employment of one long-lived capital good and the production and employment of a sequence of short-lived capital goods is unrelated to transactions balances. It can be noted in passing, however, that to the extent that long-lived captial goods are associated with early stages of production (physical plant) and short-lived capital goods are associated with the later stages (working capital), many of the implications of the Kessel–Alchian analysis are consistent with those of the Austrian analysis.

Before turning to the sort of preference changes that serve as the focus of analysis for the Austrian school, two other views about the relevant source of variation in final output can be identified. These sources, it will be seen, differ fundamentally from the ones thus far discussed (changes in leisure preferences and changes in liquidity preferences) in that they are not directly related to preferences.

In the typical treatment of macroeconomic phenomena, the variation in final output is attributed to the extent to which resources, both capital and labor, are idle. This is the standard textbook rendition of Keynesian theory. The existence of unemployed resources on an economy-wide basis is simply assumed. The resulting discrepancy between actual output and potential output is then demonstrated graphically, algebraically, and statistically. While this type of analysis has a certain internal consistency about it, the theory as a whole is methodologically unsound. If the objective is to explain the existence of idle resources, it is illegitimate to base the theory on the assumption of their existence (Hayek, 1967a, p. 34). No theoretical construct can account for its own underlying assumptions. Textbook Keynesianism may be able to show how variations in final output are related to variations in resource idleness, but it cannot explain why there should be resource idleness in the first place.[15] A methodologically sound theory of variation in final output, subjectivist or otherwise, requires that the variations be traced to some phenomenon that does not itself require an economic explanation. Tracing the variations to changes in preferences or to (unanticipated) policy changes meets this requirement; tracing the variations to resource idleness does not.

Technological change has been taken by some to be the primary source of the variation in final output. In two different contexts, both Knut Wicksell (1965) in Sweden and Joseph Schumpeter (1934) in Austria adopted this view.[16] Tracing the variation in final output to changes in technology meets the methodological requirements, but this approach has proven to be less than fruitful for several reasons.

First, from a macroeconomic point of view, the rate of technological progress – conceived in terms of blueprints for productive activity – is never the binding constraint. In the absence of new savings that would enable the implementation of the new technology, no variation in final output would result. (This point is emphasized by Rothbard, II, 1970, p. 749). Second, it is difficult to conceive of technological change that occurs truly on an economy-wide basis. By their very nature, technological changes are embodied in specific capital goods or in specific production processes. Accordingly, the analysis of the economic consequences of such changes is more in the purview of microeconomics. Third, because of the uniqueness of each technological change, there will be no predictable systematic effect on the structure of production. No general statements can be made about how an improvement in technology affects the relationships such as between capital and labor, or between long-lived capital goods and short-lived capital goods, or between capital employed in the relatively early stages of production and capital employed in the relatively late stages. Undeniably, the diverse and continual changes in technology have a dramatic influence on the particular kinds of productive activities undertaken, but technological change, in part because of its diversity, has proven to be an unsuitable focus for macroeconomic analysis.

## TIME PREFERENCES AND THE STRUCTURE OF PRODUCTION

Macroeconomic theories that satisfy basic methodological strictures focus on broadly defined changes in preferences and on the various government policies that affect (positively or negatively) the ability of the market to adjust to such changes. These changes in preferences, which correspond to the conventionally identified macroeconomic aggregates, are of the sort that have systematic and identifiable economy-wide effects. As suggested by the discussion above, both leisure preferences and liquidity preferences have served as keystones for alternative classes of macroeconomic theories. Theories that belong to the first class begin by pointing to the direct effects of a (leisure) preference change on wages and the volume of employment, and then go on to identify possible indirect effects that are brought about by the market's adjustment process; theories of the second class begin by pointing to the direct effects of a (liquidity) preference change on the price level and the volume of real cash holdings, and then go on to identify the corresponding set of indirect effects.

Given the particular preference changes that serve as the respective foci of analysis, the two classes of theories, which tell substantially different stories, are to be seen as complementary rather than contradictory. But taken together, they may fail to tell the whole story. They may even fail to tell the part of the story most relevant to the historical interpretation of government policies in the past and to policy prescriptions in the future.

The belief that these alternative classes of theories have indeed failed in this respect is what led the Austrians to consider a theory that focuses on a third broadly defined change in preferences. *Time* preferences serve as the keystone of Austrian macroeconomic theory. The analysis begins by pointing to the direct effects of a change in time preferences on the volume of savings, and then goes on to identify the subsequent effects on the level of investment in the various stages of production and on the pattern of the employment of labor. This analysis forms the basis for a theory of monetary disturbances, which involves a market process that resembles the preference-induced adjustment in its early stages but deviates from that adjustment process in critical ways during the later stages.[17]

Anticipating the arguments in chapter 9, we can note that expectations will have their effect on both the preference-induced and the policy-induced market process. To the extent that individual market participants understand the general effects of various policies, and to the extent that they anticipate policy changes, the *intended* effects of the policy will be thwarted. Entrepreneurs will attempt to base their decisions on the "real factors." This is not to say, however, that so-called "rational expectations" will eliminate all the real effects of monetary policy. Supporting these claims about expectations and the effects of policy will be the business of the following chapter.

Preliminary to such issues is an accounting of how the market adjusts to a change in time preferences in the absence of any policy disturbances. The present concern, then, is how the various markets *would have to work* if a change in time preferences on the part of consumers is to be successfully translated into a corresponding change in the pattern of productive activities. The issue of whether the markets *do* in fact work in this way (or would work in this way in the absence of debilitating government policy) is an issue that turns on our understanding of entrepreneurship. The following discussion will assume that entrepreneurs are alive and well and that they tend to discover and act upon opportunities for making profits. In other words, for the time being we are abstracting from coordination problems in order to focus on these later.

The analysis focuses on the effects of an hypothesized fall in time preferences, that is, a shift in preferences away from current consumption and toward greater consumption in the future. This task is a prerequisite to the Austrian analysis of a monetary expansion. (Detailing the effects of a rise in time preferences, which are – with some qualifications – symmetrical to the effects of a fall, would be a prerequisite to the analysis of a monetary contraction.)

Hypothesizing a fall in time preferences is equivalent to hypothesizing a decrease in the demand for consumption goods in the current period and a concomitant increase in the supply of loanable funds. That the funds not spent on consumption goods are made available in the loan market – that is, that they do not simply accumulate in cash hoards – follows from the hypothesis that the preference change involves time preferences only and not liquidity preferences or some combination of the two. Further, a fall in time preferences implies an increase in the demand for consumption goods at some time in the future. That is, the preference change does not imply a permanently lowered level of consumption and hence of production. This would be the case only if the consumers had also experienced an increase in leisure preferences. With unchanged preferences for liquidity and leisure, a change in time preferences implies only a change in the time pattern of desired consumption activity in the future. A fall in time preferences means a demand for relatively less consumption activity in the present and near future and relatively more in the more distant future.[18]

The direct effect of a fall in time preferences is a fall in the loan rate of interest and an increase in the quantity of loanable funds supplied and demanded. This result requires only that market-clearing forces prevail in the market for loanable funds. More interesting is the question of the particular ways in which this increased quantity of loanable funds is put to use. The hypothetical change in preferences implies that individuals will want to consume some assortment of consumption goods at some date in the future. Gauging what particular consumption goods to produce and when in particular to have them ready for consumption is the task of the entrepreneur. But then, this is always the task of the entrepreneur. The change in time preferences simply means that the entrepreneur is performing his task under the conditions of a lower rate of interest and a greater availability of credit. All that needs to be said here about the ability of entrepreneurs to adapt successfully to these changed credit conditions is that self-correcting forces are at work: those entrepreneurs who do successfully adapt will tend to make profits and hence will gain command over greater quantities of resources, while those who do not will tend to make losses and hence will lose command over resources.[19]

In any case, the systematic effect of the change in credit conditions can be stated independently of the particular assortment of consumption goods produced.[20] The lower rate of interest provides the incentive to allocate more capital to the relatively early stages of production. As suggested earlier the greater the amount of time separating an existing capital good from the prospective consumption good, the greater the difference in value arising from time discounting between the capital good and the prospective consumption good. Alternatively stated, the value of capital goods used in the early stages of production is more sensitive to changes in the rate of interest than is the value of capital goods used in the later stages. Thus, a lower rate of interest provides an incentive to allocate more capital to the relatively early stages of production – and even to create still earlier stages of production than had previously existed. This reallocation of capital is consistent with the increase in demand for consumption goods in the relatively distant future. The increased level of savings – that is, the decreased level of consumption in the present and near-future periods – releases resources that would otherwise have been used in the later stages of the old structure of production. These are the resources that enable the completion of the new, more time-consuming, production processes. To the extent that entrepreneurs correctly perceive and act upon profit opportunities, the allocation of capital among the stages of production in the new production process will reflect the rate of interest associated with the new time preferences.

The pattern of prospective consumption activity and the pattern of current production each contain an explicit time element. And the market process that tailors the production pattern to the prospective consumption pattern itself takes place through time. This means that expectations about the particular assortment of consumption goods demanded become concretized with the passage of time in the particular capital goods of the early stages, while the passage of time itself begins to reveal the extent to which those initial expectations were valid. Clearer perspectives on approaching periods of consumption and mounting information (via the price system and otherwise) about resource availabilities may serve to establish the validity of the initial expectations or to demonstrate their falsity. In the case of the latter, new production activities will have to be planned in the light of changed expectations and in the circumstances of a partially completed, but inappropriate, structure of production.[21] (An illuminating *gestalt* is that of buttoning together two pieces of material of unknown relative lengths. With each successive button we commit more resources to the total task and at the same time gain a better perspective on whether or not we are correctly matching the buttons and the buttonholes.)

The obstacles that stand in the way of successful entrepreneurship are substantial and multifaceted. Entrepreneurs must foresee what particular goods will be in demand and when, in particular, the consumers will demand them. They must take into account the extent to which the various consumption goods are substitutes for or complements to one another. They must decide how best to produce these goods, what capital goods should be used, and how the value of these various capital goods may change because of their relationships with other capital goods as substitutes or complements. They must base all these foresights, this accounting, and these decisions on changing information while recognizing that each new bit of information is itself the result of the passage of time and the entrepreneurs' attempts to implement their earlier production plans. Further, because few production processes are characterized by complete vertical integration, entrepreneurs must form expectations about the actions (and hence about the expectations) of other entrepreneurs who are involved in other stages of the production process.

The opportunities for entrepreneurial error are virtually infinite. Yet, there is no reason to believe that entrepreneurs will be *systematically* in error. In general, the market process should result in the production of consumption goods whose time pattern tends to correspond with the time preferences of consumers. It is expected to produce consumption goods neither systematically too early nor systematically too late. There is no reason to believe that the market process would cause the structure of production to be adjusted in such a way that resources were left idle, or that it would result in the abandonment of an attempted structural adjustment because of a lack of sufficient resources. In other words, the market process is expected to result in neither general gluts nor general shortages of resources.

But systematic errors on the part of entrepreneurs are observed historically. Particular periods in the course of history appear to be marked with "clusters" of entrepreneurial errors as revealed by economy-wide losses suffered by business firms. These clusters of errors – and of losses – constitute the downturn of the business cycle.[22] With no reason to believe that this cyclical pattern is inherent in the market process that tailors production activities to consumption activities, theorists must look outside the market itself for an explanation. And the explanation of cyclical activity is to be found in the effects of monetary policy on the structure of production. The arguments can be anticipated by recognizing one similarity and one difference between the effects of a fall in time preferences and the effects of an expansion of credit by the central bank. A fall in time preferences results in a lower rate of interest, which initiates a restructuring of productive activities and releases enough resources (from the later stages of production) to complete the new structure of production; a policy-induced expansion of credit lowers the loan rate of interest, which has an initial effect similar to that of a fall in time preferences but which does *not* release the resources required to complete the new structure of production.

Information about the activities of the central bank, anticipation of future policy changes, and an understanding on the part of entrepreneurs of the effects of credit expansion do, undeniably, have important effects on the way in which the restructuring takes place; but neither these nor any other considerations can eliminate all the real effects of credit expansion. This is the subject matter of the following chapter.

Before turning to monetary theory, it may be worthwhile to address directly several popular criticisms of Austrian capital theory and of such related notions as the period of production, the degree of roundaboutness, and the original factors of production.

## SUBJECTIVISM REVISITED

Dating from the writings of Böhm-Bawerk, the basic concepts in Austrian capital theory have met with substantial criticism. An early controversy involving Clark and Böhm-Bawerk was followed by an involved and protracted debate between Knight and Hayek.[23] Although criticism stemming from the Clark–Knight tradition continues today (see, for example, Rolph, 1980), these controversies have given way to challenges from other quarters. In the last two decades, Cambridge capital theorists, who have been largely preoccupied with the phenomena of "technique reswitching and capital reversing," have constructed multi-period models of capital-using production processes that are widely believed to have discredited the older Austrian vision.[24] The models of the more broadly conceived "classical revival" are believed to have similar implications about the theory of capital devised by Böhm-Bawerk. To provide anything like a comprehensive survey of this literature would be both tedious and unnecessary. It will serve our purposes to point out that the challenging views share a single characteristic which renders all of this criticism inapplicable to the formulation offered in the present chapter.

It was emphasized above that the concept of "stages of production" and, by implication, the related concepts of the "period of production" and the "degree of roundaboutness" are subjectively defined. That is, they are defined in terms of the prospective consumption activity that ultimately motivates a given act of production. At best, the various criticisms of Austrian capital theory are well-taken warnings against all attempts to define these concepts objectively.

The fact that the critics have seen the objectively defined concepts as their target is not entirely their own fault. Böhm-Bawerk himself, in his eagerness to make use of arithmetic examples, imbued these concepts with a distinctly objectivist flavor. But this aspect of Böhm-Bawerk's formulation has been the target of criticism from *within* the Austrian school. Mises, for instance, pointed out that one "shortcoming of Böhm-Bawerk's reasoning was his misconstruction of the concept of the period of production. He was not fully aware of the fact that the period of production is a praxeological category . . ." (Mises, 1966, p. 488). Israel Kirzner shows that Böhm-Bawerk virtually stood alone on this methodological issue (Kirzner, 1976, p. 54). Later Austrian theorists who have built upon the Böhm-Bawerkian vision have been careful to recast the basic concepts in a more consistently subjectivist mold.

In the present exposition of Austrian capital theory, certain summary-type statements have been deliberately avoided. "A fall in the rate of interest tends to increase the degree of roundaboutness." Or "the rate of interest and the period of production are inversely related." Such statements invite misinterpretation. They suggest that the degree of roundaboutness and the average period of production are measurable quantities – quantities that can be determined by, say, inspecting the blueprints that map out a given production process. And the statements would have to be true in this sense if the demonstration of technique reswitching is to constitute a refutation of Austrian capital theory.

Cambridge capital theorists have constructed models of an economy that employs one or the other of two alternative production techniques, designated as technique A and technique B. They have then demonstrated that successive reductions in the rate of interest can lead to the abandonment of technique A and the adoption of technique B followed by the abandonment of technique B and the re-adoption of technique A. This is the phenomenon of technique reswitching (Samuelson, 1966, pp. 236–8). So long as the degree of roundaboutness of the two production techniques is uniquely specified by their respective blueprints, one of the switchings has to be contrary to the summary truths of Austrian capital theory.

The possibility of technique reswitching in this Cambridge sense was recognized by Hayek in the early 1940s (Hayek, 1941, pp. 76–7, 140ff., and 191f.), but neither he nor later Austrian theorists have seen this phenomenon as a threat to Austrian capital theory. If the theory is interpreted subjectively, the Cambridge challenge misfires. The blueprint of a production technique does not, by itself, fully define the economically relevant time element of the economy's production process. If increased savings cause entrepreneurs to commit additional resources to the earlier stages of production of a given production process, then the structure as a whole is more time-consuming. The fall in the rate of interest translates the now more distant time horizons of consumers into correspondingly more distant time horizons of producers. This result is quite independent of any change in the production technique employed. In the context of the Cambridge model, the Austrians would claim that the re-adoption of technique A involves more roundaboutness than its earlier employment.

The value in the summary statements quoted above lies precisely in their ability to summarize a complex argument. They represent a shorthand for expressing the general way in which the pattern of productive activity can be expected to change in response to a change in time preferences on the part of the consumer.[25]

Finally, it can be noted that the period of production is sometimes reckoned in terms of the time that elapses between the application of the so-called original factors and the emergence of the final output. The "original factors." a phrase that is usually interpreted to mean raw land and labor, has also been avoided in the present exposition. Again, the use of such terminology invites misinterpretation. It suggests not only an objectivist conception but also an historical orientation. Any attempt to impute economic meaning to the period of time between the objectively defined original factors and the resulting consumption activity will be in vain. With a subjectivist interpretation, factors of production have meaning only in the context of prospective consumption goods and the plans formulated by the entrepreneurs to produce these goods. All factors – land, labor, *and capital* – that were in existence when the entrepreneur's plan was first formulated can rightly be thought of as original factors.[26]

Modern objections to Austrian capital theory could be countered on still other grounds (see Yeager, 1979; Garrison, 1979). In the Cambridge formulation the rate of interest is treated as an exogenous variable. The changes in the interest rate that supposedly induce technique reswitching are themselves unaccounted for. This simply makes for bad theory – theory in which changes in the level of savings are neither a cause nor a consequence of changes in the rate of interest. In the reswitching models, the only change in production activities allowed for is a change in the technique employed. A change in the rate of interest either has no effect whatever or provokes a change in the production technique. The relevance of such a model – even to Böhm-Bawerk's formulation of Austrian capital theory – is questionable. And the particular way in which the analysis is carried out raises still further questions. Despite claims to the contrary, the fundamental distinction between the comparison of alternative equilibrium states and the description of the process by which the economy is moved from one state to another is hopelessly blurred. This is a virtually inevitable consequence of the failure to specify what particular preference or policy change caused the initial change in the rate of interest. While these aspects of Cambridge capital theory are grounds for dissatisfaction with the theory itself, they have been largely overlooked in the present treatment in order that the thematic distinction between subjectivist and objectivist views of a capital-using economy could be emphasized.

## NOTES

1 Walsh and Gram (1980, pp. 122 ff. and passim) take this a-temporal resource allocation to be the defining theme of neoclassical thought.

2 A fuller accounting of the limits of neoclassical general equilibrium theory is found in Hahn (1980); see also Walsh and Gram (1980, pp. 159–61).

3 Ludwig Lachmann (1973, p. 46) identifies formalism, defined as "a style of thought according to which abstract entities are treated as though they were real," as the antithesis of subjectivism: see Lachmann (1969, pp. 95–100) for a discussion of formalism and subjectivism in the perspective of the history of economic thought.

4 In his early writings Mises (1953, p. 339) simply indicated that, while

he was making use of Böhm-Bawerk's terminology and general approach, he was not an adherent of Böhm-Bawerk's theory of interest. Mises identified and elaborated upon his dissatisfaction with the theory some years later in *Human Action* (1966).

5 Israel Kirzner sees this as the central idea in Menger's *Principles*. "Men value goods according to the value of the satisfactions that depend on possession of those goods. More generally, Menger's Law – as we may call this insight – draws attention to man's propensity *to attach the value of ends to the means* needed for their achievement."

6 Capital as a two-dimensional concept can be traced as far back as Turgot, but it is commonly associated with the writings of Jevons (1970) and Cassel (1903).

7 In Keynes' vision of the economy, the question is whether and how the investors can "defeat the dark forces of time and ignorance which envelop our future" (Keynes, 1964, p. 155).

8 This point was fully recognized by Mises but not by Böhm-Bawerk: see pp. 181 above.

9 "The mere information conveyed by technology would suffice for the performance of calculation only if all means of production – both material and human – could be perfectly substituted for one another according to definite ratios, or if they were absolutely specific" (Mises, 1966, p. 207).

10 Mises (1966, pp. 483–8) and Rothbard (1970, pp. 323–32) make the case that (positive) time preference is a logical imperative.

11 Hayek (1967a, pp. 32ff.) clearly recognizes this question as preliminary to the question about the nature of industrial flucutations. This section can be viewed as an updated and elaborated version of the first few sections of Hayek's second chapter.

12 This methodological stricture, which is typically observed in the breach by modern macroeconomic theorists, was first introduced by Hayek in a macroeconomic setting. "Before we can explain why people commit mistakes, we must first explain why they should ever be right" (1937a, p. 34).

13 Hayek (1967a, p. 33) cites Robertson's *Banking Policy and the Price Level* as the best example of reasoning based on the labor–leisure trade-off.

14 A recent survey article (Maddock and Carter, 1982, p. 42) points out that "The example most often used in the (rational expectations) literature involves the allocation of time between labor and leisure."

15 In Keynes' *General Theory*, resource idleness is caused by a blockage of some kind in the market for labor – or in the market for the capital assets to which labor is complementary (see Keynes, 1964, pp. 222–44, 257–71). The attempt to pin down the precise nature of these blockages has separated Keynes' interpreters into two camps: those who believe that Keynes was only emphasizing the possibility – long recognized by pre-

Keynesian economists – that disequilibrium wages and prices can result in resource idleness (see, for instance, Knight, 1960), and those who believe that Keynes held some truly revolutionary ideas that he was not quite able to spell out in his book (see, for instance, Clower, 1965).

16 For Schumpeter "technological change" refers to any change not spontaneously initiated by consumers; see Schumpeter (1934, pp. 65ff.), where several specific categories of such changes are itemized.

17 One of the most succinct comparisons of the preference-induced process and the corresponding policy-induced process is found in Hayek (1967a, pp. 49–60).

18 The relevance of this analysis does not depend upon the actual occurrence of the monolithic changes in time preferences on an economy-wide basis. It is enough that such changes are conceivable and that less monolithic changes do in fact occur. Hayek (1967a, p. 50) clearly recognized that he was dealing with a "strong case" that is "highly unlikely to occur in practice."

19 This reasoning implies that current production is in fact linked to future consumption plans via the interest rate and entrepreneurial activity. The existence of any such link was denied by Keynes (1964, p. 21) when he accused the orthodoxy of "fallaciously supposing that there is a nexus which unites decisions to abstain from present consumption with decisions to provide for future consumption."

20 This is the systematic effect that Hayek depicted with his triangles: see Hayek (1969, pp. 49–54) and Rothbard (1970, pp. 470–9). For an attempt at a comprehensive diagrammatical exposition of Austrian macroeconomic relationships, see Garrison (1978).

21 The idea that expectations are neither truly exogenous nor entirely endogenous is a recurring theme in the writing of Ludwig Lachmann. See for example Lachmann (1976, pp. 126–32).

22 According to Rothbard (1970, p. 16), "The main problem that a theory of depression must explain is: *why is there a sudden general cluster of business errors?*" As critics of the rational expectations school, Maddock and Carter (1982, p. 44) point out that this problem is being overlooked. "If expectations are rational, then expectation errors should be randomly distributed over time. A straightforward implication of that for this model is that the level of output (or unemployment) is uncorrelated over time. Yet everybody knows that the GNP and the unemployment series have a high degree of serial correlation. We tend to go through a series of years in which unemployment is below the 'natural rate,' and then a series of years in which it is above the 'natural rate.' It doesn't seem to be distributed very randomly. Compare the sixties and the seventies in Australia – it's the old story of business cycle expansion and contraction."

23 For a critical assessment of the Clark–Knight view, see Kirzner (1966, pp. 79–82).

24 The key article by Samuelson (1966) is reprinted in Harcourt and Laing (1971). This volume contains a number of other articles that deal with the Cambridge capital controversy.

25 This is the basis upon which Hayek (1941, p. 70) recommended that such statements be retained.

26 This point was first made by Kirzner (1966, p. 80).

# 9

# The Microanalytics of Money

Money is not a consciously created artifact, but grows out of, reflects, and in turn affects the ever-changing relationships between individuals and the society which they compose. *S. Herbert Frankel (1977, p. 12)*

## INTRODUCTION

In this chapter, we focus on two major topics: Menger's theory of the origins of money, and the Mises–Hayek theory of economic fluctuations. Each exemplifies the subjectivist approach to economic questions followed throughout this book. In his theory of the origins of money, Menger adopted a microeconomic approach to analyzing the evolution of money and monetary institutions. He viewed money as an example of an organic social institution, which, though the result of human action, was not the product of human design.

Menger applied a kind of "invisible hand" theorem to explain how a common medium of exchange emerges from individual choices. Specifically, transactors must decide in what form to hold their wealth. Their choices involve commitments in the form of commodity inventories. Menger argued that liquidity considerations would dominate these choices. If the process did not produce a unique money, it would certainly converge on a small number of media of exchange.

In their business cycle theory, Mises and Hayek also adopted microeconomic reasoning to analyze a macroeconomic problem. Their theory emphasizes the importance of the passage of real time, and the intertemporal effects of agents' making commitments in the form of fixed investments. Further, it illustrates the practical importance of the distinction between typical and unique events.

The Mises–Hayek theory of economic fluctuations analyzes the interplay between monetary disturbances, resource scarcities, and entrepreneurial expectations. It concludes that, by changing expectations, monetary shocks can influence the course of economic expansion. The resulting expansion will develop, however, in a way that is inconsistent with long-run scarcity constraints. The theory focuses on sectorial imbalances in economic expansion, imbalances producing economic fluctuations.

In this chapter we focus on points of convergence and divergence between the earlier Austrian theories and modern formulations of the problems. We emphasize the common ground between them, and in some cases try to suggest resolution of the differences. In doing this, we also highlight the policy relevance of the theories.

## MICROANALYSIS OF MONEY

The modern macroeconomic revolution is associated with Keynes' *General Theory*. We refer here to the division of economics into two major areas or fields: micro- and macrotheory. At least until the mid-1970s, the two areas evolved semi-autonomously. This theoretical isolation diminished somewhat with the quest for the microeconomic foundations of macrotheory.

Subjectivists always felt uneasy about this bifurcation. In particular, Mises and Hayek consciously sought to integrate monetary economics and microtheory. They viewed the marginal revolution basically as a microeconomic upheaval, a triumph of micro- over macroanalysis. They saw monetary theory as a backwater in which macroeconomic reasoning dominated (O'Driscoll, 1977, pp. 135–42). In other words, monetary theory was macroeconomic in its orientation before the Keynesian episode. Hayek and Mises specifically criticized the quantity theory tradition for being mechanistic and aggregative, a holdover from the macroeconomic approach of classical (Ricardian) political economy. Along with other pre-Keynesians, they recast monetary theory in light of modern microeconomics. Thus, Hicks' "Suggestion for Simplifying the Theory of Money" (1935) met with great professional acclaim precisely because it encapsulated the unifying theme or goal of these contributions. The fruits of all these efforts were swept aside by the Keynesian tide, which was a macroeconomic inundation.[1]

Hayek criticized Keynesian macroeconomics for lacking micro-foundations – indeed, for being inconsistent with micro-theory on key issues. In particular, he questioned the validity of analyzing the determination of aggregate demand and national income as distinct theoretical problems. He argued that the process of moving toward equilibrium in individual markets is identical with that of achieving full employment of resources. What is called "unemployment" equilibrium is a manifestation of *micro*economic disco-ordination. Macroeconomic phenomena can be analyzed properly only by microeconomic analysis. *There are macroeconomic effects of economic disequilibrium, but there is no distinct macroeconomic theory*. That is, there is no consistent theory of macro-aggregates that can be couched solely in terms of these aggregates or that consistently relates aggregates to each other (see Lachmann, 1973).

In terms of the literature on both micro-foundations and rational expectations, Hayek and Mises anticipated some modern theoretical arguments. Moreover, their specific theories pointed in the direction toward which important contemporary theories are evolving. For this reason, we devote some time to presenting their position and relating it to modern theoretical developments.

Hayek's monetary theory of economic fluctuations is couched in terms of changing relative prices and costs. Monetary shocks produce particular types of discoordination in markets. The process of adjusting to these shocks produces effects on aggregative variables. It is not possible, however, to analyze these effects in terms of a standard macrotheory. The level of aggregation necessarily obscures the economic phenomena being studied. If one were, for instance, to aggregate heterogeneous capital goods into "capital," the complex relationships among capital goods would be lost. The concept of "aggregate demand" is problematical because, among other things, it obscures the potentially *inverse* relationship between consumption and investment. An increase in consumption expeditures does not simply increase aggregate demand and national income: it may also decrease investment. Investment alone leads to capital formation, which provides for a future supply of output. As a result, a given quantitative increase in consumption, compared with the same increase in investment, can have qualitatively different effects on employment and real income.

Hayek's approach is ultimately as inconsistent with monetarist as it is with Keynesian macroeconomics. The precise points of contention change, but not the ultimate theoretical questions. Monetarists focus on the determination of the price level. The determination of the equilibrium price level is analyzed separately from that of relative prices. Monetarists thereby implicitly invoke a limited neutrality assumption. Unanticipated monetary shocks may cause the growth rate of output to deviate from its trend rate, but these shocks change neither relative prices nor the composition of output. Monetary shocks and concomitant price level effects are superimposed on a given structure of production and set of relative prices (O'Driscoll and Shenoy 1976, pp. 192–3). In contrast, Hayek integrated the analysis of the value of money with that of the determination of relative prices.

Modern neutrality assumptions virtually rule out the possibility of relative-price effects of monetary shocks. By integrating monetary analysis and the theory of prices, economists make it feasible to analyze relative-price effects that may exist. The former approach closes off theoretical avenues of inquiry while the latter opens them up.

Menger's theory of money similarly integrates micro- and monetary analysis. It analyzes the evolution of money and the effects of monetary development on economic activity. There is no distinction in the theory between micro- and macroanalysis. Menger does distinguish, however, between the intended and unintended consequences of human actions. This distinction is central to his analysis of monetary evolution. In his theory of monetary evolution, he treated theoretical and institutional analysis as complementary endeavors. Indeed, his approach is a model of the theoretical–institutional approach sought by the new institutional economists (Langlois, 1982a, pp. 11–17).

Menger and Hayek each adopted a microeconomic approach to traditional macroeconomic questions. Each thereby evidenced his aversion to macroeconomic reasoning. In what follows, we both explicate the theoretical basis of this attitude and develop the respective theories. We begin with Menger's seminal analysis of money and monetary institutions.

## THE ORIGIN OF MONEY

The central issue with which Menger dealt was the question of "how. . .certain commodities come to be exalted into general media of exchange?" (Jones, 1976, p. 758).[2] In distinguishing between money and nonmoney goods, analysts have traditionally highlighted intrinsic physical characteristics, such as portability and divisibility. Money and banking textbooks still repeat these explanations. Menger's contribution was to focus not on physical but on market characteristics of goods. In taking this path, Menger was being more modern than are most contemporary monetary theorists. As Robert Jones observed in his study, "analysis suggests that the rationale for using a medium of exchange in the first place might be found in the differing market characteristics of goods and the decentralized nature of exchange" (Jones, 1976, p. 775).

The evolution of money is a paradigm case of the development of an organic social institution. In his *Principles*, Menger summarized the evolutionary process in the following way:

> As *each* economizing individual becomes increasingly more aware of his economic interest, he is led by this *interest, without any agreement, without legislative compulsion,* and *even without regard to the public interest*, to give his commodities in exchange for other, more saleable, commodities, even if he does not need them for any immediate consumption purpose. With economic progress, therefore, we can everywhere observe the phenomenon of a certain number of goods, expecially those that are most easily saleable at a given time and place, becoming, under the influence of *custom*, acceptable to everyone in trade, and thus capable of being given in exchange for any other commodity. These goods were called "*Geld*" by our ancestors, a term derived from "*gelten*" which means to compensate or pay. Hence the term "*Geld*" in our language designates the means of payment as such. (Menger, 1981, p. 260)

Menger's theory is reminiscent of Adam Smith's invisible hand reasoning. He based his theory of money on his analysis of commodity-stock holdings. Economies progress from economic self-sufficiency, to production on order, to speculative production for the market. In the course of this evolutionary process, transactors increasingly hold inventories of unfinished and finished goods. They do so in order to enhance their ability to consummate future trades and to further their own consumption plans.

In committing themselves to holding commodity stocks, traders are concerned, among other things, with the marketability (*absatz-fahigkeit*) or saleability of the goods held in their inventories. Traders discover that some commodities are especially marketable and widely acceptable, while other commodities are less so. Menger was almost exhaustive in discussing the factors impeding and facilitating marketability (Menger, 1981, pp. 248–53). For the purpose of our discussion, it is sufficient to observe that such factors exist and lead to differences in the saleability of various commodities.

Overtime, entrepreneur-traders will prefer holding their wealth in more marketable commodities. This preference accentuates the differences in marketability among commodities. Those commodities perceived to be more saleable will tend to become even more so as individuals act on their perceptions. In building inventories of preferred commodities, wealth-owners create a wider and more active market for the commodity. Subjective factors thus play a crucial role in this market process, far more than is captured in arguments focusing on physical characteristics of commodities. Because the free choices of traders and the sequence of events affect the ultimate outcome, it is partly an accident of history which goods become the most marketable. This indeterminism is typical of evolutionary processes.

If a good is sufficiently marketable, particular individuals (mainly professional traders) would be willing to hold inventories of it even if they have no final demand for it. The good becomes a store of value. If the process continues, the store of value becomes a medium through which other transactions are conducted. In other words, we are describing the economic rationale for indirect exchange. Again, however, we are analyzing the productivity of indirect exchange on microeconomic grounds and in terms of a general theory of inventory holdings. Moreover, the focus is on subjective perceptions and market characteristics of goods, not on their physical attributes.

Menger initially developed this theory by observing that goods do not have a unique price, but have different buying and selling prices. Not only is there a bid-asked spread, but this spread varies for different commodities. This phenomenon was not explicable in terms of standard demand and supply theory. Menger's explanation of bid-asked spreads is essentially a transactions-cost explanation. The bid-asked spread helps compensate wealth-owners for the costs of disposing of goods, costs that vary among goods. Since money is the most liquid commodity, it alone has a unique price, there being no bid-asked spread.

Sir John Hicks has succinctly characterized liquidity preference as a desire for flexibility: "Liquidity is not a property of a single choice; it is a matter of a sequence of choices, a related sequence. It is concerned with the passage from the known to the unknown – with the knowledge that if we wait we can have more knowledge" (Hicks, 1974, pp. 38–9; cf. Shackle, 1967, p. 6). In contrast, "by holding the imperfectly liquid asset the holder has narrowed the trend of opportunities which may be open to him. . . . He has 'locked himself in' " (Hicks, 1974, pp. 43–4). Liquidity provides economic agents with flexibility, flexibility that lowers the cost of specialized production.

So large are the cost savings that the development of a complex economic order depends crucially on monetary evolution. Without the evolution of a highly liquid commodity with general acceptability, economic development would be impossible. Specialized production depends on the ability of transactors to calculate efficiently, and money alone makes this calculation possible. In our schematic analysis, we linked the progress of economic development with that of monetary evolution. Monetary evolution must be far advanced before a complex market system can evolve. In other words, a non-monetary economy must logically be a primitive one. This implication is corroborated by the notable absence of highly developed market economies utilizing barter.[3]

Modern monetary theory characterizes money as though it were in some sense invented, despite the fact that over one hundred years ago Menger realized that "money is not the product of an agreement on the part of economizing man nor the product of legislative acts. No one invented it" (Menger, 1981, p. 262). Of the modern literature on the evolution of money, Jones has commented that: "Although these works illuminate how money might overcome logistical difficulties of reaching an efficient allocation with decentralized exchange, they offer no suggestions of how a monetary pattern of trade could evolve without a centralized decision" (Jones, 1976, p. 759). Jones himself avoided this pitfall, but did not solve the problem of simultaneously determining the money good and its market value. Menger had, however, accomplished this in the *Principles* and in "*Geld.*" There, Menger noted that, since money is simply the most marketable good, it has always had an exchange value. As it evolves into the medium of exchange, demand for the good increases. This process increases the relative price of the commodity money over time.

There is, of course, no unique point at which a good becomes money, no logical or historical break in economic history. One day's price builds upon yesterday's. At some point, we recognize that a commodity has become money in the modern sense, but any arbitrariness derives from our perception, not from the historical events themselves. In very recent times, economic historians have tended to look to the enactment of legal tender laws as marking the monetization of a good. Aside from perpetuating the myth that money is the invention of the state, this approach overlooks the fact that governments have done no more than sanction the existence of what has evolved on the market. The approach embodies the error dubbed "constructivism" by Hayek.

Consider the issue of monetary reform as an application of the evolutionary principle being discussed. Monetary reform proposals are often long on lists of advantages of adopting a new standard or monetary constitution, but short on transitional details. Hall has stated that: "Experience in countless nations shows that the simple announcement of the definition of a national monetary unit, without any compulsion for its use, is sufficient to bring about almost unanimous use" (Hall, 1982, p. 2). This casual empiricism is not compelling. Consider the example of a government's introducing a new monetary unit, the "ecru." To be a clear test of the thesis, the ecru cannot be linked to another currency. If, for instance, the ecru were declared to be worth one British pound, then the country would be effectively going on a sterling standard rather than introducing a new standard: the ecru would simply be the name for a pound sterling in the hypothetical country. There are many practical legal, political, and economic problems inherent in such a change; but these are not the problems that concern us here.

Introducing the pure ecru standard raises the following analytical problem, which is Menger's central problem in another guise. No economic agent would have an incentive to accept ecrus, because no one would have any grounds for forming expectations about the ecru's future expected value. By assumption, the ecru has never existed before. Accordingly, it has no established value. Even if the government were to declare the ecru legal tender, no one would have a clue as to its market value: no one, for instance, would know the ecru-price of a pair of shoes. Until that question can be resolved, ecrus will not circulate as a medium of exchange.[4]

We are simply restating the fact that the marginal utility of money depends on its exchange value, the reverse of the ordinary relationship for goods. In general equilibrium analysis, the *equilibrium* values of all economic variables are simultaneously determined. Actual market prices are not established, however, by everyone sitting down and jointly solving a system of equations that describes the economy. The mutual determination of prices is a characteristic of general equilibrium, not a method of attaining that equilibrium. No *market mechanism* exists that could provide information to transactors as to what prices would be if *all* of them were to accept ecrus as the means of payment. The assumption to the contrary is an implicit denial that we are analyzing a decentralized system.

In the nineteenth century, Hall's "simple announcement" of a new monetary unit consisted of a country's adopting either the gold or silver standard. In the twentieth century, "new" monetary units have typically come about in one of the following two ways. First, a government may link its national currency to another major currency, such as the pound or dollar. In this case, the government has effectively adopted a sterling or dollar standard. Second, a government may institute currency reform, substituting 5, 10 or 100 units of the old currency for a unit of the new currency. If the government couples this conversion with newly found monetary stringency, then the action can have value in speeding adjustment to anti-inflationary policies.

To some extent, of course, it is a purely verbal issue whether this change is characterized as introducing a new monetary standard. Verbal issues aside, however, the success of the change depends crucially on the new standard's being defined in terms of the old standard. If it were not, the policy action would be equivalent to trying to adopt the ecru standard. With respect to the second type of currency reform, the cases of Germany in the 1920s and France in the 1950s come to mind. In each case, a new currency was defined in terms of the old. Both were successful reforms.

Following Menger, Hayek has suggested that money is an evolved social institution in the same sense that language is. The analogy in fact can help illuminate the issue at hand. Modern linguists, do not suppose that recognized languages are invented.

To suppose that they could be invented would be to involve oneself in absurdities. To convince a whole population to switch its language, one would have to assure each individual that everyone else would use the language if he did. To introduce successfully the new language, one must thus find a population already conversant with the language. The richer one makes the example, the more overwhelming the informational and organizational problems become. (What motivates anyone to play this game? In what language do they negotiate, the new or the old?)

The problems with designed linguistic innovation derive from the complexity of undesigned orders. Money and monetary institutions are largely undesigned or evolved social institutions. Policy actions do, of course, affect the evolution of institutions. Policy actions cannot precisely determine the eventual outcome, however, as is illustrated by the failure of attempts in French-speaking countries to maintain the "purity" of the language, and by the failure of the Irish government to maintain Gaelic as a living language.

We are not arguing against monetary reform or against the idea of permitting a new monetary standard to evolve. We are suggesting, however, that reform proposals ought to take account of the complexity of evolved social institutions, as well as the exigencies of decentralized social systems. Actual historical examples of monetary reform do not illustrate governmental power to implement change so much as they illuminate the constraints on reforformers. Reforms have consisted of precisely those types that we have treated as being feasible. Governments can no more alter the monetary system by mere announcement than it can change its citizens' language by fiat.

Constructivist monetary reform proposals attempt to predetermine outcomes, rather than permit these to be determined by market forces. Market-determined outcomes reflect all relevant factors, not just the comparatively small number that can be included in economic models. Constructivist reform proposals overlook the fact that markets embody more information than will ever be available to a single mind or even to a group of experts (Hayek, 1945). The proposals treat these institutions and practices as being susceptible to centralized planning. In reality, monetary institutions – indeed, money itself – are shaped by the same kind of forces affecting ordinary business practices and market institutions.

Indeed, in monetary matters generally, economists adopt procedures and theorize in ways rejected in other areas. Few economists would accept the validity of trying to reason *a priori* about the optimal qualities that should be possessed by a cup of coffee or a glass of wine. These are recognized to be things that can be determined only by market test, and which, moreover, typically show great variation across brands or trademarks. Yet most monetary economists believe that rational economic theory ought to be capable of prescribing the optimal qualities, if not the optimum quantity, of money. In part, these attitudes reflect the belief that money is "different," different in a way possessing normative significance. This belief, though long incorporated into theoretical assumptions, is yet to be convincingly substantiated. At the very least, there is an heuristic value to carrying the analysis of money as an ordinary good, generated by market forces, as far as it can carried. This would be better determine the limits of policy-making than would continued applications of *a priori* reasoning about desirable properties of money.

Economic theory can perhaps specify the likely limits of monetary reform or the range of possible institutional outcomes. The range is not, however, open-ended; monetary systems that are postulated to be the product of market processes must be the probable outcome of such processes. They must also be consistent with incentives facing individuals in the situations postulated (see O'Driscoll, 1983, p. 331).

## BUSINESS CYCLES

Cyclical variations generate profit opportunities, a fact that is most apparent in the case of unemployed resources. Unemployed resources represent a mismatching of inputs to outputs. As long as final output is scarce, versatile resources ought not to be persistently unemployed. Entrepreneurs who can reallocate resources to superior uses will earn profits. There are also profit opportunities in speculating against markets in cyclical expansions. For instance, the housing and construction boom of the 1970s should have provided as many potential arbitrage possibilities as any eighteenth-century "bubble."

We are characterizing the phases of an economic cycle as periods in which plans are persistently discoordinated. Any attempt to analyze such movements, however, presents insuperable problems for models based on general equilibrium theory. The logic of static general equilibrium theory cannot generate processes in which decentralized systems move away from equilibrium. It cannot do so even if it postulates exogenous disturbances. Even then, general equilibrium theory "can do no more than demonstrate that . . . the economic system always reacts to such changes by its well-known method of adaptation, i.e. by the formation of a new equilibrium" (Hayek, 1966, pp. 42–3).

In essence, rational expectations theorists have renewed Hayek's critique of business cycle analysis. In his own work, Lucas (1977) has explicitly referred to that critique. Rational expectations theorists have generally focused their criticism on the expectational assumptions of traditional macroeconomic models. In their own positive theory, they treat the business cycle as an "equilibrium" phenomenon, utilizing static models to analyze cyclical activity. This is one way to resolve the theoretical dilemma in question, but one that we suggest does violence to the phenomenon. In our analysis, we adopt Hayek's view of the cycle as a disequilibrium phenomenon. We restate his analysis, however, in terms of our own formulation of process theory. In particular, we argue that the distincition between typical and unique aspects of phenomena is especially useful in analyzing economic fluctuations.

Analyzing expectational equilibrium is one aspect of the more general problem of modeling error in economics. *Ex ante* error has been all but eliminated from neoclassical economics. Models can accommodate *ex post* forecast errors, so long as these do not cause agents to revise their forecasting function. In other words, there is error without regret or revision. Such errors must be uncorrelated with information available at the time decisions were implemented. In models of stochastic equilibrium, agents are correct on average. "Error" observations result from serially uncorrelated, random disturbances. Business cycles, however, represent a jarring element in this *weltanschauung.* Maddock and Carter concisely stated the issue:

> If expectations are rational, then expectation errors should be randomly distributed over time. A straightforward implication of that for this model is that the level of output (or unemployment) is uncorrelated over time. Yet everybody knows that the GNP and the unemployment series have a high degree

> of serial correlation. We tend to go through a series of years in which unemployment is below the "natural rate" and then a series of years in which it is above the "natural rate." It doesn't seem to be distributed very randomly. (Maddock and Carter, 1982, p. 44)

Any consistent theory of cyclical fluctuations must incorporate time and expectational error in the analysis. It must also explain the important sources of expectational error. As we argued in the previous chapter, it is insufficient merely to invoke uncertainty, even radical uncertainty, to explain the cycle of economic expansion and contraction. Individual firms are continuously making errors, which show up as profits and losses. Some entrepreneurs underestimate demand, resulting in an excess demand for their goods. Others overestimate demand, resulting in an excess supply of their goods. These errors tend to be negatively correlated, not because of the law of large numbers but because of the law of markets. If excess demand exists in some markets, there must be a corresponding excess supply somewhere else. Over a cycle, however, there tends to be not only serial correlation in error terms within given time series, but an observed correlation in errors across markets. In simplified terms, periods of general excess demand for commodities (accelerations in the inflation rate) alternate with periods of general excess supply of commodities (disinflation). This is the problem of the "clustering of errors" referred to in chapter 8. While the stylized facts require more precise statement, they do point up the problem of using received theory to analyze the business cycle.

In general equilibrium theory, markets always equilibrate because of the adjustment process triggered by matched purchases and sales: every sale constitutes a demand for other goods. It is in this sense that theory embodies Say's Law of markets (Hayek, 1966, p. 42n). Money alone can break the mechanical linkage of matched purchases and sales, because only money constitutes a source of demand for real goods with no corresponding supply of real goods. In the Mengerian or Hicksian sense, a demand for money expresses a preference for liquidity or generalized purchasing power, with no implied commitment to purchase any particular commodity. Similarly, variations in individuals' money stocks, whether caused by a demand or a supply shift, can cause the demand for some produced goods to increase (decrease) with no corresponding diminution in demand for other produced goods (cf. Hayek, 1966, p. 45).

The difference between a money and a barter economy is the essential ingredient in any analysis of economic fluctuations. This insight does not itself constitute a cycle theory, nor does it commit one to a monetary theory of the cycle, except in the broadest sense of the term. Though the formulation of the problem may strike one as "Keynesian," in no sense can Keynes be credited with this particular insight. If we have paraphrased anyone, it is Hayek. Hayek, however, was merely restating here a position well established in classical political economy. The existence of a variable money supply, i.e., one at least partially composed of fiduciary media, changes the "black letter" statement of the theory of value. It can be readily established that classical economists were aware of the point. For instance, after articulating what would now be called a caricature of the quantity theory, including a strong neutrality proposition, John Stuart Mill observed that:

> The proposition which we have laid down, respecting the dependence of general prices upon the quantity of money in circulation, must be understood as applying only to a state of things in which money, that is gold or silver, is the exclusive instrument of exchange, and actually passes from hand to hand at every purchase, credit in any of its shapes being unknown. When credit comes into play as a means of purchasing, distinct from money in hand, we shall hereafter find that the connection between prices and the amount of money in circulation is much less distinct and intimate, and that such connection as does exist no longer admits of so simple a mode of expression. (Mill, 1973, p. 495)

We have insisted on viewing formal economic theory as incorporating Say's Law, thereby implicitly denying the frequently repeated distinction between Say's Law and Walras' Law. There simply is no distinction, at least not at the level of generality specified here. Say's Law is a statement of the interdependency of all markets, a statement formalized but not fundamentally changed by Walras. Economists relying on Say's Law recognized that monetary factors introduced complications, as is indicated by the previous quotation from Mill. Similarly, business cycles fascinated economists, from the South Sea Bubble down through the end of the nineteenth and into the early twentieth centuries. What was missing was a consistent monetary analysis in which existing insights were woven into a story that shed light on economic cycles.

The use of money in a decentralized economy reflects the scarcity of information available to transactors, a scarcity that generates pervasive uncertainty. If money had not evolved, individuals could neither cope with this uncertainty nor solve the allocational problem confronting them. Money itself, however, can produce informational problems, causing particular types of disequilibrium. It can do so by interfering with market forces tending to produce consistency of plans. Monetary shocks can, then, discoordinate plans and economic activity. In the next section we develop these points.

## A SUBJECTIVIST THEORY OF ECONOMIC FLUCTUATIONS

The existence of business cycles evidences coordination failure. The price system fails to accomplish the task assigned to it by static economic theory. In a modern economy, any serious coordination failure disrupts entrepreneurial planning. In analyzing economic fluctuations, then, we focus on entrepreneurial expectations, particularly those embodied in decisions to utilize or abandon concrete capital goods. Expectations, coordination, and capital allocation are the analytical building blocks of a subjectivist theory of economic fluctuations.

Our analysis fits within the Thornton–Wicksell monetary tradition, a tradition focusing on the interest rate mechanism for coordinating saving and investment decisions. We follow the Austrian development of that tradition, a variant originally enunciated by Mises and Hayek. O'Driscoll (1977) restated the theory; Garrison (1978) clarified the static capital theory underlying it; and Wainhouse (1982) confronted the theory with postwar evidence.

In presenting our version or approach, we recognize that other schools have developed the Wicksellian theme differently: the Stockholm School (Lindahl, Ohlin, Myrdal), and the early Cambridge School (Hawtrey, Robertson, Keynes), presented alternative formulations of savings–investment disequilibrium (Leijonhufvud,

1981). Though the differences among these variants are important, where appropriate we draw on insights from the broad Thornton–Wicksell tradition.

We begin with the familiar loanable funds approach to the determination of market interest rates (figure 5). At an interest rate $r_0$, the plans of savers and investors are consistent in the aggregate. Planned saving equals planned investment at this rate, which is Wicksell's "natural rate." At an interest rate below $r_0$, such as $r_1$, planned investment exceeds planned saving (by $I_1 - S_1$). Only if the banking system creates additional liabilities in the course of extending credit will $r_1$ persist, and will $I_1$ be the actual or *ex post* level of investment. In this case, the supply of loanable funds is increasing by more than the supply of savings. The difference is made up by the creation of bank money or bank credit.

An interest rate of $r_0$ represents *neutral* bank policy. Bank policy is neutral if it does no more than intermediate between savers and investors. If policy is neutral, changes in the supply of credit are governed by changes in the supply of planned saving (cf. Leijonhufvud, 1981, p. 153). If policy is non-neutral, then some plans must be frustrated or go unfulfilled. The form that this frustration takes depends crucially upon the assumed sequence of events. In what follows, we specify a sequence of events.

Assume that the bank policy is adhered to for several periods, and does not merely represent a once-and-for-all shock. So long as

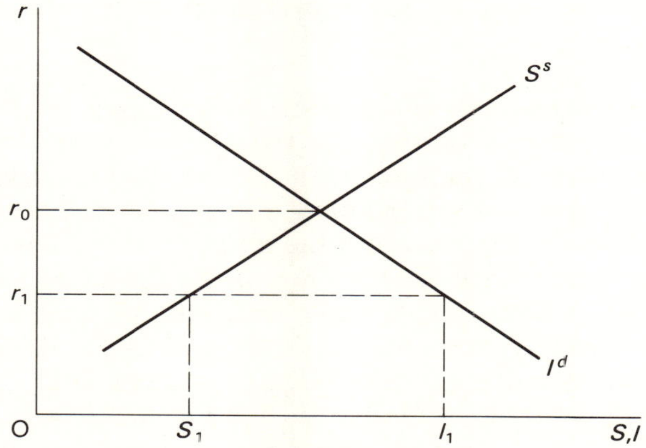


Figure 5

the policy is effective, the market or loan rate will be less than the equilibrium rate. Each period, entrepreneurs plan to invest more income than recipients plan to save. As explained in chapter 8, entrepreneurs will implement projects geared to produce greater consumption output in the more distant future, but relatively less in the near term. Consumers' plans, however, entail greater consumption in the near term, and relatively less in the more distant future (compared with producers' plans).

Something must adjust as the result of the implied intertemporal plan discoordination. In the aggregate, income recipients will be unable to acquire the consumer goods that they would wish to purchase at that income level. Consumption plans cannot all be fulfilled, since, by assumption, a smaller proportion of consumption goods is being produced at the very time that incomes are being bid up. The complete allocational and distributional stories await development of the relative-price story. What is being described here, however, corresponds to the concept of "forced saving" in nineteenth-century British monetary economics (Hayek, 1932; O'Driscoll, 1977, pp. 51–6). In real terms, consumers are compelled to consume less than planned for each period.

The assumed sequence of events is as follows.

(1) In period 1, bank money is created in the form of business credits.
(2) In period 2, entrepreneurs spend the money on factor services, bidding up incomes.
(3) In period 3, income recipients bid up the prices of consumers goods.

The transmission mechanism goes from money, to incomes, to prices, and then to output. At this point, we have linked the Thornton–Wicksell tradition with that of Richard Cantillon. As Hayek (1967a, pp. 8–9) pointed out, it is a logical connection. Cantillon argued that, because the inflation process is sequential, i.e., takes place in real time, there will be gainers and losers. Some incomes rise before others: early recipients of increased income do not confront higher prices. In the case that Cantillon adduced, owners of gold mines and those supplying them with goods clearly gained from an inflow of bullion. Their incomes rose before prices increased. In the third and fourth rounds, incomes still rose more quickly than did prices. At some point in the sequence, however, we discover consumers who face higher prices but whose incomes have not risen proportionately. They are the losers in the inflation process. So long as the inflow of bullion continues, the distribution effects will be operative. These distribution effects generate, *mutatis mutandis*, allocational effects. In Cantillon's analysis, there is no sharp distinction between the allocational and distributional effects, because there is no sharp distinction between real and monetary shocks.

For Cantillon's comparatively simple case, it was relatively easy to outline the sequence in some depth. The greater complexity of our case requires somewhat more analysis, which we develop in the following subsection.

### *Prices and Production*

A fall in interest rates, generated by monetary expansion, will not increase uniformly the value of all investment projects. The value of investment projects yielding consumption output in the more distant future rises relative to projects with more immediate payoffs. We call these projects and capital goods type 1 and type 2, respectively. Here, a "project" is defined as a set of interrelated, heterogeneous capital goods. The full impact of the fall in interest rates comprises: (1) a discount rate effect, (2) derived-demand effects, and (3) cost effects.

*Ceteris paribus*, the decline in interest rates will increase the value of all long-lived assets. This effect reflects the negative elasticity of present value with respect to the interest rate. It is, however, a partial effect, as can be seen by considering the full effect on individual capital goods. The demand for type 2 capital goods is affected more immediately by the demand for current consumption output than by current interest rates (the derived-demand effect). Consumption demand has declined, at least in relative terms. In other words, the increased demand for type 1 capital goods is equivalent to a decline in demand for type 2 goods. In terms of a standard present value (PV) formula for a capital good yielding services over n periods,

$$PV = \frac{S_1}{(1+r)} + \frac{S_2}{(1+r)^2} + \frac{S_3}{(1+r)^3} + \ldots + \frac{S_n}{(1+r)^n},$$

there are derived-demand effects for different capital goods, effects that show up in the numerator. The interest rate disturbance causes the expected stream of quasi-rents ($S_i$) accuring to capital goods to change. For type 1 goods the stream tends to rise; for type 2 goods the stream tends to fall. For some goods, therefore, the quasi-rent and interest rate effects reinforce each other; for other goods, these are offsetting effects. To calculate the full compact of the kind of disturbance being analyzed, we must also take account of cost effects.

The prices of complementary factors, which we designate "labor" and "raw materials," will be affected in this process. Entrepreneurs undertaking type 1 projects will be able to bid factors away from type 2 projects. Moreover, this occurs as the derived demand for the latter is declining. Owners of type 2 goods are thus caught in a price–cost squeeze. Of course, none of this implies that already completed type 2 projects will be abandoned. So long as depreciation is sufficient to pay the increased variable costs, these projects can be continued. The quasi-rents accruing to these projects will, however, decline. More importantly, new investment funds will tend to flow to type 1 not type 2 projects.

In any period, net investment is small relative to the value of the existing capital stock. Nonetheless, investment is a large component of each period's GNP. Moreover, shifts in investment expenditures can have substantial impact on production and employment in the affected industries. We are interested primarily in changes in the *pattern* of investment flows, not in the demand for "capital."

In analyzing the effects of changes in capital value on *users* of capital goods, it may be useful to assume the short-run fixity of capital. It is misleading to do so, however, for *producers* of capital goods. Monetary disturbances affect credit markets, which in turn cause demand for new capital goods to change. Adjustments in the capital goods industries begin as soon as the change is perceived to be permanent; or at least is long-lived enough to warrant a commitment of resources.

Our analysis involves expectational assumptions at each stage, and we now make some of these more explicit. First, we assume that all information possessed by entrepreneurs is embodied in the $I^d$ function. This includes not only future expected returns, but also information on current economic policy. Changes in entrepreneurial knowledge or beliefs show up as shifts in $I^d$. The investment demand function might, then, be specified as follows:

$I^d = (r, s, i)$

where

$r$ = relevant interest rate

$s$ = profit (quasi-rent) expectations

$i$ = a *portmanteau* information variable.

We have thus packed a great deal into $i$. We by no means wish to argue that information will remain fixed during the cumulative process: indeed, the contrary is almost surely the case. Certain factors change, *mutatis mutandis*, as the cumulative process proceeds. One could attempt to incorporate all these into the elasticity measure. We argue below, however, that at least one factor will show up as a shift effect. Moreover, as indicated above, we are not trying to present the analysis in terms of aggregate investment. So we do not pursue the analysis in each of $n$ periods in terms of stable aggregate saving and investment functions. If the reader is more comfortable in doing so, he may do so to get a "first approximation" of the theory. This would be a rough approximation at best, and one that ultimately does violence to the microeconomic approach being employed. We are not, strictly speaking, presenting an over-investment model, but one of *mal-* or *misdirected* investment (cf. Rothbard, 1963, pp. 34–5).

Second, we assume that entrepreneurs are *ex ante* profit-maximizers, making use of the best information that they have. Entrepreneurs will devote resources to acquiring relevant information, so long as they expect it to be cost-effective. To the degree that they are successful, they may modify their actions compared with what they would have done in the absence of that information. This assumption does not, however, warrant any inference that monetary policy will be ineffective. In a decentralized economy, the kind of information acquired by agents is not sufficient to insulate them completely from the effects of monetary shocks. We can outline the reasons here; we elaborate on some of these points in dealing with rational expectations.

Agents know prices and other endogenous variables, but not the structure of the system. They may have acquired information in the past about demand and supply conditions in the neighborhood of a prior, temporary equilibrium point. This information is subject to obsolescence, a process speeded up by the kind of shocks that we are analyzing here. Agents may have theories about how the system works, but, as recently clarified by Frydman (1982), theory-conflict insures that entrepreneurial error will not be eliminated. Information characteristics of decentralized economies insure that agents will disagree on the effects of policy and on the future course of events generally.

We return now to the dynamics of the expansion. Reallocation of capital and other factors is occurring, but in a manner inconsistent with preferences and opportunities (revealed, for instance, in the planned savings ($S$) and investment ($I$) functions).[5] As the output of current consumption goods declines, investment in this sector declines. Future-period consumption is being provided for at an ever increasing rate. Investment is being committed to multi-period projects, and their future output cannot be used now to satisfy consumption demand. (People cannot consume half-completed steel plants and hydroelectric dams.) Rising incomes make the satisfaction of consumption demand more urgent, but interest-rate and relative-price signals continue to make the satisfaction of future-period consumption demand seem even more profitable. At some point, *ex post* returns in consumer goods industries will begin rising. In theory, this might ameliorate or slow the process (Hayek, 1969). If it did, however, it could do so only by leading entrepreneurs in consumer goods industries (type 2 investment projects) to enter into a bidding war with the capital goods (type 1) industries. To the degree the former succeeded, some of the new projects would be rendered unprofitable.

Both practical and theoretical considerations argue against this happening, especially in earlier stages of an expansion. First, policy-makers normally view with alarm any slowdown in the recovery of business investment. One Keynesian legacy is to define economic recovery virtually in terms of the profitability of producers of capital goods (i.e., "smokestack industries"). Excessive attention to capital goods industries leads monetary authorities to respond by accelerating the rate of growth of money. Consequently, they are induced to step on the accelerator until signs of recovery in investment occur. If the past is any guide, they will kick the accelerator again at least once in any recovery, in order to maintain the strength of the recovery and thereby the growth in the capital goods sectors.

A theoretical consideration also argues against an endogenous end to a malinvestment cycle. This consideration depends on the complementarity of capital goods. The more resources that have already been sunk in the capital-intensive production methods, the greater will be the demand for additional resources that can be used to complete the projects. If a project is nearly complete, then the incremental resources needed to complete it will have a far greater value than would have been the case *ex ante. In the limit*, entrepreneurs would be willing to pay up to discounted value of the future quasi-rents accruing to the entire project in order to obtain a comparatively small additional sum needed to complete the project.

Indeed, it was precisely this consideration that led Hayek (1937b) to one of his most important analytical contributions to business cycle theory. The capital complementarity effect helps explain the pro-cyclical behavior of interest rates, *apart from any Fisher effects.* A prolonged cycle of capital investment is likely to increase the expected returns from additional borrowing and investment. Past investment raises the demand for current investable funds, driving up real market interest rates. Toward the end of a cycle, the real short-run interest rate, which would clear the market, will be higher – perhaps significantly higher – than the long-run equilibrium rate.

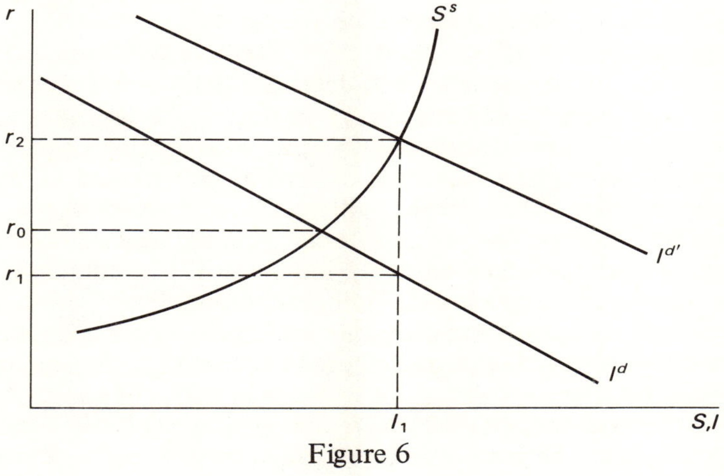


Figure 6

Consider the stylized analysis in figure 6. If the savings-investment equilibrium had been maintained throughout at an interest rate $r_0$, then investment expenditures would have remained at the correct level "in the aggregate," and would have been "efficiently allocated."[6] As a consequence of an expansionary policy, rates are driven to $r_1$. Toward the end of the cycle, therefore, the investment demand schedule will have increased to $I'$. Presumably, price inflation has accelerated by then, particularly for consumer goods. Assume that monetary authorities now wish to engage in a "tight" monetary policy. Merely to hold investment expenditures to $I'$, monetary policy would have to increase *real* rates to $r_2$. This is higher than the long-run equilibrium rate. If the inflation expectation effects are operative, nominal interest rates would have to rise by that much more.

In fact, we believe that Hayek's analysis is consistent with the basic facts of cycles. In the next section, we present evidence to support this contention. For the moment, we take it as an assumption. We suggest, further, that investment cycles typically end in a credit crunch, with a comparatively sudden and simultaneous financial "crisis" for numerous firms. At $r_2$ the interest rates is too high for long-run equilibrium. Many projects, newly undertaken, will have to be abandoned. Entrepreneurs simply will not be able to command the complementary factors to complete these projects. In particular, labor and raw materials will be prohibitively expensive for entrepreneurs to purchase at an interest rate of $r_2$. The *initial* round of unemployment and cyclical decline begins as these factors are released from type 1 projects.

How will the rest of the decline look? It will appear to be "Keynesian." Entrepreneurs will decrease their demand for investment funds, particularly for type 1 projects. The resulting unemployment will, however, eventually spill over to type 2 industries. Unemployment spreads because of income-constrained processes. Investment demand collapses: entrepreneurial expectations turn pessimistic in response to relizations of lower sales and profits. Indeed, investment demand could fall below *I*. If monetary policy does not respond quickly, a Wicksellian cumulative contraction may develop. Market interest rates are now too high; even an interest rate of $r_0$ could be temporarily too high during such a downward-adjustment phase.

Notice, however, that a Hayekian analysis (or a similar story) is needed to rationalize a quasi-Keynesian ending. Keynesian analysis begins in the middle of a cyclical story: the marginal efficiency of capital declines. This decline is either exogenous, or is predicated on a view of capital goods as all gross substitutes. Analysis predicted *purely* on exogenous shifts in expectations is objectionable on a number of grounds. If it is an accepted mode of analysis, then any story can be told with no *a priori* grounds for distinguishing among them. Further, the Keynesian story depends on waves of optimism or pessimism striking large numbers of entrepreneurs simultaneously. This latter assumption appears to be the conclusion of dubious amateur psychological reasoning.

Some analysts (e.g., Leijonhufvud, 1968) attribute a kind of Schumpeterian hypothesis to Keynes. After a long period of high investment, expected returns decline. For the reasons indicated in the previous chapter, we are not sanguine about analysis of economic cycles based on technological innovations. Such innovations surely help explain the direction that investment takes in a cycle, but are dubious as an explanation of the cyclic character of investment.

D. H. Robertson (1940) was virtually the only one to have perceived the connection between Hayek's theory of expansion and crises and Keynes' theory of contraction. By the time Robertson pointed this connection out, however, neither party to the Keynes–Hayek controversies wanted to listen to Robertson's resolution. In essence, Robertson pointed out that each had offered *part* of a complete Wicksellian theory: Hayek and Keynes wrote about different problems. In our judgment, Hayek's theory was more complete on a number of grounds, especially in his far greater attention to capital and interest theory. We do not wish, however, to press this doctrinal point here.[7]

## *Evidence*

As a result of the Keynesian revolution, economists basically lost interest in monetary analysis and monetary problems (cf. O'Driscoll, 1977, pp. 35–7). Interest in the Quantity Theory revived first, a process beginning with Milton Friedman's 1956 restatement of that tradition. The Austro–Wicksellian tradition languished in the shadow of Keynes for another decade. The Austrian revival began with Hicks' (1967) recounting of "the Hayek Story," an analysis to which Hayek (1969) responded. Buchanan (1969) restated the Austrian–subjectivist theory of cost. With Dolan (1976), a modest amount of new work in that area began to appear. While Hayek's theory of economic fluctuations received a great deal of attention, no one went back to check the consistency of the data with the predictions of the theory. Earlier works on the Great Depression by Robbins (1934) and Rothbard (1963) did not use modern statistical and econometric techniques. In addition, Robbins had repudiated his earlier views; and Rothbard's thesis won him opposition from monetarists as well as Keynesians. Part of Rothbard's thesis has since been justified by Gallaway and Vedder (1987). In a still more comprehensive study, Wainhouse (1982) systematically confronted Hayek's monetary theory of the cycle with postwar data.

Wainhouse formulated six operational propositions derived from Hayek's original statement of his theory (1967a), these consisted of three propositions about causality and three propositions about relative-price movements. Wainhouse applied causality tests to the first three propositions. He also compared actual with expected relative-price movements. He used monthly data from January 1959 to June 1981 (January 1959 being the first month that all series were available as monthly data).

His six propositions were as follows:

(1) Changes in the supply of savings are independent of changes in the supply of bank credit.
(2) Changes in the supply of credit lead to changes in rates of interest. Furthermore, changes in credit and interest rates are inversely related.
(3) Changes in the rate of change of credit lead to changes in the output of producers' goods.
(4) The ratio of producers' goods' prices to consumers' goods' prices tends to *rise* after the initiation of a credit expansion.
(5) Prices of producers' goods closest to final consumption tend to decline relative to the prices of producers' goods located further away from the consumers' goods in the production scheme (in the expansion phase of a cycle).
(6) The prices of consumers' goods rise relative to the prices of producers' goods, reversing the initial shift in relative prices.

With respect to the first three propositions, Wainhouse tested for Granger "causality." He first estimated state–space models for the variables, and then employed the equivalent Auto-regressive Moving Average (ARMA) representation of each state–space form. Proposition 1 asserts the strict independence of changes in savings and changes in credit; this is a particularly strong interpretation of Hayek's thesis. It also implies that bank policy is not neutral (see p. 203 above). Proposition 2 establishes that monetary policy initiates cyclical activity, rather than responding to real shocks. Again, a more general formulation of Hayek's theory would allow real shocks to initiate the process. Proposition 3 is an explicit statement of non-neutrality. Wainhouse found that the empirical evidence produces significant support for the three causality propositions.

Wainhouse next indentified credit cycles corresponding to Hayekian cycles (though not necessarily National Bureau of Economic Research (NBER) Reference Cycles). He examined relative-price movements after the initiation of each cycle, comparing them with price averages 24 months before the onset of the cycle. In proposition 4, Wainhouse presents Hayek's prediction of the broad pattern of relative-price movements after the initiation of the cycle. Over two-thirds of the observation are consistent with the prediction. Most of the anomalous findings are concentrated in one particular credit cycle. Again, over two-thirds of the observations confirm the broad prediction of proposition 5. Proposition 6 contains one of the most controversial aspects of Hayek's theory: the reversal of relative price movements in the contraction. It is a precise statement of the proposition that the seeds of recessions are sown in the prior expansion, suggesting the inevitability of recessions after an expansionary period. Wainhouse found evidence in the majority of cases to be consistent with this sixth proposition.

Wainhouse's results are robust, not varying significantly with alternative formulations. In his study, Wainhouse utilized state-of-the-art time series analysis. Moreover, he applied Hayek's theory to recent periods, in which the economy had changed fundamentally from the nineteenth-century institutions that Hayek (1969, p. 282) had in mind. Wainhouse's evidence not only corroborates key elements of Hayek's theory, but also suggests that further empirical research would be rewarded.

## RATIONAL EXPECTATIONS

In this section, we do not claim to present a comprehensive treatment of the rational expectations revolution. That revolution is in progress, currently doing intellectual battle with a counter-revolution. No clear resolution has yet emerged. Our concern here is to relate our theory to this controversy, and to forestall misunderstandings about what we are and are not saying.

The first problem is to define carefully what rational expectations means or implies. Definitions are often either so broad as to be almost vacuous, or so stringent as to seem like a virtual caricature of themselves. Consider the variety of formulations offered by one author, David K. H. Begg (1982), in a recent survey:

> (1) The Rational Expectations Hypothesis asserts that individuals do not make systematic mistakes in forecasting the future. (p. xi)
>
> (2) These expectations are rational in the following sense: when these expectations are fed back into the model the actual evolution of the economy will imply that there are no systematic forecasting errors which could have been discovered by individuals using information available at the date they had to form expectations. (pp. 12–13)
>
> (3) The hypothesis of Rational Expectations . . . . is concerned with incentives to acquire information and exploit profitable opportunities for revising behavior. It admits the notion of an equilibrium set of expectations, even when the economy is not in a static equilibrium. (p. 28)
>
> (4) The recent work on the hypothesis of Rational Expectations has commanded considerable attention because it seems to rely on a good optimizing principle: individuals should not make systematic mistakes in forecasting the future. It is not appealing to assume that individuals make predictable errors yet take no action to revise their rule for forming expectations, but *ad hoc* expectations assumptions typically possess this property; only under Rational Expectations is the contradiction avoided. (p. 71)

Begg's first definition sometimes appears as the contention that "rational forecasting requires that forecast errors be serially uncorrelated" (Poole, 1976, p. 465). Each formulation has been disputed. Consider the following rebuttal by Milton Friedman:

> For about five years, the future price of the Mexican peso was decidedly below the current price. And every year, while

> the Mexican government maintained the price of the peso at 8¢ a peso, the people operating in the futures market made an error in the same direction. Anybody who sold the peso short was bound to lose money. Did that mean that expectations were not rational? Not at all. What it meant was that every single year there was one chance in four that the peso was going to go down 50 percent; and that meant that it was appropriate for the future price to be 12½ percent below the current price. And that continued for 4 or 5 years. (Friedman, 1977, p. 14)

We agreed with Professor Friedman that the peso story points to the need for precision in defining rational expectations. One general implication of Friedman's parable should be noted. It will not generally be possible to infer the rationality of expectations by observing patterns of forecast error. But, conversely, *data on forecasts that were correct,* ex post, *tell us little about the optimality or rationality of these forecasts.* Agents may have been ignoring information that would have generated forecasts that, in retrospect, turned out to be incorrect. In Friedman's case, speculators were "wrong for the right reason": in the latter case, they may be "right for the wrong reason."

Begg's second definition is more precise, and, in this case, admits of a wider range of phenomena. Friedman's peso example meets the criterion of this definition: the experience of the same error year after year gave transactors no reason to revise what were optimal forecasts. This definition also points to the importance of specifying what kind of information transactors possess. We come back to this point shortly.

The third statement purports to characterize rational expectations. It is, however, precisely what the rational expectations hypothesis is *not* concerned with. Rational expectations models typically *begin* with the assumptions that all profit opportunities have been exploited and all necessary information has already been acquired. Critics (e.g. O'Driscoll, 1979) have long pointed to this deficiency. There is no analysis of the adjustment process in the rational expectations hypothesis, no theory of discovery.

The fourth statement is outrageous but useful for being so clear a statement of a view that we suspect is more often believed than articulated. The rational expectations hypothesis is neither the "only" alternative to *ad hoc* theorizing about expectations, nor the only expectational hypothesis involving optimizing behavior. While it may not be appealing to assume that individuals make errors that they themselves could have predicted (*ex ante* error), it is not obviously wrong to suppose that *others* could have predicted the errors of the first group. Any act of entrepreneurship or speculation involves trying to outguess the market, to do better than the crowd or the median asset-holder. Entrepreneurs and speculators are constantly taking actions that assume that most people make "predictable" errors (predictable by entrepreneurs).

In market economies, information is localized and specialized, implying the existence of differential returns. Because of changing circumstances and the fleeting value of information, this situation is always characteristic – indeed, is an essential characteristic – of markets. And decentralization of information is certainly an essential ingredient of any subjectivist economic theory. Any theory that begins with the elimination of profit and informational differences has assumed that the market process has come to an end.

There is another, important information difference sloughed over in the rational expectations hypothesis. That hypothesis takes it as axiomatic that there is no difference in the information possessed by the theorist, who is an ideal observer, and the human agents in the model. This assumption is thoroughly anti-subjectivist, making it difficult ultimately to reconcile rational expectations and subjectivist theories. To reiterate, we are not interested in refuting rational expectations *per se*. It may be that our objections are only to "the simplicity of the models in which rational expectations have so far been embedded" (Begg, 1982, p. 255). It does appear at this juncture, however, that rational expectations theorists are leading the profession down a garden path. From what we have seen of the trail thus far, it is a route that we are unwilling to follow.

There certainly are features or implications of rational expectations with which we agree or are in sympathy. Rational expectations theorists have correctly focused attention of the importance of expectational assumptions in macroeconomic analysis and policy-making. Though the Keynesian revolution began as an attempt to incorporate expectations more fully into economic reasoning, it paradoxically ended by suppressing expectational issues. In the *General Theory*, Keynes emphasized the exogenous aspects of entrepreneurial expectations. As a modelling technique, he assumed that they were completely exogenous in the short run. Short-run exogeneity became the static expectations of Keynesian macro-models, an assumption inhibiting further analysis (cf. Begg, 1982, pp. 19–22; Leijonhufvud, 1983a, pp. 6–11).

Extravagant claims to revolutionary character notwithstanding, the commonsense core of the rational expectations hypothesis represents a return to inherited wisdom. This core hypothesis has been referred to as "Lincoln's Law," as in the following passage:

> You can't fool all of the people all of the time. Eventually the masses come to understand the schemes of their rulers. Then the cleverly concocted plans of inflation collapse. . . . Inflation is not a monetary policy that can be considered as an alternative to a sound-money policy. It is at best a temporary makeshift. The main problem of an inflationary policy is how to stop it before the masses have seen through their rulers' artifices. It is a display of considerable naiveté to recommend openly a monetary system that can work only if its essential features are ignored by the public. (Mises, 1953, p. 419)

Mises developed the thesis that inflationary expectations emerge with a lag. Once expectations of inflation become embeded in the system, however, the effects of inflationary finance become more far-reaching and serious (Mises, 1953, pp. 418–19).

Wicksell articulated even more concisely this commonsense core of any sound expectational theory:

> Those people who prefer a continually upward moving to a stationary price level forcibly remind one of those who purposely keep their watches a little fast so as to be more certain of catching their trains. But to achieve their purpose they most not be conscious or remain conscious of the fact that their watches are fast; otherwise they become accustomed to take the extra few minutes into account and so, after all, in spite of their artfulness, arrive too late . . . . (Wicksell, 1965, pp. 3–4)

Rational expectations theorists have taught us that, in game-theoretic terminology, agents play games with policy-makers. Agents' strategy can offset the intended effects of policy actions. These will not, however, always be the games supposed in the rational expectations literature. Consider the following situation.

(1) Agents are very good predictors of policy-makers' actions.
(2) One or more endogenous variables are exclusively controlled by a policy-maker.
(3) The payoff of an action to a policy-maker depends on whether his policy will be anticipated.

In this situation, Frydman, O'Driscoll, and Schotter (1982) have shown rigorously that policy-makers may have no uniquely rational course of action to follow. Different theories suggest different optimal behavior. If no rational course of action exists for the policy-maker, agents cannot then form a rational expectation. This follows because a rational course of action must incorporate a theory of the policy-makers' behavior, and there is a conflict of theories. The situation is further complicated if, in order to forestall prediction by the public, the policy-maker engages in nonsystematic behavior. This dilemma, known as "Newcomb's Problem," depends on all parties attempting to behave rationally. In a game-theoretic setting, then, fully rational behavior may be inconsistent with the formation of rational expectations.

Frydman, O'Driscoll, and Schotter (1982) highlight the problem of conflict among theories. Rational expectations theorists assume this problem away by postulating that agents' expectations are "essentially the same as the predictions of the relevant economic theory" (Muth, 1961, p. 316). In macroeconomics, however, there is an embarassingly large number of theories claiming relevance. Applications of these theories to the same data often produce results that, from the perspective of the different theories, can be taken as corroborating rather than being inconsistent. In this case, theorists have no incentive to revise their views and converge to a single "correct" theory. Agents who interpret the world with these conflicting theories, or who purchase forecasts based on conflicting theories, may also fail to converge on a unique theory. In fact, Frydman (1982) investigated the possibility of convergence to an expectational equilibrium in some detail. His analysis led him to conclude that "the possibility of convergence to the rational expectations equilibrium appears to be remote in the context of models of decentralized competitive markets in which agents are assumed to be making individual decisions on the basis of market prices and their private information" (p. 664).

Economists have basic disagreements about macroeconomics, particularly concerning causal relationships between monetary changes and income, prices, and output. Expectational theories cannot ignore this disagreement or conflict. As Leijonhufvud (1983b, p. 5) put it, "When theorists are not sure they understand, or cannot agree, it is doubtful that they are entitled to the assumption that private sector agents understand and agree."

Frydman (1982) has offered a criterion for incorporating information into economic models that is consistent with both optimization and information decentralization.[8] In specifying the information available to individual actors, the economic modeller should include "*only information they can acquire according to the model* in the process of making individual decisions and observing market outcomes." This postulate "requires that the REH [rational expectations hypothesis] be *internally consistent* with other informational assumptions of the model" (Frydman and Phelps, 1983, p. 15). Frydman finds this criterion violated in the rational expectations models that he considers. This violation is theoretically equivalent to postulating that agents can perform actions violating the resource constraints in the model. In other words, agents are acting in ways that are strictly infeasible in terms of the model's other assumptions.

One recent development in monetary economics is both encouraging and consistent with the spirit of the Hayek/Frydman criterion. This is the new economics of monetary regimes, or what used to be called the monetary standard. Leijonhufvud has described a monetary regime as:

> a system of expectations that governs the behavior of the public and that is sustained by the consistent behavior of the policy-making authorities. . . . The present definition assumes that people understand the systematic components of the authorities' behavior in a general sort of way but avoids a linkage so tight as to build, for example, short-run neutrality or policy ineffectiveness assertions into the concept itself. Nonetheless, it is in effect an equilibrium concept. (Leijonhufvud, 1983b, p. 2)

This literature explicitly links institutions and expectations formation. Specifically, it postulates that the amount and quality of information possessed by individuals depends on the institutional environment (the "regime") within which they operate. A monetary regime or institutional environment generates patterns or regularized features among economic variables. On the basis of this pattern, agents can form reasonably firm expectations. In the course of gaining experience under a given regime, individuals learn the typical features of the monetary environment. Different regimes produce different features or relationships, possibly requiring a different theory. Changes in regimes render obsolete knowledge about typical features.

Leijonhufvud examines two regimes: one embodying a "quantity principle" (e.g., a modern fiat standard) and the other, a "convertibility principle" (e.g., a commodity standard). Macroeconomists frequently mismatch theory and regime.. Further, today's regime is not merely a hybrid, but, according to Leijonhufvud, is really no standard at all (Leijonhufvud, 1983b, p. 27).

Klein (1975) is an example of empirical work informed by analysis in terms of alternative regimes. Among other things, Klein found that public recognition of a change in monetary regimes occurs slowly and over a long period of time. Consequently, in a transition from a regime of stable prices to one of high and variable inflation, the public may be caught unaware or else may anticipate a return to the old regime. During a transition phase, inflation may be largely unanticipated. Once there is public recognition of the change in regimes, however, inflation will tend to be anticipated. If there is a great deal of unpredictability in prices, however, expectations formation will be difficult and costly. Thus, a regime in which inflation is higher on average but more predictable might, *ceteris paribus*, be preferred to a highly unpredictable but lower average inflation rate (if such a choice is possible).

The monetary regime approach may also explain why, under the gold standard, monetary growth was frequently comparatively large over periods of months and even years with no acceleration in price inflation. What would be an alarming rate of monetary growth under a pure fiduciary standard is not worrisome under a commodity standard, so as long as people believe in the government's commitment to the standard. A standard is an investment in creating public trust that rules and goals will be adhered to (cf. Klein, 1975, pp. 482–3). The investment may take the tangible form of real resources held as reserves, or it may involve legal limits on policy-makers that can be relaxed only at great cost (e.g., constitutional rules). The trust cannot, however, be obtained costlessly.

These theoretical insights cannot be incorporated into models by assuming the availability of information to all agents at low cost and independent of the character of monetary institutions. The Hayekian criterion for information, recently restated by Frydman, together with an institutional approach to monetary analysis, represents a promising avenue of analytical inquiry (cf. O'Driscoll, 1984a).

We have focused on expectational issues because they are important for any theory of economic fluctuations. The main conclusions of our theory do *not* depend, however, on expectational errors – at least not in the conventional sense. Most theories of economic fluctuations attribute deviations from trend rates of growth of economic variables to expectational error. If, for instance there is a monetary innovation, then prices accelerate, output increases, and unemployment declines. There are real effects only because transactors misperceive purely nominal changes as real changes. Workers, for example, supply more labor as wage rates rise, in the mistaken belief that real wage rates have risen. The process is reversed once expectations are revised.

Expectational errors may be sufficient, but they are surely not necessary for the existence of fluctuations in economic activity. Monetary shocks – changes in the rate of monetary growth – have real effects quite apart from those generated by expectational error. These shocks have distributional and allocational effects, which we have labelled "Cantillon effects." In the model presented in this chapter, these consequences depend on capital-theoretic considerations first adduced in the previous chapter (and simplified greatly in our type 1 and type 2 capital goods model). The profitability of alternative investment projects is affected by monetary policy. Entrepreneurs are not making errors in responding to these changes, though, of course, it may take time to discover the new opportunities. Indeed, entrepreneurs would be commiting mistakes if they ignored the profitable opportunities just because they had not resulted from what economists choose to call "real factors."

Inflation-induced economic growth is not sustainable. Nonetheless, there are profits to be made from exploiting temporary situations. U.S. postwar expansions average three to four years in length, time enough for entrepreneurs to reap profits. It is true, of course, that expansionary monetary policy tends to increase the profitability of projects having *longer* periods of investment. In the last chapter, we already noted that entrepreneurs in earlier stages of a production process can make profits selling to later stages, even if the latter eventually experience losses. And owners of non-specific resources (e.g., raw materials) can still profit from a *fully anticipated* cyclical episode (i.e., expansionary and recessionary phases of a cycle). Such a situation might reflect, however, one set of entrepreneurs benefiting at the expense of another set. Can a Hayekian cycle occur if fully anticipated by all?

To answer this question, we must distinguish between "micro" and "macro" prediction. Entrepreneurs may understand the macro-aspects of a cycle, which correspond roughly to the typical features of cycles. They understand that investment, the profitability of which depends on continued inflation of the money stock, cannot be sustained once the inflation ceases. Though entrepreneurs understand this at an abstract (or macro-) level, they cannot predict the exact features of the next cyclical expansion and contraction. That is, they do not know how the unique aspects of one cyclical episode will differ from the last such episode or from the "average" cycle. They lack the ability to make micro-preductions, even though they can predict the general sequence of events that will occur. These entrepreneurs have no reason to foreswear the temporary profits to be garnered in an inflationary episode. In the end, of course, all profits are purely temporary. And each individual investment opportunity carries with it a risk. For one thing, other entrepreneurs may be quicker. Or so many may have perceived an opportunity that there is a temporary excess supply at some point in the future.

From an individual perspective, then, an entrepreneur fully informed of the Austrian theory of economic cycles will face essentially the same uncertain world he always faced. Not theoretical or abstract knowledge of economic relationships, but knowledge of the circumstances of time and place is the source of profits. In any case, real effects of monetary expansion will be a compound of the distributional impact of the expansion and errors of prediction about inflation's impact. This case probably corresponds best to the real-world situation.

What if entrepreneurs could predict the exact sequence of

redistribution, relative price changes, and output responses resulting from a given monetary expansion? To hypothesize this case quickly gets us into the general paradoxes (including Morgenstern's and Richardson's) resulting from assuming perfect foresight. Nonetheless, this case presents no additional problems of logic or theory. Fully anticipated monetary shocks should have the same general implications as a fully anticipated change in tastes or a fully anticipated (exogenous) redistribution of income. The complexity of the case derives from the assumption of the self-reversing character of the allocational changes. And, as in other instances of perfect foresight models, one cannot begin to specify what one entrepreneur will do without also specifying what all others will do. "Perfect foresight" here, as elsewhere, implies perfect prediction of the actions of all other relevant parties. It really is the Holmes–Moriarity example multiplied to an *n*-player case. If the players were not paralyzed by their dilemma, then they presumably would make investment commitments that have a positive present value over the cycle or relevant planning horizon. They would not get caught unaware by the downturn, though they might experience accounting losses in some periods.

Let us put the case starkly, and shorn of some of the capital-theoretic issues emphasized heretofore. Assume that the Federal Open Market Committee (FOMC) decides to engage in an aggressive monetary expansion over the next two years. It breaks with tradition by immediately announcing its intentions in great detail. Included in this announcement is the statement that it is simply going to give all the newly created money to Roger Garrison. Over the next two years, the money supply will increase by 50 percent. Assume further that no one doubts the Fed's intensions, etc. (The twelve district banks post a bond equal to the proposed increase in the money supply.) Once all adjustments are made, prices will have risen approximately 50 percent.

Will the fact that the subsequent price inflation is fully anticipated make Mr Garrison other than a rich man? Surely not. (Those who do doubt this conclusion should not be willing to pay a positive price to take Garrison's place.) In fact, the openness of the procedure clarifies the way in which Garrison benefits. It also clarifies that, except for though experiments *à la* Hume or Friedman, the process of expanding the money supply involves redistribution of wealth. Though the redistribution may or may not be random and unpredictable, it is redistribution nonetheless. (The non-randomness of the redistribution constitutes the empirical content of our hypothesis.)

"Surely," says the neoclassical economist, "the anticipation of the event will offset the effects." The answer is "no," if we adhere consistently to the assumptions of economic decentralization and competition. Garrison, we assume, is either a canny Scotsman or closely related to one. He will not pay more for his purchases just because he is wealthier. Given his greater wealth, he may, of course, purchase higher-quality products. His wealth elasticity of demand is not equal to one for every good. To pursue this line of reasoning would call into questions even the long-run neutrality of money (ef. Mises, 1953), a point that we are not interested in pursuing here.

If the rest of us could get together and, as it were, gang up on Garrison, we could nullify his wealth gain. That is, every potential supplier could agree to charge Garrison – *and only Garrison* – prices that are 50 percent higher than before. We would however, no longer be describing a competitive environment. If some of us were parties to such an agreement, good neoclassical theory would remind us that the canny Scotsmen among us would cheat on the agreement. Garrison would retain his wealth gain, not because printing pieces of paper creates wealth, but because monetary expansion can transfer wealth.

The problem of anticipating monetary shocks and their effects surely exacerbates the costs of inflation (see below). Neither entrepreneurs nor the monetary authority can predict the micro-details of a given policy change. Expectational errors probably account for a significant portion of the real effects of inflation. At the theoretical level, however, it is important to distinguish between these real effects and those arising from the distributional consequences of inflation and deflation of the money stock. For one thing, the distinction helps one avoid arid debates on whether fully anticipated monetary policy matters.

In a sense, we are having our cake and eating it too. In emphasizing the importance of Cantillon effects, we can also recognize the role of the unexpected component of policy changes. Thus, we agree that, as an inflationary policy comes to be anticipated, its effects diminish. We do not follow the rational expectations theorist or even the monetarists in concluding that real effects of monetary expansion and contraction can be eliminated once agents understand the structure of the economy or the causal nexus among economic variables. This strikes as analagous to suggesting that the horrors of war would be eliminated once citizens understood the causes of war.

We are not, of course, suggesting that the FOMC meets every six weeks and decides whom to enrich the following period. To the extent that wealth and income redistributions accompany monetary accelerations and decelerations, these effects are undoubtedly no part of the intention of the members of that committee. Resulting redistributions and misallocations may be offset by other factors or benefits. Nonetheless, it is important that all the significant effects of inflation be understood before deciding to engage in some of it. Further, if we are correct, then the conventional wisdom on the "costs" of fighting inflations is fundamentally wrong.

Unsustainable monetary expansions generate resource misallocation. The pattern of investment in such expansions is self-reversing; once the growth of money ceases or even decelerates, the pattern will begin to be reversed. The "costs" have been incurred in the expansionary phase. That misallocations occur during the expansionary phase of a business cycle is one thesis of rational expectations models with which we are in complete agreement. The recession phase constitutes the recognition of costs already incurred and errors already made. Ending an inflation does not generate costs but reveals those already incurred. This is true unless an actual monetary *contraction* is imposed on the previous expansion. Of course, without specifying a regime, it is impossible to say exactly what would constitute a contractionary policy. With an endogenous component of the money supply, a fall in the stock of money may merely reflect the decreased demand for credit in a contractionary phase of the cycle. If authorities attempt to offset any decline, they may perpetuate what they are attempting to remedy.

Three basic policies have been derived from the Austrian development of Wicksell's theory. Hayek (1967a) argued for maintaining the amount of spending ($M \times V$) constant. He suggested that this would entail a rough constancy in factor prices, and, in a growing economy, a falling price level of final output. Rothbard (1963) argued for constancy in the money supply, all but insuring secular deflation. More recently, however, White (1984) has criticized any inflexible monetary rule derived from *a priori* theorizing. He argues for a system of free banking, in which the quantity of money is market-determined by the interaction of competitive suppliers (unregulated banks) and demanders (the nonbank public). From our perspective, the question is not yet settled. We do expect the renewed interest in monetary regimes to help provide a resolution, if not to offer new alternatives.

## CONCLUSION

In this chapter we have attempted to adopt a subjectivist and micro-economic approach to monetary theory. We have argued that, from Carl Menger down to contemporary figures, subjectivists have adopted a distinctive perspective on monetary questions. The distinctiveness of this position is most striking in the theory of economic fluctuations. In no other area is economics so dominated by macroeconomic and non-subjectivist reasoning. This is also an easy area to relate to modern monetary theories and models. For instance, modern rational expectations models have, paradoxically, incorporated essential features of an Austrian–subjectivist theory of the cycle, while at the same time representing an extreme example of anti-subjectivist reasoning. We have suggested that the essential truths of modern macroeconomics can be better presented and defended with a consistently subjectivist monetary theory.

Subjectivist economics involves a consistent development of methodological individualism, and hence is systematically microeconomic in its mode of analysis. The further one strays from this approach, the less subjectivist is one's theory. Monetary economics represents a test case. Economists have, by and large, accepted that there is something distinctive about the subject matter, which requires a separate theory if not a distinct set of economic "laws." Admittedly, any treatment of traditional monetary questions involves discussion of aggregates. Where a subjectivist draws the line, however, is in insisting that nothing other than microeconomic forces are at work. Among other things, this precludes analysis in terms of such hoary macroeconomic concepts as "the price level of output" or "output as a whole." Neither aggregate has any real existence, or has any direct impact on economic decision-making. As we have tried to demonstrate in the last two chapters, this conclusion does not merely follow from arcane methodological considerations. Traditional macro-models overlook important microeconomic phenomena. Nowhere is this more apparent than in the area of capital theory, and particularly where capital and monetary theories intersect. The subjectivist approach also involves an emphasis on real time and the indeterminacy of processes. As we have seen, Menger's theory of the evolution of money embodies the insight that the outcome of a process is not independent of the process itself. No one could have predicted the development of today's monetary institutions or monetary regime. In business cycle theory, Austrians have recognized that whatever applicability the rational expectations hypothesis has to the typical features of cycles, it cannot predict their unique features. Moreover, in real time economic fluctuations contain many surprises; agents will accordingly suffer disappointments. These insights are surely consistent not only with subjectivism, but also with our experience of economic cycles.

## NOTES

1 We are not suggesting that Hicks (1935) represents a consistent subjectivist analysis. This article is, however, a pioneering effort in the microeconomic analysis of money. It thus belongs to a literature, of which the subjectivist work of Mises, Hayek, and others is one part.

2 This section draws heavily from O'Driscoll (1984b).

3 Axel Leijonhufvud convinced us of the importance of this latter argument.

4 The government might try circumventing this problem by promulgating the price of one commodity, e.g., a representative pair of shoes. For this promulgation to be effective, however, transactors would have to perceive informational value in the decreed price. The price certainly would not have the same informational content as a market price, which conveys information about the exchange rate at which shoes are bought and sold on a regular basis. For this and other reasons, we suspect that this strategy would not work. We are aware that this line of reasoning calls into question the ability of the government to introduce a truly *fiat* currency, a doubt also expressed by Mises (1953).

5 As Hayek (1939) pointed out, equality between savings and investment is an imprecise and ultimately unsatisfactory way of describing intertemporal equilibrium. In his words, the "starting point" of a Wicksellian theory should be "(a) the intentions of all the consumers with respect to the way in which they wish to distribute at all the relevant dates all their resources (not merely their 'income') between current consumption and provision for

future consumption, and (b) the separate and independent decisions of the entrepreneurs with respect to the amounts of consumers' goods which they plan to provide at these various dates. Correspondence between these two groups of decisions would be characteristic of the kind of equilibrium which we now usually describe as a state where savings are equal to investment and with which the idea of an equilibrium rate of interest is connected." Hayek's microeconomic approach takes account of the complexities of the *multi-period* case sloughed over in the macroeconomic formulation that $S = I$. It also makes clear that "the" rate of interest is a shorthand for the whole set of relative prices involved in the intertemporal coordination process (and certainly not merely some loan rate of interest).

6 We do not mean to imply that, but for money, the economy would be in general equilibrium. Following the distinction made in the previous chapter, we are distinguishing between an economy characterized by normal entrepreneurial error and one subjected to persistent to monetary shocks. In the latter case, we argue that systematic errors are being made; and economic activity will be discoordinated in a systematic and predictable manner.

7 Any comparison between Hayek and Keynes depends on one's interpretation of Keynes. Leijonhufvud (1983a) offers an interpretation that makes Keynes seem more Wicksellian, and hence more attractive, than the "textbook" Keynes.

8 As Frydman and Phelps (1983, p. 15) make clear, this criterion is the very one first offered by Hayek (1937a).

# 10

# Some Unresolved Problems

> To me it is far more pleasant to agree than to differ; but it is impossible that one who has any regard for truth can long avoid protesting against doctrines which seem to him to be erroneous. There is ever a tendency of the most hurtful kind to allow opinions to crystallize into creeds . . . . A despotic calm is usually the triumph of error. In the republic of the sciences sedition and even anarchy are beneficial in the long run to the greatest happiness of the greatest number. *W. Stanley Jevons (1970, p. 260)*

> Scientific progress is a process of creative destruction. What is destroyed is the intellectual capital of other scientists whose resistance to accepting new contributions is not only understandable, but desirable; it is only by overcoming this resistance that the few genuine contributions can be separated from the more numerous invalid proposals. *Melvin W. Reder (1982, p. 20)*

At the beginning of this book, we suggested that what separates schools in science is the questions posed, not the answers given. Certainly in the history of economics, major innovations have occurred when theorists observing the same phenomena asked new questions about it. And these innovations have been opposed precisely because different questions were being asked. In the eighteenth century, students of government sought to devise policies that would achieve a pre-ordained social pattern and lead to an increase in national wealth. Adam Smith altered the nature of the inquiry by asking a different question. He speculated on how a nation of autonomous individuals, each seeking to increase his own wealth and well-being, could produce an overall order that was no part of anyone's intention. The answers to this question spawned what we now recognize as economic science.

A century later, Ricardianism had transformed economics into an arid set of laws of distribution and production, conjoined with a dubious population theory. Jevons, Menger, and, to a lesser extent, Walras posed a new question: What governs the choices of consumers? The resulting neoclassical analysis transformed economics into the science of choice. It also transformed economics from a predominantly macro- into a predominantly microanalytic discipline.

In this century, Keynes changed economics by inquiring into the determination of aggregate demand and national income. In a sense, economics had now come full circle back to macroanalysis and the study of distributional rather than allocational questions. The subsequent dilution of Keynesianism in the neoclassical synthesis is well known but does not change our interpretation of the Keynesian message.

Subjectivists do not perform constrained maximization problems differently than neoclassical theorists. Nor are subjectivists privy to a special mathematics that yields different solutions to familiar equations. Subjectivists do, however, ask different questions. To relate our philosophy of science to our concise history of economics, subjectivists try consistently to analyze economic phenomena within the framework first sketched out by Menger in the last century. This involves, *inter alia*, a focus on the goals and plans of individuals, not on the objects or instruments of these plans; the reconstruction of observed phenomena in terms of individual choices; and the analysis of overall outcomes as the unintended results of individual interactions.

We have attempted to steer a course, as it were, between Charybdis and Scylla. On the one hand, we have sought to avoid unnecessary controversy. We are certainly aware that, within the neoclassical edifice, many of the individual points that we have made in this book are recognized and incorporated in the work of at least some major figures. Indeed, wherever possible we have cited the orthodox literature to emphasize points of convergence or, alternatively, the subjectivist elements in neoclassical economics. Where we are critical, our purpose in citing specific individuals is not to foment controversy but to be precise in our criticism. In every instance, we have attempted to cite an author who is representative of the orthodox position on a particular point.

On the other hand, we have been cognizant of the necessity of clearly stating the differences that do exist between subjectivists and their neoclassical brethren. It should not be surprising if there were substantial overlap between Austrian or subjectivist economics and neoclassical orthodoxy. The Austrians were one of the three founding schools of modern economics; and, in fact, there are more Austrian elements in neoclassical economis than are recognized in textbooks (including, via Lord Robbins, the very conception of economics as the study of the allocation of scarce means among competing ends). The reader may at times wonder why we have not emphasized this overlap more. The simple reason is that the subjectivist analysis would then have been obscured. Our purpose in writing this book was to restate and advance subjectivist economics. This goal would scarcely have been promoted by presenting an exhaustive list of neoclassical propositions with which we agree.

There is a "sponginess" to neoclassical economics that enables it to absorb divergent elements around it without ever emphasizing their main points. These fringe ideas become footnotes to which theorists can refer as evidence that they have taken the ideas into account. For instance, Keynes' liquidity preference concept is incorporated in neoclassical economics as an interest-elastic demand for money. The idea has been formally incorporated, yet Keynes' main point has been lost: the *instability* of liquidity preference. Nor are the effects of an unstable liquidity preference on interest rates and capital markets adequately treated in orthodox analysis. In terms of our own ideas, we have chosen to compare them to the dominant themes of neoclassical economics and not to unrepresentative footnote presentations.

We have also attempted to strike a balance between, on the one hand, presenting theoretical and methodological abstractions and, on the other hand, offering examples or applications. We did not wish to overwhelm the reader with too much of the former, or to confuse him with too much of the latter. If, however, we were to characterize the subjectivist literature generally, we would have to admit that it has been relatively long on methodological prescriptions and short on applications. It is time to do the difficult work of applying subjectivist ideas to actual problems. We are aware that most of our applications involve only a sketchy analysis of a particular problem. In almost every case, more work needs to be done. We believe, however, that the time is ripe for applying subjectivist insights to current economic problems. Accordingly, we outline here some areas where we think the returns would be particularly high.

First, we would mention the whole area of law and economics. We do so not only because we have each have written in this area, but because it is a field that virtually demands the theoretical–institutional approach advocated by subjectivists. If any area involves a blending of theoretical and institutional analysis, it is law and economics. Nowhere else is an institutionless analysis less fruitful and more destructive. For instance, a good bit of ink has been spilled on the question of the efficiency of common law. This view, first of all, treats an undesigned order as if it were the creation of individuals; and, second, it puts the theoretical cart before the horse. What is efficient depends on the institutional environment. One can inquire whether a particular institution is consistent with a whole set of institutions (as when one analyzes the consistency of a common-law doctrine with all others). It is quite meaningless, however, to ask whether an entire set of institutions – like the property rights structure – is efficient. This question treats as "givens" conditions, that change *mutatis mutandis* as property rights evolve (Rizzo, 1980b; O'Driscoll, 1980). Of course, having made this point, we have only opened up a research program, not completed one. Needless to say, an important aspect of that program involves a theory of these institutions that does not treat them as the outcome of a collective constrained-maximization problem. The next item on our subjectivist research agenda is a suggestion for a start in this direction.

The analysis of money as an evolved social institution is a quintessential subjectivist topic. Viewing money as the unintended outcome of a market process involves thinking about money in a fundamentally different way (Frankel, 1977). Money then becomes not something that individuals can shape or control, but an institution or order to which they must accommodate themselves. In this process of accommodation, individuals will inadvertently affect the monetary order. The resulting monetary "innovations" will not, however, be changes that individuals have deliberately adopted: rather, these changes will represent evolutionary adaptation. Even when dramatic choices are made, as when a gold standard is substituted for a fiat money system, or fixed exchange rates are substituted for flexible exchange rates, policy-makers have not created new monetary institutions so much as they have moved the country from one given environment or regime to another. Policy-makers do not necessarily have a great deal of explicit control over the characteristics of either environment. They may surely take actions that affect their environment, but this does not imply that they can control the outcome. If we may suggest an analogy, we each have options with respect to which kind of climate we live in. We choose by moving from one climate to another, however, not by altering the climate of the area in which we presently live. The sum total of individual actions may affect the climatic environment, but even collective action will not enable individuals to effect a desired outcome.

The monetary approach suggested here has policy implications, of which two can be mentioned. The first concerns the nature of monetary rules. Every monetary system has or can be described by rules, including rules governing the growth of the supply of money. If a monetary system is an evolved economic order, then it is difficult to imagine how these rules could be externally imposed or chosen exogenously. The rules themselves, including the money growth rules, must be the product of an evolutionary process – a process of economic adaptation. Macroeconomic planning for a fixed rate of growth of the money supply has all the allure of microeconomic planning – and all the pitfalls, if recent history is any guide.

The second implication is more specific, though it is related to the first one. If the monetary institutions and money itself are part of the market system, then it is difficult to imagine how the quantity of money could be exogenous or independent of individual choices. Empirical evidence aside, there are strong *a priori* reasons to suspect the endogeneity of the money supply. Of course, empirically we may recognize that monetary questions have historically become political questions, and that political intervention leads to exogenous influences on the quantity or rate of growth of the money supply. This recognition puts the question of the exogeneity of the money supply in quite a different light, however, than that produced by, say, monetarist analysis. In the evolutionary view, money is a market institution and its supply is endogenously determined. There may be exogenous factors, as there are exogenous factors like fortuitous inventions in economic growth. An unexpected discovery of new sources of base money would be an example of a exogenous monetary change. For the supply of money to be strictly exogenous, however, it must be transformed from an economic or market institution into one subject to rigid political control. And market forces will constantly be at work offsetting the effects of these controls.

We think that an evolutionary approach to money has more explanatory power for analyzing recent financial market innovations, including the multiplication of close money substitutes (if not money themselves), than a positive theory of exogenous money determination.

Finally, we turn once again to the topic of competition. Economists analyzing competition as a process need to develop a theory of nonprice information structures. Neoclassical formulations rely almost exclusively on prices to convey information. This is untenable as soon as one incorporates real time and expectations in the analysis. Spot-price movements no longer convey unambiguous signals. Even were futures markets to be "complete," the passage of time would upset any temporary intertemporal equilibrium. Not only do producers require information about trade-offs, but they need to know how other producers will react to these prices. No matter how rich the array of futures markets producers confront Keynes' beauty-contest problem.

Entrepreneurs are not, of course, paralyzed by this informational void. Their ability to plan in a tolerably stable environment indicates the existence of other, nonprice, sources of information. There must be market institutions and rules of thumb that "fill in" some of the information not provided by prices. This realization requires, however, that we rethink our attitude toward familiar institutions and practices. For some of the required information will be about product characteristics, production plans, and even prices charged by competitors. Competition may, then, depend on the existence of institutions and practices presently regarded as non-competitive or anti-competitive.

In chapter 5 we discussed endogenous uncertainty in the guise of Keynes' beauty contest and the Holmes–Moriarity story. We saw there that, as long as independent decision-making remains independent, the search for more knowledge does not reduce uncertainty. It merely heightens the level of guessing and counterguessing. In this sense, then, endogenous uncertainty is ineradicable. On the other hand, as we have previously intimated, endogenous uncertainty can be reduced or eliminated if actors (agree to) follow "arbitrary conventions." Independent firms, for example, face endogenous uncertainty in the form of trying to guess the price decisions of their rivals. In "oligopolistic" markets, the price that any given firm should charge will depend, in part, on the prices that he expects other firms to charge. Their decisions will in turn depend on what he is expected to decide. Thus, the expected price distributions faced by firms are endogenous; that is, they arise from the very operation of the market process. One "arbitrary convention" or institution that can reduce this form of uncertainty is the exchange of reliable price information among the rival firms.

Firms are subject to both exogenous and endogenous uncertainty. While exogenous risk may be transformed, by definition nothing can be done to eliminate it. Endogenous uncertainty arises from the very operation of the market. At least in principle, some actions can be taken to lessen this type of uncertainty. Consider uncertainty about what price to charge. At any given moment, firms observe a distribution of prices charged by their competitors, a distribution that need by no means be normal. Firm owners are aware, moreover, that they do not have complete information about prices. The variance of prices reflects *inter alia*, temporary cost advantages, special discounting, and product differentiation.

Each firm owner desires information that will improve his planning ability. This would include information about the mean and variance of the price distribution, product characteristics, amounts sold at these prices, etc. All of this information is either given or superfluous in perfectly competitive models, but is available only at some cost in competitive markets. Though he would never describe it in this way, the entrepreneur is seeking information about equilibrium conditions in his market. Though he may have quite different uses in mind for this information, a competitive firm owner requires much of the same information needed by a cartel.

By reducing price uncertainty, information-sharing arrangements may reduce the variance of prices. If firms are risk-averse, this may also reduce the mean of the price distribution. This latter point is emphasized in Dewey (1979), while Rizzo (1984) presents the more general argument.

None of this sanctions other aspects of collusive arrangements, especially not legal barriers to entry. Indeed, the existence or absence of legal blockages to competition would surely be crucial in ascertaining empirically whether an exchange of information were facilitating collusion or abetting competition.

We are not arguing that the exchange of price information would be generally characteristic of competitive industries, though some of it probably occurs in every industry (including among economists). We are suggesting, however, that competitive markets will generally rely on institutions and practices to generate information assumed in neoclassical analysis to be given by price signals alone. Sharing of price information may be one of these practices, which may also be institutionalized. A theory leaving no room for these nonprice sources of information is an impoverished – indeed, a biased – analysis of competition.

In conclusion, we have attempted in this book to offer a sample of research topics whose development would especially benefit from a consistent application of subjectivist economics. This sample is certainly not meant to be exhaustive, reflecting, as it does, the constraints both of space and of the authors' own interests. We will count this book a success if readers begin adding their own items to the research agenda.

# Bibliography


Ackerman, R. (1976) *The Philosophy of Karl Popper* Amherst, Mass.: University of Massachusetts Press.

Alchian, A. A. and Demsetz, H. (1972) "Production, Information Costs and Economic Organization." *American Economic Review* 62: 777–95. Reprinted in *Economic Forces at Work: Selected Works by Armen A. Alchian* Indianapolis: Liberty Press, 1977.

Allais, M. (1966) "A Restatement of the Quantity Theory of Money." *American Economic Review* 56: 1123–57.

Allen, P. M. (1994) "Evolutionary Complex Systems: Models of Technology Change." In L. Leydesdorff and P. van der Besselaar (eds.) *Evolutionary Economics and Chaos Theory* New York: St. Martin's Press.

Arrow, K. J. (1959) "Toward a Theory of Price Adjustment." In M. Abramovitz *et al.* (eds.) *The Allocation of Economic Resources* Stanford, Cal.: Stanford University Press.

Arrow, K. J. (1968) "Economic Equilibrium." In D. L. Sills (ed.) *International Encyclopedia of the Social Sciences* 4: 376–88. London and New York: Macmillan and Free Press.

Arrow, K. J. (1974) *The Limits of Organization* New York: W. W. Norton & Company.

Arrow, K. J. and Hahn, F. H. (1971) *General Competitive Analysis* San Francisco: Holden-Day.

Arthur, B. (1990) "Positive Feedbacks in the Economy" *Scientific American* 262: 92–9.

Barreto, H. (1989) *The Entrepreneur in Microeconomic Theory: Disappearance and Explanation* London: Routledge.

Baumol, W. J. (1965) *Economic Theory and Operations Analysis* (2nd edn.) Englewood Cliffs, NJ: Prentice-Hall.

Baumol, W. J. (1972) "On Taxation and the Control of Externalities." *American Economic Review* 62: 307–22.

Bausor, R. (1981) "Time and the Structure of Economic Analysis." Unpublished paper, University of Massachusetts at Amherst.

Becker, G. S. (1965) "A Theory of the Allocation of Time." *Economic Journal* 75: 493–517.

Becker, G. S. (1971) *Economic Theory* New York: Alfred A. Knopf.

Becker, G. S. (1976a) *The Economic Approach to Human Behavior* Chicago: University of Chicago Press.

Becker, G. S. (1976b) "Toward a More General Theory of Regulation: Comment." *Journal of Law and Economics* 19: 211–40.

Begg, D. K. H. (1982) *The Rational Expectations Revolution in Macroeconomics. Theories and Evidence* Baltimore: Johns Hopkins University Press.

Berger, P. L. and Luckmann, T. (1966) *The Social Construction of Reality* New York: Anchor Books, Doubleday & Co.

Bergson, H. (1910) *Time and Free Will: An Essay on the Immediate Data of Consciousness* Trans. F. L. Pogson, London: George & Allen Unwin.

Bergson, H. (1911) *Creative Evolution* New York: Henry Holt.

Bergson, H. (1920) *Mind-Energy* New York: Henry Holt.

Bergson, H. (1946) "The Possible and the Real." In *The Creative Mind* Trans. Mabel L. Andison. Westport, Conn.: Greenwood Press.

Birner, J. and van Zijp, R. (eds.) (1994) *Hayek, Coordination, and Evolution* London: Routledge.

Blackstone, W. (1803) *Commentaries on the Laws of England* Book 4, London: T. Codell and W. Davies.

Boettke, P. J. (1990a) "Institutions and Individuals: A Review of Geoffrey Hodgson, *Economics and Institutions*." *Critical Review* 4: 10–26.

Boettke, P. J. (1990b) "Interpretive Reasoning and the Study of Social Life." *Methodus: Bulletin of the International Network for Economic Method* 2: 35–45.

Boettke, P. J. (1990c) *The Political Economy of Soviet Socialism: The Formative Years, 1918–1928* Boston: Kluwer Academic Press.

Boettke, P. J. (1993) *Why Perestroika Failed: The Politics and Economics of Socialist Transformation* London: Routledge.

Boettke, P. J. (1994) "The Reform Trap in Politics and Economics in the Former Communist Economies." *Journal des Economistes et des Etudes Humaines* 5: 267–93.

Boettke, P. J. Horwitz, S. and Prychitko, D. L. (1994) "Beyond

Equilibrium Economics: Reflections on the Uniqueness of the Austrian Tradition." In P. J. Boettke and D. L. Prychitko (eds.) *The Market Process: Essays in Contemporary Austrian Economics* Aldershot, England: Edward Elgar.

Böhm-Bawerk, E. v. (1959 [1889]) *Capital and Interest*, 3 vols. Trans. G. D. Huncke and H. F. Sennholz. South Holland, Ill.: Libertarian Press.

Bork, R. H. (1978) *The Antitrust Paradox: A Policy at War with Itself* New York: Basic Books.

Boulding, K. E. (1966) "The Economics of Knowledge and the Knowledge of Economics." *American Economic Review, Papers and Proceedings* 56: 1–13.

Briggs, J. A. (1981) "Fly Me, I'm Little." *Forbes* 27 April: 112–18.

Buchanan, J. M. (1969) *Cost and Choice* Chicago: Markham.

Buchanan, J. M. (1979) "Natural and Artifactual Man." In *What Should Economists Do?* Indianapolis: Liberty Press.

Buchanan, J. M. (1982a) "The Domain of Subjective Economics: Between Predictive Science and Moral Philosophy." In I. M. Kirzner (ed.) *Method, Process, and Austrian Economics: Essays in Honor of Ludwig von Mises* Lexington, Mass.: Lexington Books, D. C. Heath & Co.

Buchanan, J. M. (1982b) "Order Defined in the Process of its Emergence." *Literature of Liberty* 5: 5.

Buchanan, J. M. (1986) "Order Defined in the Process of Its Emergence." In *Liberty, Market and State: Political Economy in the 1980s* New York: New York University Press.

Burczak, T. A. (1994) "The Postmodern Moments of F. A. Hayek's Economics." *Economics and Philosophy* 10: 31–58.

Butos, W. and Koppl, R. (1993) "Hayekian Expectations: Theory and Empirical Applications." *Constitutional Political Economy* 4: 303–29.

Caldwell, B. J. (1982) *Beyond Positivism: Economic Methodology in the Twentieth Century* London: George Allen & Unwin.

Capek, M. (1961) *The Philosophical Impact of Contemporary Physics* Princeton: D. Van Nostrand.

Capek, M. (1971) *Bergson and Modern Physics* Boston Studies in the Philosophy of Science, vol. VIII, Dordrecht, Holland: D. Reidel.

Cassel, G. (1903) *The Nature and Necessity of Interest* London: Macmillan.

Choi, Y. B. (1993) *Paradigms and Conventions* Ann Arbor: University of Michigan Press.

Clair, R. T. and O'Driscoll, G. P. Jr. (1993) "Learning from One Another: The U.S. and European Banking Experience." *Journal of Multinational Management* 2: 33–52.

Clower, R. W. (1965) "The Keynesian Counter-Revolution: A Theoretical Appraisal." In F. H. Hahn and F. P. R. Brechling (eds.) *The Theory of Interest Rates* London: Macmillan. Also in R. W. Clower (ed.) *Monetary Theory* Harmondsworth, Middlesex: Penguin Books, 1969.

Coase, R. H. (1937) "The Nature of the Firm." *Economica* n. s. 4: 386–405.

Coase, R. H. (1960) "The Problem of Social Cost." *Journal of Law and Economics* 3: 1–40.

Coddington, A. (1975) "Creaking Semaphore and Beyond: A Consideration of Shackle's 'Epistemics and Economics'." *British Journal for the Philosophy of Science* 26: 151–63.

Cohen, L. J. (1977) *The Probable and the Provable* Oxford: Clarendon Press.

Colonna, M. and Hagemann, H. (eds.) (1994a) *Money and Business Cycles: The Economics of F. A. Hayek* vol. 1, Aldershot, England: Edward Elgar.

Colonna, M. and Hagemann, H. (eds.) (1994b) *Capitalism, Socialism and Knowledge: The Economics of F. A. Hayek* vol. 2, Aldershot, England: Edward Elgar.

Comte, A. (1988 [1855]) *Introduction to Positive Philosophy* Trans. F. Ferre. Indianapolis, IN: Hackett.

Cowan, R. and Rizzo, M. (1995) "The Causal-Genetic Tradition and Economic Theory." Unpublished Manuscript at the University of Western Ontario and New York University.

Cowen, T. and Kroszner, R. (1994) *Explorations in the New Monetary Economics* Oxford: Basil Blackwell.

Dahrendorf, R. (1968) *Essays in the Theory of Society* Stanford: Stanford University Press.

Davidson, P. (1981) "Post Keynesian Economics: Solving the Crises in Economic Theory." *The Public Interest*, Special Issue: 123–38.

Demsetz, H. (1969) "Information and Efficiency: Another Viewpoint." *Journal of Law and Economics* 12: 1–22.

Demsetz, H. (1982) "Barriers to Entry." *American Economic Review* 72: 45–57.

Denzau, A. T. and North, D. C. (1994) "Shared Mental Models: Ideologies and Institutions." *Kyklos* 47: 3–31.

Dewey, D. (1979) "Information, Entry and Welfare: The Case for

Collusion." *American Economic Review* 69: 587–94.

Dolan, E. G. (ed.) (1976) *The Foundations of Modern Austrian Economics* Kansas City: Sheed & Ward.

Doty, L. (1977) "New Pacts Reflect Commuter Success." *Aviation Week & Space Technology* 4 April: 38.

Epstein, R. A. (1982) "Private Property and the Public Domain: The Case of Antitrust." In J. R. Pennock and J. W. Chapman (eds.) *Ethics, Economics and the Law* New York: Nomos, New York University Press.

Faber, M. (ed.) (1986) *Studies in Austrian Capital Theory, Investment and Time* Berlin: Springer-Verlag.

Fetter, F. A. (1977) *Capital, Interest, and Rent: Essays in the Theory of Distribution* (ed.) M. N. Rothbard. Kansas City: Sheed Andrews & McMeel.

Feyerabend, P. K. (1975) *Against Method* London: Verso.

Fisher, F. M. (1983) *Disequilibrium Foundations of Equilibrium Economics* Cambridge: Cambridge University Press.

Frankel, S. H. (1977) *Money: Two Philosophies* Oxford: Basil Blackwell.

Friedman, M. (1953) "The Methodology of Positive Economics." In *Essays in Positive* Economics Chicago: University of Chicago Press.

Friedman, M. (1977) "The Monetarist Controversy: Discussions by Milton Friedman and Franco Modigliani." *Federal Reserve Bank of San Francisco Economic Review Supplement.*

Frydman, R. (1982) "Towards an Understanding of Market Processes: Individual Expectations, Learning, and Convergence to Rational Expectations Equilibrium." *American Economic Review* 72: 652–68.

Frydman, R., O'Driscoll, G. P. Jr. and Schotter, A. (1982) "Rational Expectations of Government Policy: An Application of Newcomb's Problem." *Southern Economic Journal* 49: 311–19.

Frydman, R. and Phelps, (eds.) (1983) *Individual Forecasting and Aggregate Outcomes: "Rational Expectations" Examined* New York: Cambridge University Press.

Gallaway, L. and Vedder, R. (1987) "Wages, Prices and Employment: Von Mises and the Progressives." *Review of Austrian Economics* 2: 33–80.

Garrison, R. W. (1978) "Austrian Macroeconomics: A Diagrammatical Exposition." In L. M. Spadaro (ed.) *New Directions in Austrian Economics* Kansas City: Sheed Andrews & McMeel.

Garrison, R. W. (1979) "Comment: Waiting in Vienna." In M. J. Rizzo (ed.) *Time, Uncertainty, and Disequilibrium* Lexington, Mass.: Lexington Books, D. C. Heath & Co.

Garrison, R. W. (1984) "Time and Money: The Universals of Macroeconomic Theorizing." *Journal of Macroeconomics* (forthcoming).

Gjertsen, D. (1989) *Science and Philosophy: Past and Present* London: Penguin.

Gordon, D. F. and Hynes, A. (1970) "On the Theory of Price Dynamics." In E. S. Phelps (ed.) *Microeconomic Foundations of Employment and Inflation Theory* New York: W. W. Norton.

Grossman, S. J. (1976) "On the Efficiency of Competitive Stock Markets Where Traders Have Diverse Information." *Journal of Finance* 31: 573–85.

Grossman, S. J. (1977) "The Existence of Futures Markets, Noisy Rational Expectations and Informational Externalities." *Review of Economic Studies* 44: 431–49.

Grossman, S. J. and Stiglitz, J. E. (1976) "Information and Competitive Price Systems." *American Economic Review* 66: 246–53.

Hahn, F. H. (1952) "Expectations and Equilibrium." *Economic Journal* 62: 802–19.

Hahn, F. H. (1973) *On the Notion of Equilibrium in Economics* Cambridge University Inaugural Lecture. Cambridge: Cambridge : University Press.

Hahn, F. H. (1980) "General Equilibrium Theory." *The Public Interest*, Special Issue: 123–38.

Hall, R. E. (1982) "The Government and the Monetary Unit." NBER *Working Paper* no. 159 Stanford: Stanford University Press.

Harcourt, G. C. and Laing, N. F. (eds.) (1971) *Capital and Interest* Harmondsworth, Middlesex: Penguin Books.

Harper, D. (1994) "A New Approach to Modelling Endogenous Learning Processes in Economic Theory.' In Peter Boettke and Mario Rizzo (eds.) *Advances in Austrian Economics*, vol. 1 Greenwich, CT: JAI Press.

Harper, D. (1996) *Entrepreneurship and the Market Process: An Inquiry into the Growth of Knowledge* London and New York: Routledge.

Hausman, D. M. (1981) *Capital, Profits, and Prices* New York: Columbia University Press.

Hayek, F. A. (1932) "A Note on the Development of the Doctrine of

'Forced Savings'." *Quarterly Journal of Economics* 47: 123–33. Reprinted in *Profits, Interest and Investment; and Other Essays on the Theory of Industrial Fluctuations* London: George Routledge & Sons, 1939. This volume reprinted in Clifton, NJ by Augustus M. Kelley, 1975.

Hayek, F. A. (1935a) "The Nature and History of the Problem." In F. A. Hayek (ed.) *Collectivist Economic Planning: Critical Studies on the Possibilities of Socialism* London: Routledge & Kegan Paul. This volume reprinted in Clifton, NJ by Augustus M. Kelly, 1975. This essay also appears in *Individualism and Economic Order* Chicago: University of Chicago Press, 1948.

Hayek, F. A. (1935b) "The State of the Debate (1935)." In F. A. Hayek (ed.) *Collectivist Economic Planning: Critical Studies on the Possibilities of Socialism* London: Routledge & Kegan Paul. This volume reprinted in Clifton, NJ by Augustus M. Kelly, 1975. This essay also appears in *Individualism and Economic Order* Chicago: University of Chicago Press, 1948.

Hayek, F. A. (1937a) "Economics and Knowledge." *Economica* n.s. 4: 33–54. Reprinted in *Individualism and Economic Order* Chicago: University of Chicago Press, 1948.

Hayek, F. A. (1937b) "Investment that Raises the Demand for Capital." *Review of Economic Statistics* 19: 174–7. Reprinted in *Profits, Interest and Investment; and Other Essays on the Theory of Industrial Fluctuations* London: George Routledge & Sons, 1939. This volume reprinted in Clifton, NJ by Augustus M. Kelley, 1975.

Hayek, F. A. (1939) "Price Expectations, Monetary Disturbances and Malinvestment." In *Profits, Interest and Investment; and Other Essays on the Theory of Industrial Fluctuations* London: George Routledge & Sons. This volume reprinted in Clifton, NJ by Augustus M. Kelley, 1975.

Hayek, F. A. (1940) "Socialist Calculation: The Competitive 'Solution'." *Economica* n.s. 7: 125–49. Reprinted in *Individualism and Economic Order* Chicago: University of Chicago Press, 1948.

Hayek, F. A. (1941) *The Pure Theory of Capital* Chicago: University of Chicago Press.

Hayek, F. A. (1944) *The Road to Serfdom* Chicago: University of Chicago Press.

Hayek, F. A. (1945) "The Use of Knowledge in Society." *American Economic Review* 35: 519–30. Reprinted in *Individualism and Economic Order* Chicago: University of Chicago Press, 1948.

Hayek, F. A. (1948a) "The Meaning of Competition." In

*Individualism and Economic Order Chicago*: University of Chicago Press.

Hayek, F. A (1948b) “The Use of Knowledge in Society.” In *Individualism and Economic Order* Chicago: University of Chicago Press.

Hayek, F. A. (1955) *The Counter-Revolution of Science* Glencoe, Ill.: Free Press.

Hayek, F. A. (1965) “Kinds of Rationalism.” *The Economic Studies Quarterly* (Tokyo) vol. 15, no. 3. Reprinted in *Studies in Philosophy, Politics and Economics* Chicago: University of Chicago Press, 1967.

Hayek, F. A. (1966 [1933]) *Monetary Theory and the Trade Cycle* New York: Augustus M. Kelley.

Hayek, F. A. (1967a [1935]) *Prices and Production* (2nd edn.) New York: Augustus M. Kelly.

Hayek, F. A. (1967b) “Degrees of Explanation.” In *Studies in Philosophy, Politics and Economics* Chicago: University of Chicago Press.

Hayek, F. A. (1967c) “The Theory of Complex Phenomena.” In *Studies in Philosophy, Politics and Economics* Chicago: University of Chicago Press.

Hayek, F. A. (1969) “Three Elucidations of the Ricardo Effect.” *Journal of Political Economy*, 77: 274–85. Reprinted in New Studies in *Philosophy, Politics, Economics and the History of Ideas* Chicago: University of Chicago Press, 1978.

Hayek, F A. (1973) *Law, Legislation and Liberty: Rules and Order*, vol. 1. Chicago: University of Chicago Press.

Hayek, F. A. (1976) *Law, Legislation and Liberty: The Mirage of Social Justice*, vol. 2. Chicago: University of Chicago Press.

Hayek, F. A. (1978) “Competition as a Discovery Procedure.” In *New Studies in Philosophy, Politics, Economics and the History of Ideas* Chicago: University of Chicago Press.

Hayek, F. A. (1988) *The Fatal Conceit* Chicago: University of Chicago Press.

Heiner, R. (1983) “The Origin of Predictable Behavior.” *American Economic Review*, 73: 560–95.

Hempel, C. G. and Oppenheim, P. (1965) “Studies in the Logic of Explanation.” In C. G. Hempel, *Aspects of Scientific Explanation* Glencoe, Ill.: Free Press.

Hey, J. D. (1981) *Economics in Disequilibrium* New York: New York University Press.

Hicks, J. (1935) "A Suggestion for Simplifying the Theory of money." *Economica* n.s. 2: 1–19.

Hick, J. R. (1965) *Capital Growth* Oxford: Oxford University Press.

Hicks, J. R. (1967) "The Hayek Story." In *Critical Essays in Monetary Theory* Oxford: Clarendon Press.

Hicks, J. R. (1974) *The Crisis in Keynesian Economics* New York: Basic Books.

Hicks, J. R. (1976) "Some Questions of Time in Economics." In A. M. Tan, F. M. Westfield and J. S. Worley (eds.) *Evolution, Welfare, and Time in Economics* Lexington, Mass.: Lexington Books, D. C. Heath & Co.

High, J. (1986). "Equilibration and Disequilibration in the Market Process." In Israel M. Kirzner (ed.) *Subjectivism, Intelligibility and Economic Understanding: Essays in Honor of Ludwig Lachmann* New York: NYU Press.

Hood, W. C. (1948) "Some Aspects of the Treatment of Time in Economic Theory." *Canadian Journal of Economics Political Science* 14: 453–68.

Horwitz, S. (1992) *Monetary Evolution, Free Banking and Economic Order* Boulder: Westview Press.

Horwitz, S. (1993) "Spontaneity and Design in the Evolution of Institutions." *Journal des Economistes et des Etudes Humaines* 4: 571–88.

Horwitz, S. (1994) "Subjectivism." In P. J. Boettke (ed.) *The Elgar Companion to Austrian Economics* Aldershot, England: Edward Elgar.

Howard, R. A. (1971) *Dynamic Probabilistic Systems*, 2 vols New York: John Wiley.

Hurwicz, L. (1973) "The Design of Mechanisms for Resource Allocation," *American Economic Review, Papers and Proceedings* 63: 1–30.

Husserl, E. (1964) *The Phenomenology of Internal Time-Consciousness*. Trans. J. S. Churchill, Bloomington: University of Indiana Press.

Ikeda, S. (1990) "Market-Process Theory and 'Dynamic' Theories of the Market." *Southern Economic Journal* 57: 75–92.

Ikeda, S. (forthcoming) *Dynamics of the Mixed Economy: Toward a Theory of Interventionism* London: Routledge.

James, W. (1890) *The Principles of Psychology*, vol. 1. New York: Henry Holt & Company.

Jevons, W. S. (1970 [1871]) *The Theory of Political Economy* (ed.) R. D. C. Black. New York: Penguin Books.

Jones, R. (1976) "The Origin and Development of Media of Exchange." *Journal of Political Economy* 84: 757–75 .

Kaldor, N. (1934) "A Classification Note on the Determinateness of Equilibrium." *Review of Economic Studies* 1: 122–36.

Kessel, R. A. and Alchian, A. A. (1962) "Effects of Inflation." *Journal of Political Economy* 70: 521–37. Reprinted in *Economic Forces at Work: Selected Works by Armen A. Alchian* Indianapolis: Liberty Press, 1977.

Keynes, J. M. (1964 [1936]) *The General Theory of Employment, Interest, and Money* New York: Harcourt, Brace & World.

Keynes, J. M. (1973) *Collected Writings XIV* (ed.) D. Moggridge. New York: St. Martin's Press.

Kirzner, I. M (1966) *An Essay on Capital* New York: Augustus M. Kelly.

Kirzner, I. M. (1973) *Competition and Entrepreneurship* Chicago: University of Chicago Press.

Kirzner, I. M. (1976) "Ludwig von Mises and the Theory of Capital and Interest." In L. S. Moss (ed.) *The Economics of Ludwig von Mises* Kansas City: Sheed & Ward.

Kirzner, I. M. (1976b) "Equilibrium versus Market Process." In E. G. Dolan (ed.) *The Foundations of Modern Austrian Economics* Kansas City: Sheed & Ward, Inc.

Kirzner, I. M. (1979a) *Perception, Opportunity, and Profit* Chicago: University of Chicago Press.

Kirzner, I. M. (1982) "Uncertainty, Discovery, and Human Action." In I. M. Kirzner (ed.) *Method, Process, and Austrian Economics: Essays in Honor of Ludwig von Mises* Lexington, Mass.: Lexington Books, D. C. Heath & Co.

Kirzner, I. M. (1984) "Prices, the Communication of Knowledge and the Discovery Process," unpublished manuscript.

Kirzner I. M. (1992) "Market Process Theory: In Defence of the Austrian Middle Ground." In *The Meaning of Market Process: Essays in the Development of Modern Austrian Economics* London and New York: Routledge.

Klein, B. (1975) "Our New Monetary Standard: The Measurement and Effects of Price Uncertainty, 1880–1973." *Economic Inquiry* 13: 461–84.

Klein, B. H. (1977) *Dynamic Economics* Cambridge, Mass.: Harvard University Press.

Knight, F. H. (1934) "Capital, Time, and the Interest Rate." *Economica* n.s. 1: 257–86.

Knight, F. H. (1946) "Capital and Interest." *Encyclopedia Brittanica* (14th ed.) 4: 799–801. Reprinted in American Economic Association, *Readings in the Theory of Income Distribution* Philadelphia: Blakiston.

Knight, F. H. (1960 [1937]) "Unemployment: And Mr Keynes's Revolution in Economic Theory." In H. Hazlitt (ed.) *The Critics of Keynesian Economics* New Rochelle, New York: Arlington House.

Knight, F. H. (1971 [1921]) *Risk, Uncertainty, and Profit* Chicago: University of Chicago Press.

Kolko, G. (1967) *The Triumph of Conservatism: A Reinterpretation of American History, 1900–1916* Chicago: Quadrangle.

Koppl, R. and Langlois, R. (1994) "When do Ideas Matter? A Study in the Natural Selection of Social Games." In P. Boettke and M. Rizzo (eds.) *Advances in Austrian Economics* vol. 1, Greenwich, CT: JAI Press.

Koppl, R. and Yeager, L. (1994) "Big Players and the Russian Ruble: Lessons from the Nineteenth Century." Unpublished manuscript at Fairleigh Dickinson University and Auburn University.

Kornai, J. (1971) *Anti-Equilibrium: An Economic Systems Theory and the Tasks of Research* Amsterdam: North-Holland.

Kornai, J. (1992) *The Socialist System: The Political Economy of Communism* Princeton: Princeton University Press.

Kuhn, T. S. (1970) *The Structure of Scientific Revolutions* (2nd edn.) Chicago: University of Chicago Press.

Lachmann, L. M. (1943) "The Role of Expectations in Economics as a Social Science." *Economica* n.s. 10: 12–23. Reprinted in Walker E. Grinder (ed.) *Capital, Expectations, and the Market Process* Kansas City: Sheed Andrews & McMeel.

Lachmann, L. M. (1956) *Capital and Its Structure* London: G. Bell & Sons.

Lachmann, L. M. (1959) "Professor Shackle and the Economic Significance of Time." *Metroeconomica* 11: 64–73.

Lachmann, L. M. (1969) "Methodological Individualism and the Market Process." In E. Streissler et al. (eds.) *Roads to Freedom: Essays in Honor of Friedrich von Hayek* London: Routledge & Kegan Paul.

Lachmann, L. M. (1971) *The Legacy of Max Weber* Berkeley, Cal.: Glendessary Press.

Lachmann, L. M. (1973) "*Macro-economic Thinking and the Market Economy* London: Institute of Economic Affairs, Hobart Paper no. 56.

Lachmann, L. M. (1976) "On the Central Concept of Austrian Economics: Market Process." In E. G. Dolan (ed.) *The Foundations of Modern Austrian Economics* Kansas City: Sheed & Ward.

Lachmann, L. M. (1977) "Ludwig von Mises and the Market Process." In Walter Grinder (ed.) *Capital, Expectations and the Market Process* Kansas City: Sheed, Andrews & McMeel.

Lachmann, L. M. (1978) "An Austrian Stocktaking: Unsettled Questions and Tentative Answers." In L. M. Spadaro (ed.) *New Directions in Austrian Economics* Kansas City: Sheed Andrews & McMeel.

Lachmann, L. M. (1984) "Economic Theory in Tempestuous Season." Trans. C. Dorfschmid. Unpublished (in English) manuscript, New York University.

Lachmann, L. M. (1986) *The Market as an Economic Process* Oxford: Basil Blackwell.

Lakatos, I. (1970) "Falsification and the Methodology of Scientific Research Programmes." In I. Lakatos and A. Musgrave (eds.) *Criticism and the Growth of Knowledge* Cambridge: Cambridge University Press.

Lancaster, K. J. (1966) "A New Approach to Consumer Theory." *Journal of Political Economy* 74: 132–57.

Langlois, R. N. (1982a) "Economics as a Process: Notes on the 'New Institutional Economices'." *C. V. Starr Center for Applied Economics Working Paper No. 82–21* New York University.

Langlois, R. N. (1982b) "Subjective Probability and Subjective Economics." Unpublished paper, New York University.

Langlois, R. N. (1984) "Internal Organization in a Dynamic Context." In M. Jasawalla and H. Ebenfield (eds.) *Communication and Information Economics: New Perspectives* Amsterdam: North-Holland.

Langlois, R. N. (1992) "Transaction-cost Economics in Real Time." *Industrial and Corporate Change* 1: 99–127.

Langlois, R. N. and Koppl R. (1984) "Fritz Machlup and Marginalism: A Reevaluation." Unpublished manuscript.

Lavoie, D. C. (1985) *Rivalry and Central Planning: Socialist Calculation Debate Reconsidered* Cambridge: Cambridge University Press.

Lawson, T. (1994a) "Critical Realism and the Analysis of Choice, Explanation and Change." In P. Boettke and M. Rizzo (eds.) *Advances in Austrian Economics*, vol. 1 Greenwich, CT: JAI Press.

Lawson, T. (1994b) "The Nature of Post Keynesianism and Its Links to Other Traditions: A Realist Perspective." *Journal of Post Keynesian Economics* 16: 503–38.

Lawson, T. (1994c) "Realism, Philosophical." In G. Hodgson, W. Samuels and M. Tool (eds.) *The Elgar Companion to Evolutionary and Institutional Economics*, vol. 2 Aldershot, England: Edward Elgar.

Leijonhufvud, A. (1968) *On Keynesian Economics and the Economics of Keynes* New York: Oxford University Press.

Leijonhufvud, A. (1981a) "The Wicksell Connection: Variations on a Theme." In *Information and Coordination* Oxford: Oxford University Press.

Leijonhufvud, A. (1981b) "Effective Demand Failures." In *Information and Coordination* Oxford: Oxford University Press.

Leijonhufvud, A. (1983a) "What Would Keynes Have Thought of Rational Expectations?" *UCLA Department of Economics Discussion Paper no. 299* Los Angeles: UCLA.

Leijonhufvud, A. (1983b) "Rational Expectations and Monetary Institutions." *UCLA Department of Economics Discussion Paper no. 302* Los Angeles: UCLA.

Leoni, B. (1961) *Freedom and the Law* Princeton, NJ: D. Van Nostrand.

Letwin, W. (1965) *Law and Economic Policy in America: The Evolution of the Sherman Antitrust Act* New York: Random House.

Lewin, P. (1982) "Perspectives on the Costs of Inflation." *Southern Economic Journal* 48: 627–41.

Lindahl, E. (1939) *Studies in the Theory of Money and Capital* London: George Allen & Unwin.

Littlechild, S. C. (1977) *Change Rules, O. K.?* Birmingham: University of Birmingham.

Littlechild, S. C. (1979) *The Fallacy of the Mixed Economy* San Francisco: Cato Institute.

Loasby, B. J. (1976) *Choice, Complexity, and Ignorance* Cambridge: Cambridge University Press.

Loasby, B. J. (1991) *Equilibrium and Evolution* Manchester: Manchester University Press.

Lucas, R. E. Jr. (1973) "Some International Evidence on Out-put Inflation Tradeoffs." American Economic Review 63: 326–34.

Lucas, R. E. Jr. (1975) "An Equilibrium Model of the Business Cycle." *Journal of Political Economy* 83: 1113–44.

Lucas, R. E. Jr. (1977) "Understanding Business Cycles." In K. Brunner and A. H. Meltzer (eds.) *Stabilization of the Domestic and International Economy* Amsterdam: North-Holland.

Machlup, F. (1958) "Equilibrium and Disequilibrium: Misplaced Concreteness and Disguised Politics." *Economic Journal* 68: 1–24. Reprinted in *Essays in Economic Semantics* New York: W. W. Norton, 1967. Also reprinted in *International Payments. Debts, and Gold* (2nd edn.) New York: New York University Press, 1976.

Machlup, F. (1978a) "The Ideal Type: A Bad Name for a Good Construct." In *Methodology of Economics and Other Social Sciences* New York: Academic Press.

Machlup, F. (1978b) "Spiro Latsis on Situational Determinism." In *Methodology of Economics and Other Social Sciences* New York: Academic Press.

Maddock, R. and Carter, M. (1982) "A Child's Guide to Rational Expectations." *Journal of Economic Literature* 20: 39–51.

Mäki, U. (1990) "Scientific Realism and Austrian Explanation." In *Review of Political Economy* 2: 310–44.

Marshall, A. (1961) *Principles of Economics*, 9th edn. London: Macmillan for the Royal Economic Society.

Mayer, H. (1994 [1932]) "The Cognitive Value of Functional Price Theory." In Israel M. Kirzner (ed.) *Classics in Austrian Economics*, vol. 2, *The Interwar Period* London: Pickering and Chatto.

Menger, C. (1892) "On the Origin of Money." Trans. C. A. Foley. *Economic Journal* 2: 238–55.

Menger, C. (1963 [1883]) *Problems of Economics and Sociology* (ed.) L. Schneider and trans. F. J. Nock. Urbana, Ill.: University of Illinois Press.

Menger, C. (1981 [1871]) *Principles of Economics* (ed.) J. Dingwall and trans. B. F. Hoselitz. New York: New York University Press.

Mill, J. S. (1973 [1848]) *Principles of Political Economy, with Some of Their Applications to Social Philosophy* New York: Augustus M. Kelley.

Mirowski, P. (1989) *More Heat than Light* Cambridge: Cambridge University Press.

Mises, L. v. (1953 1912]) *The Theory of Money and Credit* Trans. H. E. Batson. New Haven: Yale University Press.

Mises, L. v. (1966) *Human Action: A Treatise on Economics* (3rd ed.) New York: Henry Regnery & Co.

Morgenstern, O. (1935) "Perfect Foresight and Economic Equilibrium." *Zeitschrift für Nationalökonomie* 6 (part 3). Trans. F. H. Knight in A. Schotter (ed.), *Selected Writings of Oskar Morgenstern* New York: New York University Press, 1976.

Morgenstern, O. (1972) "Descriptive, Predictive, and Normative Theory." *Kyklos* 25: 699–714.

Muth, J. F. (1961) "Rational Expectations and the Theory of Price Movements." *Econometrica* 29: 315–35.

Myrdal, G. (1939) *Monetary Equilibrium* London: William Hodge.

Nelson, R. R. and Winter, S. G. (1982) *An Evolutionary Theory of Economic Change* Cambridge, Mass.: Harvard University Press, The Belknap Press.

O'Connor, D. J. (1957) "Determinism and Predictability." *British Journal for the Philosophy of Science* 7: 310–15.

O'Driscoll, G. P. Jr. (1977) *Economics as a Coordination Problem: The Contributions of Friedrich A. Hayek* Kansas City: Sheed Andrews & McMeel.

O'Driscoll, G. P. Jr. (1979) "Rational Expectations, Politics, and Stagflation." In M. J. Rizzo (ed.) *Time, Uncertainty, and Disequilibrium* Lexington, Mass.: Lexington Books, D. C. Heath and Co.

O'Driscoll, G. P. Jr. (1980) "Justice, Efficiency, and the Economic Analysis of Law: Comment on Fried." *Journal of Legal Studies* 9: 355–66.

O'Driscoll, G. P. Jr. (1981) "Knowing, Expecting, and Theorizing." *C. V. Starr Center for Applied Economics Working Paper no. 81–82*, New York University.

O'Driscoll, G. P. Jr. (1982) "Monopoly in Theory and Practice." In I. M. Kirzner (ed.) *Method, Process, and Austrian Economics: Essays in Honor of Ludwig von Mises* Lexington, Mass.: Lexington Books, D. C. Heath & Co.

O'Driscoll, G. P. Jr. (1983) "A Free-Market Money: Comment on Yeager." *The Cato Journal* 3: 327–33.

O'Driscoll, G. P. Jr. (1984a) "Expectations and Monetary Regimes." Federal Reserve Bank of Dallas *Economic Review*, September 1984.

O'Driscoll, G. P. Jr. (1984b) "Carl Menger and Modern Economics." Unpublished manuscript.

O'Driscoll, G. P. Jr. (1989) "A Tribute to F. A. Hayek." *The Cato Journal* 9: 345–52.

O'Driscoll, G. P. Jr. and Shenoy, S. R. (1976) "Inflation, Recession, and Stagflation." In E. G. Dolan (ed.) *The Foundations of Modern Austrian Economics* Kansas City: Sheed & Ward.

O'Hear, A. (1980) *Karl Popper* London: Routledge & Kegan Paul.

Patinkin, D. (1965) *Money, Interest, and Prices* (2nd edn.) New York: Harper & Row.

Peltzman, S. (1976) “Toward a More General Theory of Regulation.” *Journal of Law and Economics* 19: 211–40.

Plant, A. (1934) “The Economic Theory Concerning Patents for Inventions.” *Economica* n.s. 1: 30–51.

Polanyi, M. (1962) *Personal Knowledge:. Towards a Post-critical Philosophy* Chicago: University of Chicago Press.

Poole, W. (1976) “Rational Expectations in the Macro Model.” *Brookings Papers on Economic Activity* 2: 463–514.

Popper, K. R. (1950) “Indeterminism in Quantum Physics and in Classical Physics.” *British Journal for the Philosophy of Science* 1: 117–33, 173–95.

Popper, K. R. (1959) “The Propensity Interpretation of Probability.” *British Journal for the Philosophy of Science* 10: 25–42.

Popper, K. R. (1964) *The Poverty of Historicism* New York: Harper Torchbooks.

Popper, K. R. (1965 [1934]) *The Logic of Scientific Discovery* New York: Harper Torchbooks, Harper & Row.

Popper, K. R. (1979a) “Of Clouds and Clocks.” In *Objective Knowledge* Oxford: Oxford University Press.

Popper, K. R. (1979b) “On the Theory of the Objective Mind.” In *Objective Knowledge* Oxford: Clarendon Press.

Posner, R. A. (1975) “The Social Costs of Monopoly and Regulation.” *Journal of Political Economy* 83: 807–27.

Posner, R. A. (1977) *Economic Analysis of Law* Boston: Little, Brown.

Posner, R. A. (1979) “The Chicago School of Antitrust Analysis.” University of Pennsylvania Law Review 127: 925–48.

Prigogine, I. and Stengers, I. (1984) *Order Out of Chaos* New York: Bantam Books.

Prychitko, D. (1991) *Marxism and Workers’ Self-Management: The Essential Tension* New York: Greenwood Press.

Prychitko, D. L. (1993a) “After Davidson, Who Needs the Austrians?” *Critical Review* 7: 371–80.

Prychitko, D. L. (1993b) “Formalism in Austrian-School Welfare Economics: Another Pretense of Knowledge?” *Critical Review* 7: 567–92.

Pye, R. (1978) “A Formal Decision-Theoretical Approach to Flexibility and Robustness.” *Journal of the Operational Research Society* 29: 215–27.

Radner, R. (1970) “Problems in the Theory of Markets Under Uncertainty.” *American Economic Review, Papers and Proceedings*

60: 454–60. Reprinted in R. E. Neel (ed.) *Readings in Price Theory* Cincinnati, Ohio: South-Western Publishing, 1973.

Radner, R. (1975) "A Behavioral Model of Cost Reduction." *Bell Journal of Economics* 6: 195–215.

Rawls, J. (1963) *Constitutional Liberty and the Concept of Justice* New York: Nomos, New York University Press.

Reder, M . (1982) "Chicago Economics: Permanence and Change." *Journal of Economic Literature* 20: 1–38.

Richardson, G. B. (1960) *Information and Investment* Oxford: Oxford University Press.

Rizzo, M. J. (1979) "Disequilibrium and All That." In M. J. Rizzo (ed.) *Time, Uncertainty, and Disequilibrium* Lexington, Mass.: Lexington Books, D. C. Heath & Co.

Rizzo, M. J. (1980a) "Law Amid Flux: The Economics of Negligence and Strict Liability in Tort." *Journal of Legal Studies* 9: 291–318.

Rizzo, M. J. (1980b) "The Mirage of Efficiency." *Hofstra Law Review* 8: 641–58.

Rizzo, M. J. (1981) "The Imputation Theory of Proximate Cause: An Economic Framework." *Georgia Law Review* 15: 1007–38.

Rizzo, M. J. (1984) "Re-examination of the Rules Against Horizontal Collusive Arrangements: An Outline." Unpublished manuscript, New York University.

Rizzo, M. J. (1985) "Rules versus Cost–Benefit Analysis in the Common Law." *Cato Journal* 4: 865–84.

Rizzo, M. J. (1990) "Hayek's Four Tendencies Towards Equilibrium." *Cultural Dynamics* 3: 12–31.

Rizzo, M. J. (1992) "Austrian Economics for the Twenty-First Century." In B. J. Caldwell and S. Boehm (eds.) *Austrian Economics: Tensions and New Directions*, Boston: Kluwer.

Rizzo, M. J. and Arnold, F. S. (1980) "Causal Apportionment in the Law of Torts: An Economic Theory." *Columbia Law Review* 80: 1399–429.

Robbins, L. (1934) *The Great Depression* London: Macmillan.

Robertson, D. H. (1940) "Industrial Fluctuations and the Natural Rate of Interest." In *Essays in Monetary Theory* London: P. S. King & Son.

Robertson, D. H. (1949 [1926]) *Banking Policy and the Price Level* New York: Augustus M. Kelley.

Robinson, J. (1971 [1953–54]) "The Production Function and the Theory of Capital." In G. C. Harcourt and N. F. Laing (eds.), *Capital and Growth* Middlesex, England: Penguin.

Robinson, J. (1977) "What are the Questions?" *Journal of Economic Literature* 15: 1318–39.

Rolph, E. R. (1980) "On the Austrian Theory of Capital: A comment." *Economic Inquiry* 18: 501–3.

Rosenberg, N. (1969) "The Direction of Technological Change: Inducement Mechanisms and Focusing Devices." *Economic Development and Cultural Change* 18: 1–24.

Rothbard, M. N. (1963) *America's Great Depression*. Princeton, New Jersey: D. Van Nostrand.

Rothbard, M. N. (1970 [1962]) *Man, Economy, and State*, 2 vols. Los Angeles: Nash.

Ryle, G. (1949) "Knowing How and Knowing That." In *The Concept of Mind* London: Hutchinson's University Library.

Samuelson, P. A. (1966) "A Summing Up." *Quarterly Journal of Economics* 80: 568–83.

Savage, L. J. (1972) *The Foundations of Statistics*, (2nd edn.) New York: Dover Publications.

Schick, F. (15179) "Self-Knowledge, Uncertainty, and Choice." *British Journal for the Philosophy of Science* 30: 235–52.

Schotter, A. (1981) *The Theory of Economic Institutions* Cambridge: Cambridge University Press.

Schumpeter, J. A. (1934) *The Theory of Economic Development* Trans. R. Opie. Cambridge, Mass.: Harvard University Press.

Schumpeter, J. A. (1954) *History of Economic Analysis* Ed. E. B. Schumpeter from manuscript. Oxford: Oxford University Press.

Schutz, A. (1945) "On Multiple Realities." *Philosophy and Phenomenological Research* 5: 533–76. Reprinted in Maurice Natanson (ed.), *Collected Papers I: The Problem of Social Reality* The Hague: Martinus Nijhoff, 1964.

Schutz, A. (1953) "Common-Sense and Scientific Interpretation of Human Action." *Philosophy and Phenomenological Research*. 14: 1–38. Reprinted in Maurice Natanson (ed.) *Philosophy of the Social Sciences* New York: Random House, 1963. Also reprinted in Maurice Natanson (ed.) *Collected Papers I: The Problem of Social Reality* The Hague: Martinus Nijhoff, 1964.

Schutz, A. (1954) "Concept and Theory Formation in the Social Sciences." *Journal of Philosophy* 51: 257–73. Reprinted in Maurice Natanson (ed.) *Philosophy of the Social Sciences* New York: Random House, 1963. Also reprinted in Maurice Natanson (ed.) *Collected Papers I: The Problem of Social Reality* The Hague: Martinus Nijhoff, 1964.

Schutz, A. (1967) *The Phenomenology of the Social World* Trans. George Walsh and Frederick Lehnert. Evanston, Ill.: North-western University Press.

Schutz, A. and Luckmann, T. (1973) *The Structures of the Life World* Evanston, Ill.: Northwestern University Press.

Selgin, G. A. (1988) *The Theory of Free Banking* Totowa, New Jersey: Rowman and Littlefield.

Selgin, G. A. and White, L. H. (1994) "How Would the Invisible Hand Handle Money?" *Journal of Economic Literature* 32: 1718–49.

Shackle, G. L. S. (1958) *Time in Economics* Amsterdam: North-Holland.

Shackle, G. L. S. (1967) *The Years of High Theory* Cambridge: Cambridge University Press.

Shackle, G. L. S. (1969) *Decision, Order, and Time in Human Affairs*, (2nd edn.) Cambridge: Cambridge University Press.

Shackle, G. L. S. (1970) *Expectation, Enterprise and Profit: The Theory of the Firm* Chicago: Aldine.

Shackle, G. L. S. (1972) *Epistemics and Economics* Cambridge: Cambridge University Press.

Shackle, G. L. S. (1979) "Imagination, Formalism, and Choice" In Mario J. Rizzo (ed.) *Time, Uncertainty, and Disequilibrium*, Lexington, Mass.: Lexington Book, D. C. Heath and Co.

Short, E. D. and O'Driscoll, G. P. Jr. (1983) "Deposit Insurance and Financial Stability." *Business Forum* Summer: 10–13.

Smith, A. (1937 [1776]) *An Inquiry into the Nature and Causes of the Wealth of Nations* (ed.) E. Cannan. New York: Modern Library.

Snowdon, B., Vane, H. and Wynarczyk, P. (1994) *A Modern Guide to Macroeconomics* Aldershot, England: Edward Elgar.

Sowell, T. (1980) *Knowledge and Decisions* New York: Basic Books.

Spencer, H. (1888) *A System of Synthetic Philosophy*, vol. 1: *First Principles* (4th edn.) New York: D. Appleton & Company.

Sraffa, P. (1960) *The Production of Commodities by Means of Commodities: A Prelude to a Critique of Economic Theory* Cambridge: Cambridge University Press.

Starbuck, W. H. and Milliken, F. J. (1988) "Executives' Perceptual Filters: What They Notice and How They Make Sense." In D. Hambrick (ed.) *The Executive Effect: Concepts and Methods for Studying Top Managers* Greenwich, CT: JAI Press.

Stigler, G. J. (1966) *The Theory of Price* (3rd edn.) New York: Macmillan & Co.

Stigler, G. J. (1982) "Economists and Public Policy." *Regulation* 6: 13–17.

Stigler, G. J. and Becker, G. S. (1977) "De Gustibus Non Est Disputandum." *American Economic Review* 67: 76–90.

Streissler, E. and Weber, W. (1973) "The Mengerian Tradition." In J. R. Hicks and W. Weber (eds.) *Carl Menger and the Austrian School of Economics* Oxford: Clarendon Press.

Thirlby, G. F (1973) "Economists' Cost Rules and Equilibrium Theory." In J. Buchanan and G. F. Thirlby (eds.) *LSE Essays on Cost* London: Weidenfeld and Nicolson.

Tullock, G. (1967) "The Welfare Costs of Tariffs, Monopolies, and Theft." *Western Economic Journal* 5: 224–32.

Vaughn, K. I. (1994) *Austrian Economics in America: The Migration of a Tradition* Cambridge: Cambridge University Press.

von Neumann, J. and Morgenstern, O. (1947) *Theory of Games and Economic Behavior* Princeton: Princeton University Press.

Wagner, R. E. (1979) "Comment: Politics, Monetary Control, and Economic Performance." In M. J. Rizzo (ed.) *Time, Uncertainty, and Disequilibrium* Lexington, Mass.: Lexington Books, D. C. Heath and Co.

Wainhouse, C. W. (1982) "Hayek's Theory of the Trade Cycle: The Evidence from the Time Series." PhD dissertation, New York University.

Walsh, V. and Gram, H. (1980) *Classical and Neoclassical Theories of General Equilibrium: Historical Origins and Mathematical Structure* New York: Oxford University Press.

Weintraub, E. R. (1979) *Microfoundations: The Compatibility of Microeconomics and Macroeconomics* Cambridge: Cambridge University Press.

White, L. H. (1978) "Entrepreneurial Price Adjustment." Unpublished manuscript, New York University.

White, L. H. (1984) *Free Banking in Britain* Cambridge: Cambridge University Press.

White, L. H. (1989) *Competition and Currency: Essays on Free Banking and Money* New York: New York University Press.

Whitehead, A. N. (1939) *An Introduction to Mathematics* New York: Henry Holt.

Whitehead, A. N. (1961) "Time." In R. N. Anshen (ed.) *Alfred North Whitehead: His Reflections on Man and Nature* New York: Harper & Brothers.

Wicksell, K. (1965 [1898]) *Interest and Prices: A Study of the Causes*

*Regulating the Value of Money* Trans. R. F. Kahn. New York: Augustus M. Kelley.

Wicksteed, P. H. (1967 [1910] *The Common Sense of Political Economy*, vol. 1. New York: Augustus M. Kelly.

Winter, S. (1971) "Satisficing, Selection, and the Innovating Remnant." *Quarterly Journal of Economics* 85: 237–61.

Witt, U. (1992) "Turning Austrian Economics into an Evolutionary Theory." In B. J. Caldwell and S. Boehm (eds.) *Austrian Economics: Tensions and New Directions* Boston: Kluwer Academic Publishers.

Yeager, L. B. (1979) "Capital Paradoxes and the Concept of Waiting." In M. J. Rizzo (ed.) *Time, Uncertainty, and Disequilibrium* Lexington, Mass.: Lexington Books, D. C. Heath & Co.

Yolton, J. W. (1959) "Explanation." *British Journal for the Philosophy of Science* 10: 194–208.

# Index